INDO-SAARC TRADE

Emerging Trends and Potential

INDO-SAARC TRADE

Emerging Trends and Potential

DR. SANDEEP KAUR
Assistant Professor
Centre for South and Central Asian Studies
School of Global Relations
Central University of Punjab, Bathinda (Punjab)

Foreword by

DR. (MRS.) PARAMJIT NANDA
Professor of Economics
Punjab School of Economics
Guru Nanak Dev University, Amritsar (Punjab)

DEEP & DEEP PUBLICATIONS PVT. LTD.
F-159, Rajouri Garden, New Delhi - 110 027

INDO-SAARC TRADE
Emerging Trends and Potential

ISBN 978-81-8450-439-2

Printed in India at MAYUR ENTERPRISES
WZ Plot No. 3, Gujjar Market, Tihar Village, New Delhi - 110 018

Published by DEEP & DEEP PUBLICATIONS PVT. LTD.
F-159, Rajouri Garden, New Delhi - 110 027 • Phone : 25435369, 25440916
E-mail : ddpubs@gmail.com • ddpubs@yahoo.com
Showroom :
2/13, Ansari Road, Daryaganj, New Delhi - 110 002 • Telefax : 23245122

Dedicated to

MY DEAR

PARENTS

Contents

Foreword

The GATT was established in 1947 to facilitate Most Favoured Nation (MFN) principle, i.e. principle of non-discrimination which is the cornerstone of the multilateral trading system (MTS). However, GATT also made provision of Escape Clauses to MFN principle (Article XXIV) which incorporates rules regarding the establishment of regional trading arrangements (RTAs) in the form of Custom Unions and Free Trade Areas (FTAs). Taking advantage of these clauses, 143 RTAs were notified during GATT period (1948-94). Of these, only 91 RTAs were in force. Afterwards, there has been a mushroom growth of RTAs since World Trade Organisation (WTO) came in to existence on 1st Jan. 1995. Presently, total 457 RTAs had been notified to WTO/GATT. Of these, 266 RTAs were in force and remaining 191 RTAs were inactive. In 2010, 90 percent of the global trade took place with in RTAs. Because the WTO has further made important exceptions to RTAs under Article XXIV, GATS Article V and Enabling Clause. It provides MFN treatment to all its member countries and has also allowed 100 percent discrimination under RTAs along with reduced concessional arrangements for developing countries under tariff and subsidy reduction programmes. Since 1948, these RTAs have been moving from "North-North", "South-South" to "North-South" arrangements from "closed regionalism" to "open regionalism" and from "narrow regionalism" to "deep regionalism". As a result, debate has arisen among economists that whether RTAs are "Stepping Stones" towards global free trade or "Stumbling Blocks". The GATT framers wanted RTAs to be vehicle that would ultimately lead to free trade agreements and will pave the way for further liberalization in the multilateral trade. Trade creating effects will exceed the trade diverting effects. However, some persons argue that there is danger to the larger world trade system because true multilateral trade gets lost in vacuum of conflicting rules of world 457 RTAs. No doubt, RTAs and multilateralism are completely opposing approaches but they can complement each other by leading to better allocation of resources; improving the quality and quantity of factor inputs; increasing production; there by leading to better exploitation of economies of scale resulting in higher output.

As the regionalism efforts were intensified, SAARC was also formed on Dec. 1985 with seven member-countries of Bangladesh, Bhutan, India, Maldives, Nepal, Pakistan and Sri Lanka to accelerate the process of economic and social development. Afghanistan also joined SAARC in 2007. Even after more than twenty years, intra-South Asian trade and economic linkages are still very low (less than four percent) as compared to European Union and North America Free Trade Area (NAFTA). Intra-regional exports of NAFTA amount to 47.5 percent of total exports and of EU 61.5 percent. As a result, other regions, especially South Asia has not been able to take full advantage of EU's cumulative rules of origin concession, generalized system of preferences and benefits of common investment and technology regimes dispute redressed mechanism and coordinated approach on issues in the context of WTO, World Bank, International Monetary Fund (IMF) and in dealings with other groupings such as EU, NAFTA and ASEAN. Now the recent initiatives taken by Coalition for Action on South Asian Countries (CASAC) made positive approach by undertaking measures to create South Asian Economic Union (SAEU) by the end of 2020. In first step, South Asia Free Trade Area (SAFTA) will be formed by the end of 2010, then South Asian Custom Union (SACU) by 2015, which would lead to Economic Union by 2020 as South Asian Economic Union.

Keeping in view the low shares of exports of SAARC in world's exports and efforts to form South Economic Union by 2020, the comprehensive study by Dr. Sandeep Kaur to examine issues relating to 'Regionalism Versus Multilateralism'; static and dynamic effects of SAARC; competitiveness on complementarities in production and trade among SAARC nations, patterns of intra-regional trade in SAARC; and India's trade trends and potentials with other SAARC nations is to be welcomed. These issues have been examined by testing various hypothesis, i.e. (existence of complementarities in production and trade among SAARC nations; geographical diversification of trade of SAARC nations; high trade intensity of India with all other SAARC nations, existence of India's export potential with other SAARC nations and existence of other static and dynamic effects leading to rapid rate of growth of SAARC nations). All these hypotheses have been tested with the help of data for different variables for the whole period 1985-2005 and two sub-periods, i.e. Pre-WTO period (1985-94) and Post-WTO period (1995-2004). Empirical findings of the book reveal that there exist lack of complementarities in production and trade among SAARC nations. Further, the dynamic effects of SAARC integration could not explain the rapid rates of growth experienced by members of regional integration. SAARC did not affect the growth of their member countries directly but it had a significant positive influence on investment. There is large room for export expansion for Maldives, Bhutan, Pakistan and Nepal. In the chapter on India's trade with SAARC, the author points out that there was no structural shift in direction of India's exports as well imports from SAARC. There was no stable partnership in India's trade with SAARC. Further, India has not exploited all the export potential in trading with SAARC members. But India's exports to SAARC countries converged towards the estimated export potential. Based on the findings of the study; very useful policy implications have been derived. The author suggests that regional countries should develop technological capacity to produce different product varieties at declining average costs to achieve increased level of intra-industry trade. Trade complementarities can be developed within region, if countries achieve vertical specialization through product sharing arrangements. India can be as a source of potential investment and technology and a major market for products from all other SAARC members.

I congratulate Dr. Sandeep Kaur for bringing out an excellent, up-to-date and immensely useful book for the students, teachers, researchers and those are interested in International Economics.

DR. (MRS.) PARAMJIT NANDA
Professor of Economics
Punjab School of Economics
Guru Nanak Dev University, Amritsar

Preface

Regional Trade agreements have proliferated since the 1990's particularly after the completion of the Uruguay Round. Such agreements have been concluded among high income countries, low-income countries and more recently starting with between high income and developing countries. Through the structure of regional agreements varies, but the objective is common i.e. to reduce barriers to trade between member countries. By the time, WTO was established on 1st January 1995; nearly all members of the WTO belonged to one or more RTAs. About 421 RTAs have been notified to the GATT/ WTO up to December 2008. Of these, 324 RTAs were notified under Article XXIV of the GATT 1947 or GATT 1994; 29 under the Enabling Clause; and 68 under Article V of the GATS. At the same time, 230 agreements were in force. Almost 400 RTAs which are in force, but have not been notified, those signed, but not yet in force, those currently being negotiated, and those in the proposal stage, which are scheduled to be implemented by the end of 2010. Of these RTAs, FTAs account for over 90% while Custom Union for less than 10% (www.wto.org)

SAARC (South Asia Association for Regional Cooperation) is one of these RTAs. In South Asian region, trade retains a marginal character. EU constituted 38.2% share in total world exports followed by NAFTA with 13.88%, ASEAN with 6.3%, and MERCOSUR with 1.6% and SAARC with Just 1.3% share. Thus the share of SAARC in world exports is minimum as compared to other regional trading blocs (World Development

Indicators, 2006). However, it can play a crucial role in the development of region by promoting the welfare of the worlds' down trodden and poverty stricken people living in this region. Keeping in view the magnitude and seriousness of the problem regarding trade in the region, a comprehensive study is needed covering pattern of intra-regional trade in SAARC, in relation to other forms of regional integration and to suggest measures to strengthen it.

The objective of the book is to study the trends and growth of Indo-SAARC trade and their potential. For this, the book has examined the positive as well as negative effects of regional trading agreements. It has studied competitiveness or complementarities in production and trade among SAARC nations and pattern of intra-regional trade in SAARC and analyzed India's trade trends with the other member-countries of SAARC. Using panel data methodology, the book has studied static trade effects (in terms of trade creation and trade diversion) and dynamic effects (in terms of investment and technical change) of SAARC and examined the potential of India's exports with the other member countries of SAARC.

On the basis of the analysis carried out in the study, the study found out that Trade of SAARC nation is geographically diversified. India's trade is not intense with all other SAARC nations. There is a potential of India's exports to other SAARC nations. India's exports to SAARC nations have converged towards the estimated equilibrium. The hypothesis i.e. complementarities in production and trade exists among SAARC nations is not conclusively accepted or rejected as complementarities in production and trade among these nations do not exist at broad level. However, at commodity level, complementarities are found. Another hypothesis, i.e. dynamic effects of SAARC can explain the rapid rates of growth experienced by its members is not accepted as these effects cannot explain the rapid rates of growth experienced by members of SAARC. The study suggested that India is the only SAARC member that shares land border with four members and sea border with two. No other SAARC country shares a common border with each other. In terms of trade, commerce, investments, etc., India is a source of potential investment and technology and a major market for products from all other

SAARC members. Therefore, it is essentially in India's interest to put her weight behind SAARC.

Now, I take this opportunity to pay a small tribute to all the persons who have been instrumental in the completion of my book.

What appeared initially to me, Almighty God for His kind blessings, without which I would not have been able to accomplish this work. I express gratitude to my "Great Lord", the spiritual pillar in this life and the one, with whose grace and warm blessings, I have been able to complete another chapter of my life.

A formidable and impossible undertaking, was made possible because of my revered teacher Dr. (Mrs.) Paramjit Kaur Nanda, Professor, Punjab School of Economics, G.N.D. University, Amritsar. I do not have sufficient words to express my gratitude to her, who spared so much of her valuable time and had immense amount of patience for me. I consider myself fortunate that I got this opportunity to work under her guidance and will always admire her commitment, her vast knowledge and untiring zeal for work. She took great pain in the completion of this work and gave top priority to my work. Moreover, she encouraged me to complete this work whenever I lost confidence. I cannot forget her contribution and will always be indebted to her.

I would like to take this opportunity to thank Dr. P.S. Raikhy, Professor, G.N.D. University for his kind support and valuable suggestions during the study. My special thanks are due to Dr A.S. Sethi, Professor, Punjab School of Economics, G.N.D. University, Amritsar, for providing technical advise from time to time. I have been supported by a number of people within the Punjab School of Economics, G.N.D. University. I am thankful to Dr. Kuldeep Kaur and Prof. Sharanjit Singh Dhillon to encourage me to do this work.

I am grateful to S. Sukhdev Singh, Asst Programmer of Computer Centre, G.N.D. University, Amritsar, for providing technical assistance in data processing and use of computer software.

This book would not have been possible without the active support and assistance of the library staff of Panjab University, Chandigarh and G.N.D. University, Amritsar. My special thanks are due to S. Mukhtar Singh, librarian and S. Bakhtawar Singh, restorer of Punjab School of Economics, G.N.D. University library, who provide all support and help to me.

Of course, this work would not have been completed without the encouragement and prayers of my family. My father S. Surjit Singh provided constant encouragement and unflagging support throughout the period of this work. My mother Mrs. Bhupinder Kaur motivated me on to complete the work with tender words of love. The blessings and prayers of my parents inspired me and gave me the strength and courage to complete this arduous task. I also thank my sisters, Ms. Simran Kaur and Ms. Tajinder Pal Kaur and my youngest brother S. Mankirat Singh who have also given me the confidence to pursue my dreams. I also want to thank my brother in law, S. Kulwinder Singh and my nephew, S. Sukirat Singh. However, the one more person from my family who made it possible for me to pursue this dream is my grandmother Smt. Parkash Kaur, who has also encouraged me to complete this work.

Last but not least, I am truly grateful to my colleagues and friends who have helped me to realize my goal. Noteworthy among them are Dr. Manjit Singh, Dr. Tilak Raj, Mr. Nitin, Ms. Arvinder Kaur, Ms. Jyoti, Mr. Gaurav and Mrs. Anu Yadav.

SANDEEP KAUR

1

Introduction

Regional integration among various countries, particularly among developing countries has assumed increasing significance during the last two decades because regional integration provides an opportunity for industries that have not yet been established as well as for those that have to take advantage of the economies of large-scale production made possible by expanded markets. Such integration encourages a rational division of labour among a group of countries. In the absence of integration, each separate country may not provide a sufficiently large domestic market to enable local industries to lower their production costs by reaping economies of scale. In such cases, import substituting industrialization will result, leading to the establishment of cost inefficient local industries. Another dynamic rationale for regional integration is the possibility of creation of the coordinated industrial planning by removing barriers to trade. This arises especially in those industries where economies of scale are likely to exist such as fertilizers and petrochemical plants, heavy industries like iron and steel, capital goods and machine tool industries, etc. The same industry may be set-up in two or more adjoining small nations. Each will be operating at less than optimal capacity but will be protected against the imports of the other by high tariff or quota barriers from the third country(which results in wastage of scarce resources and consumers will have to pay higher price for the product) (Todaro and Smith, 2004).

Besides these two long-terms dynamic arguments for integration, the other consideration for integration are 'trade creation' and 'trade diversion'. Trade creation will lead to shift in production from high to low cost member states. Trade diversion means the production and consumption of one of member states to shift from least-cost non-member sources of supply (e.g. from a developed country) to higher cost member producers. Trade diversion is normally considered undesirable since both the world and member states are perceived to be worse-off as a result of the diversion of production from more efficient foreign suppliers to the less efficient domestic industries of members' states. But with potential economies of scale, the creation of local jobs and circular flow of income within the integrated region, static trade diversion may turn out to be dynamic trade creation (Todaro and Smith, 2004). There may generally be another distributional effect associated with a Regional Trade Agreement (RTA). If all prices are left unchanged, tariffs eliminated on RTA members but maintained on other countries, will lead to increase in consumption of member countries. Each RTA country will substitute away from consumption of her own goods, and all RTA countries will substitute away from consumption of good purchased from non-member countries. The net effect on the demand of each RTA country is ambiguous (since own demand has fallen but member demand has increased). If goods are sufficiently strong substitutes, the demand for third party goods will decrease. Thus in order to clear markets, the price of third party goods will have to fall which (as long as no member country's price decreases too much) will create a positive terms of trade effect for the member countries (Mundell, 1964).

Further, the need to attract foreign investment is increasingly cited as an impetus for RTAs. RTAs can stimulate investment flows both between its constituent member countries and from outside the RTA, in a number of ways:

By reducing distortions in production within two countries and by engaging in tariff jumping (i.e. of common external tariff is higher than pre-existing tariff), it can increase the overall quantity of investment made by investors in member countries.

Thus, regional integration promotes trade and development by increasing intra-bloc trade and by an increase in intra-bloc foreign direct investment (Fernandez, 1997).

The most significant provision of the policy regime under WTO and its predecessor-GATT is the provision of non-discrimination as explained in Article 1 (Most Favoured Nation clause or MFN) and Article III (National Treatment on internal taxation and regulation (NT). Article I, on most favoured nation (MFN) treatment, requires that "members of the WTO (contracting parties in GATT terminology) shall extend unconditionally to all other members any advantage, favour, privilege or community affecting customs, duties, charges rules and procedures that they give to members". Yet GATT/ WTO articles permitted exceptions to the MFN treatment for Custom Unions (CUs) and Free Trade Areas (FTAs).

(a) It permits the formulation of custom union or the free trade areas to promote economic integration provided that (i) such arrangement covers the bulk of trade between the participating countries, (ii) a definite time table is set for eventual removal of tariff, and (iii) the contracting parties are satisfied that the final common tariff is no more restrictive than the average of member countries' pre-union tariffs.

(b) It permits members to adopt measures against counter dumping and export subsides, provided these measures are limited to offending countries (www.wto.org).

Taking advantage of exception to MFN, regional integrations have been increasing since 1950s in various forms:

(a) Preferential Trade Area (PTA)

A preferential trade area is a trading bloc which gives preferential access to certain products from the participatory countries. This is done by reducing tariffs, but not by abolishing them completely. This is the first stage of regional integration.

(b) Free Trade Area (FTA)

A free trade area consists of a group of countries that have removed artificial barriers to trade within the group. Each of the member countries maintains its own tariff schedule and quotas with respect to non-member countries.

(c) Custom Union (CU)

Custom unions, like FTAs seek to eliminate tariff and quota restrictions on intra-union trade. In addition, the countries comprising the union agree on a common tariff schedule that will apply to all non-members' countries desiring to trade with the members.

(d) Common Market (CM)

A common market is characterized not only by removal of internal tariffs and the existence of a common external tariff but it also features the free movement of capital and labour. Thus, goods, services and the factors of production are to move freely within the common market.

(e) Economic Union (EU)

An economic union requires the member's countries to harmonize their economic policies especially monetary and fiscal policy.

(f) Political Union (PU)

A political union is an economically and politically integrated nation, usually as federation with varying degrees of integration possible.

PTA, FTA and CU are called "shallow integration" arrangements in trade literature. Common Market and Economic Union are known as "deep integration" arrangements. Among the Regional Trade Agreements, a large majority of the arrangements are shallow integration arrangements, i.e. they are mostly PTAs or FTAs. In contrast, there are only a handful of Custom Unions, Common Markets and Economic Unions world-wide. Most of these deep integration arrangements are found in Europe, e.g., the Maastricht Treaty and the EU Single Market Programme are examples of deep integration schemes. The Andean Pact and the

Central American Common Market (CACM) are examples of Preferential Trade Agreements. However, most of the new PTAs tend to be free trade areas. ASEAN Free Trade Area, AFTA) and North American Free Trade Area are examples of FTAs (Pal, 2006).

Taking advantage of exception to GATT principle (MFN Clause), regionalism led by European arrangements spread across Latin America, Africa and the Middle-east during Post-World War II. After laying dormant throughout the seventies, regional arrangements emerged again in the eighties. The process has heated up in the early nineties with new initiatives almost every month. Most developing countries had independently engaged in substantial unilateral trade liberalization (UTL) and applied simultaneously for GATT membership. Now developing countries have been associating themselves with large developed countries partners (North-South) to ensure market access. As a consequence, the concept of RTAs changed its face. In some cases, it is of the North-South variety rather than of the North-North and South-South variety which were predominant arrangement of the first wave of RTAs. Trade arrangement among industrial countries (North-North) included Australia-New Zealand Closer Economic Arrangement (ANZCERTA), European Commission (EC), The European Free Trade Association (EFTA), Canada-United States Free Trade Agreement (US-CANADA FTA), which have gone beyond trade liberalization in goods that are subject of GATT negotiations by including some liberalization in services and investment, technical and regulatory standards as well as customs formalities and government procurement policies. The North-South agreements (new wave of regionalism) under the enterprise for the American initiative (EAI) among Latin American countries are quite different from past arrangements since they are outward rather than inward-oriented (first wave of regional integration). Partners in the new wave of regionalism are from the developed and developing world (Melo, Montenegro and Panagariya, 1992).

By the time, WTO was established on 1st January 1995; nearly all members of the WTO belonged to one or more RTAs. About 421 RTAs have been notified to the GATT/WTO up to December 2008. Of these, 324 RTAs were notified under Article

XXIV of the GATT 1947 or GATT 1994; 29 under the Enabling Clause; and 68 under Article V of the GATS. At the same time, 230 agreements were in force. Almost 400 RTAs which are in force, but have not been notified, those signed, but not yet in force, those currently being negotiated, and those in the proposal stage, which are scheduled to be implemented by the end of 2010. Of these RTAs, FTAs account for over 90% while Custom Union for less than 10% (www.wto.org)

With the adoption of new international economic order, and with the desire to have regional development in South Asia through regional cooperation in core areas, president Zia-ur-Rehman of Bangladesh initiated the formation of a regional body in the late seventies. Bangladesh's proposal to hold a summit level meeting of the South Asian countries was warmly welcomed by Maldives, Nepal, Bhutan and Sri Lanka while India and Pakistan accepted it with hesitation. The first meeting of the seven countries at the level of their foreign secretaries was held in Colombo on April 21-23, 1981. At this meeting the fundamental framework with which regional cooperation was to be built up was finalized with both caution and optimism. It also identified the various areas of cooperation such as agriculture, rural development, meteorology, health and population activity and appointed study groups of experts and nominated a coordinating country for each. Later the foreign secretaries of these seven countries met in November 1981, August 1982, March 1983 and July 1983. At the standing committee of South Asia Association Regional Cooperation (SAARC), the foreign secretaries met twice in 1984 and once in 1985 to review the progress made in the implementation of the various decisions which had been adopted in the previous meetings.

SAARC countries account for about 22 percent of world population and only 3.5 percent of total land area. However, their share in world output is mere 2.77 percent (World Bank, 2007). The following are the main objectives of SAARC:

(a) To promote the socio-economic welfare and cultural development of the people in the region,
(b) To achieve the goal of collective self-reliance,
(c) To encourage active collaboration in the economic,

social, technical and scientific fields among the grouping nations,

(d) To strengthen overall cooperation and harmonious economic and political relations among the countries of SAARC,

(e) To facilitate optimum utilization of human and material resources, and

(f) To develop free regional trade and to stimulate investment flows and accelerate space of economic development

The region has an internal problem of underdevelopment and the SAARC countries are considered to be the least developed countries of the world and need regional cooperation especially in the core economic areas. There are certain problems which can be solved through regional cooperation in trade and production. Till Dec. 2008, 15 SAARC Summits have been held. The first SAARC Summit was held in Dhaka on 7th and 8th of December 1985. The Heads of State reaffirmed the fundamental goal of accelerating the process of economic and social development in the region through the optimum use of available resources, their commitment to the UN Charter, principles of sovereign equality of states, peaceful settlement of disputes, and non-interference in the internal affairs of the member countries. The second SAARC Summit was held in Bangalore on 16th and 17th of November 1986. The memorandum of understanding (MOU) was signed by the council of ministers on the establishment of permanent SAARC secretariat in Kathmandu and it was welcomed by the Heads of State or government at this summit, so that it could assist in the co-ordination of SAARC activities and more fruitful implementation of its programs and projects. The third Summit of SAARC was held in Kathmandu on 2nd of April 1987. The SAARC Audio Visual Exchange (SAVE) programme, SAARC Chairs, fellowships and scholarships, tourism among member countries, etc. were some of the outcomes of this summit. The fourth Summit meeting of the Heads of State and Government of South Asian countries was held at Islamabad from 29 to 31st December 1988. The need for preserving and liberalizing the multilateral trading system was reiterated by the Heads of State or Government at this Summit both with in and outside the Uruguay round of Multilateral Trade Negotiations. The fifth Summit of Heads of State or Government of SAARC countries were held at Mali, capital of Maldives Islands from November 21 to 23, 1990. To enhance cooperation among the SAARC countries, the Summit decided to immediately initiate steps for launching joint ventures in the field of cottage industries and handicrafts to get the stage for promoting collective self-reliance in the region. The leaders decided to observe the year 1989 as the "SAARC year for combating Drug Abuse and Drug Trafficking", 1992 as the "SAARC year of Environment" and also decided to launch the SAARC travel document scheme. The sixth Summit of SAARC was held in Colombo, Sri Lanka on 21st December, 1991. The Summit decided to set-up an independent South Asian Commission. The State or Government of member countries also set-up SAARC fund for regional projects (SFRP) for identification and development of regional projects managed by Regional Council of Development financing institutions of member countries. The seventh Summit of SAARC was held at Dhaka on 10th and 11th April 1993. During the Summit, the Council of Ministers of SAARC countries agreed for South Asian Preferential Trade Agreement (SAPTA) to usher a new era of economic cooperation in South Asia by liberalizing intra-regional trade and they expressed general desire to implement it by 1995. The eighth Summit of SAARC was held at New Delhi, India on 2-4 May 1995. The member countries decided to declare 1995 'as the SAARC year of Poverty Eradication' and 1996 as the "SAARC year of Literacy". The ninth Summit of the SAARC was held at Mali, Maldives on 12-14 May 1997. The Heads of State or Government reaffirmed their determination to strengthening of intra-SAARC links in key areas of trade, investment and finance. They decided that a Group of Eminent persons (GEP), comprising of one representing from each member state, would undertake a comprehensive appraisal of SAARC and identify measures to enhance the effectiveness of the association in achieving its objectives. They recognized the importance of achieving a free trade area by the year 2001 A.D. and decided to designate 1997 as the "SAARC Year of Participatory Governance". The tenth Summit of Heads of State or Government of SAARC countries was held at Colombo from

July 29 to 31, 1998 and the eleventh Summit of Heads of State or Government of SAARC countries was held in Kathmandu, Nepal from 4 to 6 January 2002. The Twelfth Summit meeting of the SAARC was held in Islamabad, Pakistan on 4-6 January, 2004. In this Summit, the signing of the frameworks agreement on SAFTA was a milestone. To promote tourism within South Asia and to commemorate the twentieth year of the establishment of SAARC, the year 2005 is designated as "South Asia Tourism year". Prospects for setting up of South Asian Development Bank were to be examined by the SAARC Finance through the council of ministers. The thirteenth Summit meeting of SAARC was held in Dhaka, Bangladesh on 12-13 November, 2005 and in this the Heads of State or Government stressed the importance of the entry into force of the SAFTA agreement as the scheduled date, i.e. 1 January, 2006. This would mark an important milestone on the road to a South Asian Economic union. The 14th SAARC Summit of the SAARC was held in New Delhi, India on April 3-4, 2007. Under this, Afghanistan was welcomed as a new member of SAARC and People's Republic of China, Japan, European Union, Republic of Korea, Islamic Republic of Iran and United States of America were associated as observers to SAARC. The fifteen SAARC Summit was held on August 2nd and 3rd, 2008 in Sri Lanka. The theme of SAARC was 'Partnership for our People' focused on the launch of The SAARC Development Fund, establishing a South Asian Regional Standard Organization and developing cooperation among SAARC nations with regard to criminal offenses (www.saarc-sec.org). The broad thrust of all SAARC meetings has been to encourage trade and investment.

In South Asian region, trade retains a marginal character. EU constituted 38.2% share in total world exports followed by NAFTA with 13.88%, ASEAN with 6.3%, and MERCOSUR with 1.6% and SAARC with just 1.3% share. Thus the share of SAARC in world exports is minimum as compared to other regional trading blocs (World Development Indicators, 2006). However, it can play a crucial role in the development of region by promoting the welfare of the worlds' down trodden and poverty stricken people living in this region.

Keeping in view the magnitude and seriousness of the problem regarding trade in the region, a comprehensive study is needed covering pattern of intra-regional trade in SAARC, in relation to other forms of regional integration and to suggest measures to strengthen it.

OBJECTIVES OF THE STUDY

In the light of above issues, the present study has been undertaken with the following specific objectives:

(1) To examine the positive as well as negative effects of regional trading agreements.
(2) To study competitiveness or complementarities in production and trade among SAARC nations and pattern of intra-regional trade in SAARC.
(3) To analyze India's trade trends with the other member countries of SAARC.
(4) To study static trade effects (in terms of trade creation and trade diversion) and dynamic effects (in terms of investment and technical change) of SAARC.
(5) To examine the potential of India's exports with the other member countries of SAARC.
(6) To analyze various problems faced by member countries in enhancing the trade of South Asian region.
(7) To suggest a coordinated strategy of development of trade in the region.

HYPOTHESES OF THE STUDY

In the light of above-mentioned objectives, the study attempts to test the following hypotheses:

1. Complementarities in production and trade exist among SAARC countries.
2. Trade of SAARC nations is geographically diversified.
3. India's trade is not intense with all other SAARC nations.
4. The dynamic effects, i.e. increasing investment and technical change can explain the rapid rates of growth experienced by members of regional integration.

5. There exists sufficient potential of India's exports to other SAARC nations.
6. India's exports to SAARC countries have converged towards the estimated export potential.

PLAN OF THE STUDY

The study has been divided into nine chapters including the present one. Second chapter explains positive as well as negative effects of regional integration. Third chapter reviews empirical studies. Fourth chapter explains the data base and methodology. Fifth chapter measures the production and trade structure among SAARC countries. Sixth chapter analyses the trends and growth of India's trade with other SAARC countries. Seventh chapter quantifies the static and dynamic effects of SAARC. Eighth chapter identifies the potential exports of India to other SAARC countries using gravity model and last chapter summarizes the results and derives policy implications.

2

Regional Integration
Building Blocks or Stumbling Blocks

The post-World War II era has witnessed the emergence and growing importance of regional economic groupings in many different parts of the world to overcome obstacles to international trade and to isolate the region from the fluctuations of the world economy. The process of regional economic cooperation was initiated by Western Europe in the late 1940s (first wave of regionalism) with the formation of the European Coal and Steel Community and subsequently the Treaty of Rome in 1957 that established the European Economic Community (EEC). The formation of the EEC encouraged some other countries outside the EEC to form the European Free Trade Area (EFTA). The spectacular success of the EEC in the immediate aftermath provided an added impetus to the growing tide of regional integration. Actually second wave of regional integration started during roughly the second half of the 1960s. The origin of this regionalism has been attributed to the drawn out nature and slow progress of GATT Uruguay Round negotiations, to the apparent success and fears aroused by the EU's initiative aimed at establishing a Single European

Market, and to the conversion of United States to regionalism with its negotiation of the North American Free Trade Agreement (NAFTA) (Matthews, 2003).

However, this second wave of regionalism was weak and did not go far. Regional Trade Agreements (RTAs) of this period were neither large in number nor as successful as those of recent years. One of the important reasons was that US, the largest trading economy, was philosophically opposed to regionalism. During 1990s, regionalism returned with a vengeance. The third wave of regionalism surfaced during late 1980s, with the weakening of American regionalism, breakdown of USSR in 1991 and uprisings and regional conflicts in Africa and South East Asia. This third global wave of regionalism has also come to known as "New Regionalism". It had elements of North-South integration (NAFTA, enlargement of EC in 1986 by incorporating Greece, Portugal and Spain) whereas regional integration in 1950s and 1960s consisted of regional arrangements that were either North-North or South type (EC, EFTA industrial countries), CACM, ANDEAN Pact, ASEAN and ECOWAS (developing countries). Recent regionalism is entirely different from traditional regionalism in the sense that new regional arrangements are taking place among countries who are more open, export and market-oriented and private-sector dominated (Galal, 2003).

The early years of 21st century have witnessed profound changes in the international economic environment. The period has been marked by a sharp growth in the number of regional trading agreements. During this period, on the one hand, there is a WTO move towards multilateral liberalization based on the principle of most-favoured nations, requiring member countries to open up and liberalise their economies by reducing trade barriers and to undertake policy reforms, to remove market and trade distortions. On the other hand, more and more countries are opting for various sorts of trading agreements that provide preferential access to the members and discriminate against non-members. This helps not only in general trade promotion among the countries that constitute the trading blocks but also helps to create protection against outside member while liberalizing on a selective basis. Conversely, this puts the other countries, not part of the trading bloc in a disadvantageous position in terms of access to the markets of countries operating in a Preferential Trade Area (PTA) *vis-à-vis* the countries with in the PTA. Also the countries that do not form part of the trading bloc are unable to go in for selective liberalization with some countries. These seem to be the compelling reasons for proliferation of regional trading agreements. Thus, when serious moves towards multilateral trade liberalization are being initiated and institutionalized through formation of the WTO, many economists are trying to identify the economic and political reasons which are pushing towards increased regionalism. Traditionally, regional trade agreements are explained by theories which discuss welfare effects of regional trade liberalization and the consequently gains from trade at a regional level. But these theories do not explain the new wave of regionalism of the 1990s. Most economists attribute the current surge in regionalism to lopsided nature of the current multilateral trade regime and the dissatisfaction associated with it. On the one hand regionalism is considered an obstacle to the liberalization of the international economy (stumbling blocks) while on other hand, it is being regarded as a positive factor in progress towards international economic integration (building blocks).

REGIONAL INTEGRATION : BUILDING BLOCKS

I. Welfare Impact of RTAS

The traditional theory of gains from trade allows consumers and producers to purchase from the cheapest and most competitive source of supply with removal of trade barriers. This not only enhances efficiency but also increases welfare. It was traditionally believed that regional trade blocs should generate gains from trade as member countries reduce trade barriers among themselves. This view point was first challenged by Viner in his 1950 book titled 'The Custom Union Issue'. Viner, introduced the concepts of "trade creation" and "trade diversion" and found that that net effect of trade liberalization on a regional basis is not unambiguously positive. Viner pointed out that RTAs can lead to trade creation if, due to formation of the regional agreement, RTA members switch from inefficient domestic producers to efficient members of the RTA.

In this case, efficiency gains arise from with production efficiency and consumption efficiency. On the other hand, trade diversion takes place if, because of the RTA, members switch imports from least cost producers from the rest of the world and import more from higher cost producers in the partner countries. Trade diversion lowers welfare of not only the partner countries but the rest of the world also (Pal, 2006). In Viner's own words, "where the trade diverting effect is predominant, at least one of the member countries is bound to be injured, the two combined will suffer a net injury and there will be injury to the outside world and to the world at large" (Viner, 1950).

Viner's analysis shows that trade creation and trade diversion have opposite welfare implications and the net effect will depend upon which of these two effects dominate. However, the net welfare effect of RTAs had not been unequivocally established by Viner. Interestingly, Viner's conclusion that trade diverting RTAs are necessarily welfare reducing, have been challenged by Gherels (1956-57), Lipsey (1957) and Bhagwati (1971). These studies have shown that demand of supply elasticities of the trading countries play a very crucial role about the outcome of Viner's model. It has also been shown by these authors that relaxation of some of his key assumption about demand and supply elasticities can alter the results so much that a trade diverting regional trade agreement can infact, become welfare enhancing. One more study has added another dimension to this debate by suggesting that if the members of the PTA are themselves "large", then trade diversion can be beneficial due to improvement in the terms of trade. Conversely by the same argument, trade creation can lead to welfare loss because of deterioration in the member countries's term of trade (Pangariya, 2000). A number of studies introduced dynamic effects into the model to address the net welfare effects of PTA. There is a big debate among the trade theorists about the relative dominance of these two effects. A group of economists led by Summers (1991) are of the opinion that regional trade agreements are likely to be more welfare enhancing because, trade diversion is likely to have only a benign impact on the member countries. Lipsey (1957) and Summers also argue that if the member countries are geographically close and have very high trade dependence among each other (Natural trading partners), then the risk of trade diversion is minimal. Expressing similar views, Krugman (1991) is of the opinion that beneficial effect of a regional trade agreement will depend on whether there is enough "inherent regionalism" in the transport costs between the member countries of the RTA. Frankel (1997), Stein and Wei (1995) have also expressed similar views (Pal, 2006).

Lizano (2000) argued that the costs of trade diversion have fallen over time due to several reasons like (i) the unilateral decline of protectionism has been very marked in most counties, (ii) from the economic viewpoint, the scale of regional economic integrations (REI) schemes has increased substantially (EU, NAFTA, FTAA). The risk of trade diversion, therefore, has tended to diminish both for the member countries of REI schemes and for the rest of the world. There is a greater prospect that trade creation will outweigh trade diversion.

II. Increased Returns and Increased Competition

It has been argued that with in a tiny market, there may be a trade-off between economies of scale and competition. Market enlargement removes this trade-off and makes possible the existence of (i) larger firms with greater productive efficiency for any industry with economies of scale, and (ii) increased competition that induces firms to cut prices, expand sales and reduce internal efficiencies. Therefore, RTAs would allow firms in some sectors to exploit more fully economies of scale through market enlargement and competition. However, pro-competitive effects will be larger if low external tariff allows for a significant degree of import competition from firms outside the zone. Otherwise, the more developed countries within the regional integration scheme would most probably dominate the market because they may have a head start. On the other hand, current technology may be obsolete in these countries compared to current and future needs of the regional market. Firms may then decide to re-deploy new technology and relocate in other areas depending on factor costs. In this case, countries with the most cost effective infrastructure and human resources would be beneficiaries (Kritzinger, 2005). Chand (2006) argued that regional integration provides opportunities to exploit economies of scale and specialization to promote long-run growth. These arguments formed the main basis for the basis of regionalism during the 1960s and 1970s (old regionalism).

III. Increased Progress at a Multilateral Level

As modern trade barriers are much more complicated to negotiate in a multilateral forum, most countries find it easier to deal with these issues on bilateral or regional level. In the post-Uruguay round era, the concerns about multilateral trading system have intensified. Most counties, particularly developing countries are dissatisfied with the progress of the WTO because most of the promises of the Uruguay Round agreement to expand global trade have not been materialized in practice. Particularly, for developing counties, the promised expansion of trade in three key areas of agriculture, textile and services has been dismal. Moreover, protectionism and lack of willingness among developed countries to provide market access on a multilateral basis has prompted many developing countries to look for regional alternatives (Pal, 2006).

The North-South divide which is appearing in the WTO Ministerial meets is strengthening the apprehension of the developing countries about the prospect of trade expansion under the WTO regime. This has induced many countries to adopt regionalism as an alternative option for expanding their markets. Mansfield and Reinhardt (2003) argued that multilateral trade negotiations, infact, motivate countries to conclude RTAs. This is so because as the WTO membership expands, individual country's ability to influence the content and pace of MFN liberalization reduces and the large membership makes it difficult for countries to have a coordinated strategy. As formation of regional blocs lead to increased negotiating power at multilateral level, countries want to become a part of a regional grouping to increase their leverage in the multilateral negotiations. Schott (2004) also expressed the similar view by taking an example of US. US has pursued bilateral trade arguments over the last decades to complement and cajole (fair) progress at multilateral level (Pal, 2006).

IV. Reciprocal Access to the Markets

Regional Integration guarantees reciprocal access to the

markets of the member countries thereby providing a significant advantage that is not attainable through unilateral opening. However, the importance of unilaterally eliminating obstacles to external trade as a means of fostering economic development is not to be disregarded. This is mainly true for those RTAs based on import substitution and whose external tariff is very often excessively high. In the early stages of protectionism, unilateral action plays a very important role. Its basic aim is to ensure a better allocation of the factors of the production with a view to increasing productivity later, when the external tariff has fallen significantly, regional and multilateral action acquires crucial significance in the search for access to the new markets (Lizano, 2000). Lloyd and Macleren (2004) introduced the terms hub and spokes to explain the relevance of regional agreements. According to him, a hub is a country which is a member of two or more distinct RTAs. Spokes arise when a hub country forms a bilateral RTA with another country. Hub enjoys access to all its spokes on a preferential basis due to formation of an RTA of a hub country with another trading bloc. As most hubs are developed countries, most gains of PTAs have gone to them. On the other hand, each spoke enjoys preferential access only to the hub. Therefore, spokes have less market access than the hub. This has led to the acceleration in bilateral agreement at the present time (Pal, 2006).

V. Benefits to the Developing/Small Countries

Bhagwati (1993), Panagariya (1996) and Bergsten (1996) pointed out many big developed countries like the US and the EU are increasingly getting involved of forming Free Trade Area (FTA) with developing countries on a bilateral or regional level. This has prompted many developing counties to seek participation in free trade agreements with developed countries as a defensive necessity against a possible exclusion from these markets. The motivation to go for an FTA with a developed country will be particularly strong for a developing country if other countries, with which it is competing to supply goods to the developed market, are part of a preferential trade agreement with the developed country. If these non-member countries cannot form on FTA with the developed country, they attempt to create their own market by joining a regional trade agreement among excluded members. According to Lizano (2000), small countries gain a very important advantage in RTA since regionalism entails market access commitments by all members, including the bigger members. There is thus a significant decline in managed trade by large countries within the integration areas. This guarantee of market access is undoubtedly of great advantage for small countries.

VI. Attraction of Foreign Direct Investment

Kritziner (2000) is of the opinion that RTAs may attract FDI both from within and outside the regional trade agreements as a result of market enlargement and product rationalization (reduced distortion and lower marginal cost in production). Enlarging a sub-regional market will also bring direct foreign investment, which will be beneficial provided that the incentive for foreign investors is not to engage in "tariff-jumping". This advocates for the necessity to reduce protection and more specifically external tariffs.

VII. Lock in to Domestic Reforms

Regional Trade Agreements (RTAs) work best as a commitment mechanism for trade policy. Kritzinger (2005) argued RTAs can also serve to lock the country into micro and macro-economic reforms or democracy if (i) those policies or rules are stipulated within the agreement (deeper integration arrangement), and (ii) underlying incentives have changed following the implementation of the RTA. RTAs may be an instrument for joint commitment to a reform agenda, but their effectiveness may be limited by low cost of exist and difficulties in implementing rules and administering punishment. In other words, RTAs strengthens internal economic policy. Exploiting the opportunities offered by regionalism and meeting its challenges demand a certain degree of macro-economic discipline as well as an appropriate foreign policy, in order to promote competitiveness and comparative advantage. There is a close reciprocal link between structural adjustment policies and economic liberalization on the one hand and regionalism, on the other. These two processes mutually nourish and strengthen each other in such a manner that progress is facilitated and the benefits multiply (Iglesias, 2000).

VIII. Encourage Monetary Stability as well as Financial Stability

When RTAs include monetary agreements (reserve funds, currency swaps, etc.) it lessens the member countries vulnerability to internal or external monetary and financial phenomenon. At the same time, greater financial stability has positive effects on the member countries and on international financial markets (on non-members) depending on the importance of regional integration program.

IX. Stimulate Peace and Security

RTA allows interest groups to form. Once they have won benefits from the widening of the market they are willing to offer political support to successive market enlargements. In other words they are geared towards multilateralism (Lizano, 2000). The similar views have been expressed by Polachek (1992), Kritzinger (2005) and Pal (2006). Polachek (1992) argued that entering RTAs may increase intra-regional trade and investment and also link countries in a web of positive interactions and interdependency. This is likely to build trust, raise the opportunity cost of war and hence reduce the risk of conflicts between countries (Pal, 2006). This gave importance to political factors for increasing regionalism. According to him, RTAs are used as a strategic move to consolidate peace and increase regional security among member countries. RTAs are often used by developed countries to forge geopolitical alliances and build up diplomatic ties. By providing increased discriminatory access to a large market these countries seek to garner increased support on political front. Kritzinger (2005) suggested that cooperation is extended to common defence or mutual military assistance, it will increase the global security.

X. More Bargaining Power and Coordination

RTAs became a real geopolitical instrument by increasing its member capacity to embark on negotiations with other countries or other integration schemes. Within the RTAs, coordination may be easier than through multilateral agreements since negotiation rule accustom countries to a give and take approach, which makes trade-offs between different policy areas possible. Since RTAs enable the member countries to coordinate their positions, they will stand in multilateral negotiations with at least more visibility and possibility stronger bargaining power (Lizano, 2000).

XI. Broader and Faster Agreements

Regionalism offers some significant advantages in the form of (i) faster progress, because reaching agreement in the WTO among more than a hundred countries with very disparate interests and viewpoints is much more difficult that reaching agreement among a small number, (ii) the programs are broader since they involve a variety of issues which are beyond commercial matter and it would be very difficult to include those issues on the multilateral agenda, and (iii) in regional agreements member countries often assume commitments that are broader than those assumed in the WTO (Lizano, 2000).

REGIONAL INTEGRATION : STUMBLING BLOCKS

I. Trade Diversion

Trade diversion will happen when the country with the comparative advantage is denied his comparative status. This runs counter to the general free trade and efficiency principles. It distorts the efficient allocation of resources. The inefficient producer within the RTA is artificially benefiting at the expense of the efficient producer outside of the RTA. Kim (2003) argued that additional gains from RTAs that are generated through trade creation are exaggerated because tariff rates on a whole have dramatically declined. Average tariff rates have dropped from 40% since World War II to less than 4% after the Uruguay Rounds in 1994. Similarly, the prospects for intra-regional trade expansion are not as good as imagined because of the similarity of natural endowments of countries within a given region. Usually coming from the same geographical regions, they do not have sufficient differences to benefit each other.

Viner (1950) also argued that regional schemes trigger trade diversion. This harms economic actors in the integration area by raising the cost of final and intermediate goods, since supply shifts from sources outside the area to others within it. This also harms non-member countries because they suffer losses as their exports to the members of the integration area decline.

Bhagwati (1995) and Panagariya (1996) are of the view that trade diversion is more likely to dominate trade creation in most situations. According to them, when trade is multilateral, i.e. when countries import from and export to union members as well as outside countries, trade diversion is inevitable. Also, if the members of the RTA are small in relation to the outside world, very little trade creation will take place. As a result, under these conditions, trade diversion is likely to be having more dominant effect. Actually, the negative effects of trade diversion assumes full employment if the assumption of full employment is relaxed, the welfare effects of trade diversion are ambiguous and may be even positive. In fact, research during the 1980s has shown that if the full employment and perfect competition assumption are relaxed, then trade models can lead to a totally different set of results than predicted by traditional models.

II. Deepens Factionalism

Regionalism is a direct threat to multilateralism. Trade liberalization might occur in a piecemeal fashion through RTAs, but will become a losing proposition in the end without a coordinated effort by all members. The few trading blocs that emerge from regionalism will become more stubborn (inflexible) to compromise. The larger a bloc becomes the more vested interests it has to represent, which makes it much more difficult to reach a general agreement. The EU is cited as an example but they are exceptional outliers because they share a unique symmetry in terms of size and resources and historical and political considerations. Countries that are lured to join RTAs will have little incentive to unilaterally push the RTA to expand. Larger the RTA becomes, the more it will seek to extract concession from the new parties.

Some countries as in those in Africa and Central Asia maintain two or more overlapping plurilateral RTAs at the same time. In addition to the difficulty of sustaining membership in two or more overlapping plurilateral RTAs, this could lead to the consolidation of RTAs and rationalization among participants who may be forced to align themselves with one or other regional grouping against their natural inclinations. Similarly, on a foreign policy level, regionalism leads countries to play favourites among their trading partners. Those that are excluded are abandoned and it therefore reduces international relations to a mutually self-destructive factionalism (Kim, 2003).

III. Slippery Slope of Exceptions

RTAs represent a second best option. The ultimate goal remains trade liberalization for all countries on a global basis. Yet, RTAs are the most conspicuous exception to one of the most important WTO obligation of MFN. If multilateral trade liberalization is our ultimate goal, then regional-based approaches merely delays this inevitable process. It exacts an unnecessary transaction cost because it acts as stumbling block on the way. The dedication of resources to the negotiation and maintenance of agreements at the regional level may obviously divert attention from negotiations that should clearly proceed at the multilateral level. RTAs grant a comprehensive exception from MFN covering all goods and services between the member countries involved, thus, weakening the stature and authority of the WTO and the commitment to multilateral problem-solving as a result (Kim, 2003). Bhagwati and Kruger (1995) are of the view that increased regionalism is dangerous because it not only leads to inter-bloc trade wars and domination of small countries by bigger partners in the regional blocs but also reduces the enthusiasm for participation in the multilateral trade regime.

IV. Spaghetti Bowl Problem

The proliferation of bilateral, sub-regional and regional trade agreements gradually creates a swarm (a large group of people especially when they are moving in same direction) of intertwined relationships (Spaghetti bowl). Their administration is very expensive and unmanageable, e.g. custom officials in developing countries face serious difficulties in determining the valuation of shirts from five or six countries with which their own country has trade agreements. The technical decision is not simple, because the rules of origin are based on such considerations as the value-added, the source of the raw materials and other inputs and the degree of processing. When this procedure has to be applied to hundreds of inputs, it is easy to imagine the enormous difficulties of customs administration in these countries from the view point of efficiency and the frequent lack of transparency (corruption) (Lizano, 2000). Bhagwati (1994) also argued that the growing number of RTAs may lead to a complex system of regulatory structures and preferences whereas market access for all products in one particular country will vary widely depending on their alleged origin. This phenomenon known the 'Spaghetti bowl' problem may lead to complexity and lack of transparency in the global trading system. Bhagwati and Panagariya (2003) argued that by pushing aggressive trade treaties on a bilateral basis, developed countries are weakening the power of developing countries in multilateral trade negotiations. In a PTA between a developed and a developing country, the developed country often manages to include aggressive trade liberalization clauses, investment protection clauses and extraneous issues in the treaty. Having abandoned objections about these issues on a bilateral level, the developing country cannot resist these issues on a multilateral platform. This not only help the developed countries push these issues in WTO, but it also breaks the alliance of developing countries in the multilateral negotiations (Pal, 2006).

V. Other Negative Effects

Moreover, there are other negative effects explained by Lizano (2000).

(i) RTAs do not meet its goals because the regional market, although enlarged remains too small to offer a satisfactory basis (economies of scale and agglomeration) for hastening economic development in the participating countries.

(ii) RTAs foster the formation of interest groups in the region. To defend their own interests, such groups will oppose the future enlargements of RTA, either through the accession of new members or through negotiations with other regional schemes. This places a sizable obstacle on the path leading from regionalism to multilateralism.

(iii) Human resources trained in trade negotiations are very scarce in most developing countries. In as much as those resources concentrate on the negotiation of bilateral, sub-regional or regional agreements, they have little time to attend to multilateral accords.

(iv) If regionalism is presented as an option that averts the cost of national protectionism and the risk of multilateralism there is a risks that political support of the countries involved will centre on regionalism. Consequently, multilateralism is downgraded to a subordinate and perhaps disregarded level since it lacks the necessary political support.

(v) Often, RTAs have failed to deliver the results expected of it. Indeed, the commitments assumed in regional and sub-regional agreements are frequently ignored in practice. The gap between the letter of the law and what actually happens is wide. This discredits the process of external opening and economic integration and being a poor example, it brings the idea of multilateralism into disrepute. Often, RTA programs are hostage to the members' domestic policies. The issue is sometimes used to divert attention from internal problems facing political leaders or in other circumstances, to strengthen the national political position of the ruling government. Many policy commitments are assumed despite the fact that it is known beforehand they will not be compiled with because they are incompatible with everyday circumstances.

In the light of above arguments it is worth concluding with the following points—

RTA is a fact and here to stay [Frankel (1997), Devlin and French Davis (1998)].

The current problems of RTAs must be resolved if the potential benefits of regionalism are to be realized. The main issues on which emphasis should be as follows:

Due attention should also be paid to the prospect of changing the rules, in at least three significant areas:

(i) To allow partial trade liberalization within the integration area and not to insist on the complete elimination of obstacles to intra-regional trade as the only possibility.

(ii) To make open access for non-member countries a condition for the approval of RTAs.

(iii) To establish a set of instructions of the regional scheme's common external tariff, on the basis of lowest rate among the member countries.

There must be a permanent endeavor for reducing the cost of trade diversion. For this, there is a need of continuing the process of unilateral commercial opening. In many countries, there is still appreciable scope for continuing with such policies. This gradually becomes a significant requirement if RTAs are to work effectively and move forward. A certain degree of 'spontaneous' harmonization occurs over time. There is a broad scope for moving towards "managed" harmonization. This is related to macro-economic policy issues (monetary and exchange rate policies), fiscal and tax policies, strategies to attract foreign investment. In view of the varying development levels of the member countries, policy harmonization generally becomes a process of gradual convergence within which some countries meet the goals faster than others. RTAs are not viable if they benefit only some member countries, in such a case they have not future. Until recently, RTAs were basically geared to cutting the tariffs on intra-zone trade and establishing a common external tariff (old regionalism). Today the aim is to faster "open regionalism". This entails a substantial expansion of the issue areas covered by integration schemes and the inclusion of three different but closely related areas: (i) economic issue, (ii) political issues, (iii) environmental and other issues. This will increase the potential benefits of RTA though measures that simultaneously combine integration, cooperation and regional inter-dependence (Lizano, 2000).

Thus various studies show road ahead is long and complicated. The obstacles and difficulties in the form of political, social, economic and cultural are numerous. There can be no doubt that it is very tough to determine the most appropriate solution and decide on the best way to put them into practice.

Historically, the "old" regionalism failed to deliver the results expected of it because : (i) RTAs were part of an import substitution development model and the prospects of success were light; (ii) RTAs were generally limited to intra-zone tariff reduction and the external tariff; and (iii) the member countries often failed to comply with the stipulations of RTAs.

However, open regionalism offers more encouraging prospects. It is more encouraging because : (i) there are not "closed" programs but rather as the name implies, they are outward-oriented, open and seek insertion in the international economy, (ii) such regionalism takes account of the negative experiences of national experiences of national protectionism and of the "old" regionalism, and (iii) it bears in mind the vast current difficulties in moving towards multilateralism (Lizano, 2000).

Thus, it is a matter of globalizing regionalism rather than of regionalizing globalization.

3

SAARC and Regional Integration Schemes

Studies Made

This chapter reviews empirical studies relating to different aspects of various regional integrations. For this purpose, chapter has been divided into two sections. First section reviews the studies of SAARC region and SAARC members. Second section covers the studies of regional integration schemes other than SAARC.

I

Jayarama (1978) estimated effects of integration in the Indian sub-continent in terms of static effects of a hypothetical custom union by using partial equilibrium approach. The results revealed that hypothetical custom union in the Indian sub-continent proves beneficial only under one common lowest pre-union external tariff rate among all countries for each Standard International Trade Classification (SITC) section. However, the trade gain happened to be of small magnitude (i.e. less than one percent of the total GNP of the countries involved). While for individual countries, the gains are slightly over one percent (for Bangladesh and Sri Lanka). They are well below one percent in the case of other three members (India, Nepal and Pakistan).

Ram (1979) examined only static effects of the South Asian custom union by taking the assumption that tariffs are the only barrier to trade. The study revealed that complementarities among South Asian countries were low and the establishment of joint projects in certain areas would create conditions for complementarities.

Rahman (1980) estimated the static benefits in the context of a custom union of Pakistan, Bangladesh, India and Sri Lanka. The study showed that region as a whole would drive welfare gains to the extent of only 0.07 percent of total regional income. Thus, the study concluded that static benefits are of little relevance in the context of developing countries and it is the dynamic benefit of trade liberalization which increased growth of their national incomes.

Reddy and Devi (1984) analyzed revealed comparative advantage among the South Asian countries and identified complementarities among the South Asian countries during the period 1973-78. The Study concluded that competition among the South Asian countries was restricted to mainly agricultural and agro-based manufacturing processes. Pakistan was the main competitor to India for chemical, basic manufactures and machines and transport equipment. In the sphere of machinery and transport equipment, India dominated among other South Asian countries. On the basis of revealed comparative advantage among the South Asian countries the study revealed that these countries do not possess a diversified trade structure.

Naqvi (1986) explored the possibilities of intra-regional trade expansion among Pakistan, India, Bangladesh and Sri Lanka with the help of econometric trade model. The study showed that some policy actions resulted in the expansion of intra-regional trade as well as the growth of the GNP of member countries during the study period (1975-84).

Modwel and Pandey (1987) analyzed the possibilities of expansion and diversification between SAARC and ASEAN during the period 1980-85. The study found that the intra-ASEAN-SAARC proportions in total exports and imports of the countries had improved slightly from 17.6 percent and 13.1 percent in 1980 to 18.0 percent and 14.9 percent in 1985 respectively. According to the study, the complementarities in different economies of the region had increased because of the varying pace and patterns of industrialization. Due to the existence of complementarities in different countries of the region, mostly SAARC-ASEAN countries depend on outside sources for meeting their requirements. Therefore, the study suggested that lower trade barriers should be made within the region. Product by product targets must also be set within the region.

Ahuja and Bhattacharya (1989) examined the potential for economic cooperation among South Asian and ASEAN countries during the period 1980-84 by using trade complementarity index of these economies. The study revealed that overall trade complementarity index among these economies had been generally low, i.e. (0.4). Nepal and Pakistan had the index values greater than 0.4. Therefore, the study suggested that there is a need to coordinate and plan investment and production activities in these countries in such a way so as to generate stronger trade complementarity over the long-run.

Debroy (1989) analyzed the potential of intra-regional trade in the SAARC region during the period 1972-86 by using simple regression model. The study revealed that intra-regional trade within the SAARC region accounted for a very small proportion of total trade flows. There was high instability of India's exports to Bangladesh and Sri Lanka. Pakistan's exports to the world displayed a high degree of instability. Sri Lanka exports to Bangladesh, Bangladesh's exports to India and Nepal and Nepal's exports to India and Pakistan displayed a higher degree of instability during the study period. The study suggested that there must be harmonization and coordination of trade policies and coordination to boost intra-regional trade.

Devi (1989) assessed how trade liberalization would affect the trade structure of South Asian countries in case of economic cooperation among them by using the concept of comparative advantage. The study indicated that India had nearest competition in several items of SITC sections 7 and 8. India's non-traditional exports have obtained high rankings indicating superiority over the other countries in the region, and traditional exports (except iron ore, tobacco and coffee) have got low rankings indicating that smaller countries have advantage in these items.

Chawla (1991) examined the effects of two integration schemes namely SAARC and ASEAN on the volume of intra-regional trade by means of gravity model of trade for the years 1972, 1976, 1978 and 1984. The study revealed that effects of trade preference on integration were influenced by the level of development of integrating countries. The effect of per capita income was significant for all the years of the study. The study concluded that SAARC countries were immune to external factors than ASEAN countries indicating that SAARC region have greater potential of effective integration than the ASEAN. Although, the potential and prospects of intra-regional trade was enormous in SAARC region but the share of intra-regional trade to total world trade was minimal. It was only 3.56 percent in the case of exports and 1.97 percent in the case of imports for the year 1986.

Aggarwal and Pandey (1992) explored the prospects of trade expansion in the South Asian region during the period 1970-90. The study revealed that food items dominated the intra-regional trade compared to other categories of goods during the study period. Low level of intra-regional trade in the SAARC region is due to inward-oriented import substitution policies and a high level of tariff and non-tariff barriers. The study suggested that intra-regional countries in the region have reduced the trade barriers and other government interventions in the production structure.

Srinivasan (1994) examined the benefits of regional integration (SAARC) by using gravity model. The study suggested that unilateral trade liberalization, rather than preferential liberalization would yield the greatest trade gain for the region. The small economies of the region would gain more from the region integration and also from intra-regional trade liberalization with other regions. It projected that effect of removing all tariffs, combined with low transportation costs would be to increase the total trade between 3 percent of GDP for India, 21 percent for Bangladesh and 59 percent for Nepal.

Bhattacharya and Mukhopadhyay (1996) studied the perspectives and consequences of total abolition of tariffs by

India on the goods importing from the SAARC's member countries as a preferential treatment during the period 1985 to 1996. The study revealed that major export products of India to SAARC countries were in the category of primary products. The study estimated that aggregate revenue loss on account of custom duty was Rs. 1434.3 million in 1995-96 by applying duty free access to all imports from SAARC countries. The study suggested that elimination of tariffs would most probably increase the competitiveness of products which currently are not being exported by the SAARC countries to India.

World Bank (1997) analyzed the static welfare consequences of preferential liberalization of SAARC economy by using an integrated general equilibrium model. The study revealed that regional trade liberalization would increase the welfare between 0.5 percent of GDP for India and one percent for rest of South Asia. The welfare gains from regional liberalization are the sum of trade creation effects (increased trade between countries in the region) from lower barriers minus trade diversion losses caused by replacing non-South Asian imports with non-preferred South Asian goods plus the terms of trade gains associated with increased access to each other's still protected markets. The benefits to the rest of South Asia were larger than to India because the former gained free access to many highly protected markets of latter which resulted in a significant improvement in terms of trade.

Chaudhri (1997) examined whether SAARC region (India, Pakistan, Bangladesh and Sri Lanka) was helping to achieve a long-run relationship between exchange rate and price level by taking a monthly data from June 1973 to December 1993. Author has used both US and India as base country to examine whether regional integration is helpful to establish 'PPP' (Purchasing Power Parity). The study revealed that though regional integration is helping to attain in a long-run relationship, but it does not necessarily improve the presence of PPP significantly between countries in SAARC. Trade barriers, transportation costs as well as presence of real shocks could be some of the plausible reasons for these outcomes.

Mukherji (1997) measured the structural changes in India's exports to the SAARC region during the period 1990-91 to 1994-95. The share of textiles and textile products remained predominant at nearly 29 percent, while that of primary products declined marginally to 8.5 percent during the study period. The share of value-added manufactured products remained more or less the same. The only change to be seen was decline in the share of machinery and an increasing share of basic metals reflecting an increasing share of intermediate capital goods exports to meet the growing aspiration for industrialization in South Asian countries.

Banik (1998) examined growth prospects of India's exports to Sri Lanka during the pre-liberalization period (1985-90) and post-liberalization period (1990-95). The study revealed that there is a wide scope of trade expansion as Indian exports featured both high income and price elasticity. Low supply had highlighted the need for diversification from traditional Indian exports to non-traditional Indian exports and towards unexplored pockets of Sri Lanka market.

Madaan (1998) studied the trade relations between SAARC members during the period 1975-95. The study revealed that India's trade with SAARC was only 2.8 percent. However, it was 8.6 percent for Bangladesh and 1.1 percent for Maldives. The study revealed that Bangladesh was experiencing trade deficit in SAARC. Among the SAARC countries, India and Pakistan had been the major trading partners with Sri Lanka. Pakistan's trade with SAARC has declined over the period due to the restrictive trade policies. The study suggested promotion of exports through its diversification to improve trade among SAARC members.

Upadhyaya (1998) examined the effect of devaluation in eliminating the trade deficits in four South Asian countries, namely: India, Pakistan, Nepal and Srilanka by fitting linear regression model in the first difference form for the period 1963 to 1993. The study revealed that a domestic income did not have a significant effect on the trade balance in India, Nepal and Sri Lanka. Rising domestic income deteriorated the trade balance in Pakistan. Foreign income was not significant in explaining the change in the trade balance in India, Pakistan and Sri Lanka. In case of Nepal, it carried a negative and a significant coefficient, i.e. an increase in foreign real output led to higher level of import to Nepal. Devaluations did not improve the trade balance in the long-run in any of the country under study.

Chaudhary and Kiyoshi (2000) reviewed and analyzed trade policies and linkages between Pakistan, Japan and ASEAN trade. Pakistan's trade relations with Japan were strong when Japan provided aid to Pakistan due to deficit trade account of Pakistan with Japan. But when Japanese investment in Pakistan started to remain limited, their relations weakened. Therefore, the study suggested that Japan should invest in the areas of agriculture, electronics, textile and food processing industries, energy, etc. Japanese surplus capital and management should explore possibilities of cheap labour, raw material and energy in Pakistan. It can manufacture cheaply in Pakistan and export to other countries.

Ghuman and Madaan (2000) analysed and discussed the emerging trends of Indo-SAARC trade Scenario during 1975-95. The study revealed that India's exports to SAARC countries as well to the world registered an upward trend both in pre-SAARC and post-SAARC period. The study also highlighted the basic fact that India's capacity of exports to SAARC was much higher than the SAARC's capacity of exports to India. During the pre-SAARC period, the growth rate of India's total trade with SAARC has been lower than that of its global trade. However, during the post-SAARC era, the situation got reversed. From the view point of intra-SAARC trade, India was the major exporter and minor importer as her share in intra-regional SAARC exports was more than 3 times than that of imports during 1975-95. India's exports for each member of SAARC had been higher than her imports from them. Consequently, trade balances of India with these countries had been by and large favourable to India. By estimating the gains from trade of India with SAARC countries, the study revealed that India had been a net gainer with its trade with SAARC countries and enjoyed more favourable terms of trade with SAARC countries than with the world. India's balance of trade with almost all the SAARC countries had been highly favourable except the Pakistan throughout the period under study.

Guru Gharana (2000) explained the macro-economic structure of South Asian economies and costs and benefits of increased economic integration in the region during the period 1979 to 1996 by using common macro-econometric framework.

The study revealed that wealth effect had not clearly been reflected in capital and money markets. The study simulated that South Asian countries would be dramatically benefitted by following intra-SAARC trade expansion and other prudent expansion and of the prudent macro-policies such as population control, increased foreign assistance, increased bank credit to private sector, increased FDI, etc. Therefore, study suggested that increased economic integration should not emphasize free trade and SAFTA but also include analysis of increased intra-regional private investment and increased mobility of labour and capital.

Hassan (2001) estimated a gravity model of international trade in case of SAARC to examine whether intra-SAARC is lower or higher than what is predicted by an economic model for the year 1996 and 1997. The results suggested that SAARC member countries are yet to achieve trade creating benefits. Liberalization of trade in SAARC offered significant gains for all the economies in the region. Efforts should be made to liberalize border trade and strengthen bilateral trade relations through the removal of tariff and non-tariff barriers in SAFTA.

Majumdar and Chakraborthy (2001) compared the production structures of selected SAARC countries (India, Bangladesh, Pakistan and Sri Lanka) by taking data of India (1991-92), Bangladesh (1992-93), Sri Lanka (1986) and Pakistan (1989-90) by using input-output table technique. The study concluded that a similarity in the structures of production existed between India, Bangladesh and Pakistan, but to a greater extent between India and Pakistan. India-Pakistan would be regarded as most comparable pair of countries. Sri Lanka was the least comparable country comparing to other three economies. A country-wise study showed that India-Pakistan were the most similar in respect of all sectors except rice, metal products, non-metal mineral products, other manufacturing, trade and transport and services. On the other hand, Bangladesh-Sri Lanka, Pakistan-Sri Lanka and India-Sri Lanka were most dissimilar in comparison of input coefficients. There was maximum number of sectors for which the pattern of inter-industry use was most similar, while for Sri Lanka when paired with other three economies, this was minimum. There was existence of a relatively stronger similarity in inter-country production structures regarding the pattern of intermediate use of commodities and input coefficients between India and Pakistan while Sri Lanka was totally incomparable with the rest of the economies. Bangladesh to greater extent was comparable with India and Pakistan in their structure of production.

Ahmed (2002) investigated the issue of multivariate causality among money, interest rates, prices and output in selected SAARC economies namely, Bangladesh, India and Pakistan in a multivariate framework. The study revealed that interest rate deserved to be a good policy variable in Bangladesh and Pakistan while money deserved to be a good policy variable in India. A bi-directional causality existed between money and prices in Bangladesh and Pakistan. Interest rate and money affected output in Bangladesh at 6 percent and 7 percent level of significance. So monetary policy played a role in output determination in Bangladesh. But this was not the case in other two countries. Block causality tests for Bangladesh showed that interest rate and money affected output and price as a block. But output and price did not affect interest rate and money. The situation was reversed for India and Pakistan. The role of monetary policy was more obvious in Bangladesh compared to India and Pakistan.

Nori and Patnaik (2002) studied the synchronization between the SAARC and European Union during the period 1980 to 2000. The study showed that SAARC countries had been exporting mainly to EU countries in comparison to other industrialized countries like USA and Japan. Though SAARC countries were taking advantage with the EU's offer of special preferences and increasing the market access to EU countries. However, the SAARC region could not be benefited due to restrictive trade policies of EU.

Hirantha (2003) evaluated the performance of SAARC regional economic grouping under SAFTA by applying the gravity model analysis during the period 1996-2002. The study revealed that there was trade creation in the region under SAPTA with no trade diversion during the study period. The study supported the proposition that further regional integration may bring about substantial benefits to SAARC region and SAFTA (South Asian Free Trade Area) is most likely to promote intra-regional trade through further dismantling of tariff and other non-tariff barriers to trade among members.

Sarkar (2003) quantified the impact of duty free access of India's market to the SAARC economies. The study found that if India gives free access to other members, it would lose non-significant revenues but significant positive impact on exports to member countries. Pakistan, the second largest economy in the SAARC, in terms of share in total export of individual SAARC countries would provide highest gain to Nepal. The study concluded that such policy would leave very little impact in the share of India's imports originating from SAARC in India's total global import. SAFTA alone is not sufficient to solve to problems of low-level of intra-SAARC trade as well as huge trade deficit of other SAARC countries.

Sriwardna (2003) explored two plausible trade policy scenarios for free trade on South Asia: the establishment of Free Trade Area (FTA) and a Custom Union. The study quantified the effects of these two alternatives for the region by simulation GTAP (Global Trade Analysis Project) model for the period 1980-2000. The study revealed that trade liberalization benefits South Asian Countries in terms of both GDP and welfare gains. The extent of the benefits varied among the members with Sri Lanka appearing to reap the most in both scenarios. The gains for all economies in the regions had markedly increased under a custom union although India stood to gain the least in relative terms. Due to the FTA, the effects of trade creation were likely to outweigh the effects of trade diversion leading to a net expansion of trade in the entire region. Under a custom union, both trade creation and trade diversion would bring positive outcomes with the effect of trade diversion dominating the net expansion in trade. The study suggested that neither FTA nor a custom union in South Asia would have a discernible impact on non-member countries.

Amjad and Khan (2004) reviewed the prospects of extended economic cooperation of Pakistan with the member countries of South Asian Association for regional cooperation (SAARC) during the period 1972-2001. They used the two stage least square method and found that external sector was having important influences on growth in the SAARC region countries during the study period. There was positive relationship between economic growth (GDP) and investment in the SAARC region. The study also projected the growth of the major destinations of Pakistan's exports during the study period.

Batra (2004) estimated global trade potential for India using the OLS technique for the year 2000. The study revealed that the magnitude of India's trade potential was highest with Asia-Pacific region followed by Western Europe and North America. Countries like China, United Kingdom, Italy and France revealed maximum potential for expansion of trade with India. Among specific country groupings trade arrangements, India's trade potential was revealed as highest with Pakistan in SAARC and with Philippines and Cambodia in the ASEAN for year 2000.

Bhattacharya (2004) outlined the broad trading pattern and analysed the transition from SAPTA's to SAFTA between India and Bangladesh. The study used gravity model by taking data from 1995-96 to 2001-02 and also simulated the increase in India-Bangladesh bilateral trade under four hypothetical scenarios under differing tariff rate cuts. The study revealed that coverage ratio was much higher in SAPTA III than the earlier two rounds. This was due to the replacement of the sector approach by commodity approach. Complete removal of tariff had a significant impact on India's exports to Bangladesh both in value and percentage terms. But it was not at all that significant for Bangladesh's exports to India because of their very low base value. Therefore, other factors like non-tariff barriers, marketing, and technology upgradation, product diversification and change in the commodity composition of exports should be taken into account. Interactions with several Bangladeshi exporters and manufacturers revealed that their exports were not essentially perturbed by India's tariff. In some goods, this was obviously high; the removal of high tariffs or duty free trade would certainly help them to get market access in India.

Bhattacharyya and Benerjee (2004) applied the gravity model to the panel consisting of India's yearly bilateral trade data with all its trading partners in the second half of twentieth century. The study revealed that gravity model can explain around 43 percent of the fluctuations in India's direction of trade. India's trade responds less than proportionally to size and more than proportionally to distance. India trades more with developed rather than developing countries. Size has more determining influence on India's trade than the level of development of the trading partner.

Joshi et al (2004) examined the extent, nature and speed of agricultural diversification, identified determinants of agricultural diversification and assessed implications of agricultural diversification on food security, employment and sustainable use of natural resources in South Asian Countries (Bangladesh, India, Pakistan, Sri Lanka, Bhutan, Nepal in general and India in particular) during the period 1981-82 to 1998-99. The study revealed that agricultural sector in South Asia was gradually diversifying in favour of high value commodities namely, fruits, vegetables and live stock and fish value products. Countries like Bangladesh, India and Sri Lanka had achieved food self-sufficiency at the national level, but the emphasis was still on increasing production of rice and wheat. Countries like Bhutan, Nepal and Pakistan which are still deficit in foodgrain production are making serious attempts in augmenting their production. During 1980s, the production of high value commodities was attributed to rise in their yield level and during 1990s, the production increase of these commodities came from area augmentation. By using generalised least square method to estimate the determinants of diversification of agriculture in India, the study revealed that markets and roads were the key determinants. Higher the technology in adoption of cereals (particularly irrigation) less was the diversification in favour of high value commodities. Diversification in favour of horticultural and live stock commodities was more pronounced in rainfed areas, which were by-passed during the green revolution but now could take advantage of agricultural diversification. The study also confirmed that the regions which were diversifying in favour of non-cereals, had accomplished better growth performance as compared to those specialising in cereals. Besides, relative profitability of high-value commodities in relations to other crops also played important role in determining status of diversification. This calls for strengthening R and D effects for improving the productivity in a sustainable manner. Food security was not adversely affected as a consequence of agricultural diversification. High-value crops had substantial potential for generating employment opportunities and also witnessed good performance in the international trade.

Musleh-ud Din (2004) examined the export-led growth hypothesis for the five largest economies of South Asian region using a multivariate time series framework during the period 1960-2002. The study found long-run equilibrium relationship among exports, imports and output for Bangladesh and Pakistan. However, for India, Nepal and Sri Lanka, no evidence of a long-run relationship among the relevant variables was found.

Nanda and Raikhy (2004) analyzed trends between India and SAARC during the study period 1990-97 to 2002-03. The study revealed that India's volume of trade was very low with SAARC countries (merely 5 percent of India's total trade). India had favourable trade balance with SAARC region (except Nepal). But other members also want to have balance trade with India in the era of multilateral trade. Therefore, the study suggested that India as well as other SAARC members should try to identify more and more items which India can import (especially the items which involve low transport and transshipment costs).

Sarkar (2004) constructed a suitable trade linkage system for SAARC, presented the impact of SAFTA on member's countries and studied the trade relation with non-SAARC countries during the period 1976-97. The study revealed that trade linkage system for SAARC had performed very well. Price did not play an important role in intra-SAARC trade flows except India. The bilateral export equations in the trade link sub-system had registered relatively lower value of R^2 than that in the direct linkage bloc. The reasons could be attributed towards the dominant non-economic factors rather than economic factors in the determination of intra-SAARC trade.

Sarkar (2004) constructed a trade linkage model for SAARC countries with ASEAN region during the period 1980-97 by trade allocation approach. The results showed that an expenditure effect (imports) on foreign commodity demand was positive in most cases. The ASEAN financial crisis led to its adverse impact on ASEAN imports. As the market in ASEAN region shrinked, the adverse impact of ASEAN crisis did not remain just within the region but even in the SAARC region.

The adverse impact of the ASEAN currency crisis on the SAARC region was significant.

Chowdhury (2005) measured the intra and international trade competitiveness for SAARC nations by calculating real exchange rate indices of during 1960-2000. The study revealed that smaller countries namely, Bangladesh and Sri Lanka reap higher gains from openness, whereas trade with other international partners, it took India and Bangladesh to gain international competitiveness until mid-1990s. Pakistan and Sri Lanka trade liberalization efforts did not seen to have much positive impact in terms of international trade.

Rahman (2005) examined the macro-economic structure of SAARC countries viz. Bangladesh, India, Nepal, Pakistan and Sri Lanka and also explored the possibilities of trade expansion among these countries by examining macro-economic and regional trade link models based on time series data of 28 years. The study concluded that there were inter -country differences in production and consumption patterns, investment behaviour and tax and non-tax structure in the SAARC countries. Hence, there is a considerable scope for trade expansion among the SAARC countries based on comparative advantages. The study also confirmed that aggregate regional consumption and regional GNP increased significantly with the increase of aggregate regional trade. The study also explored that the GNP of Bangladesh, Nepal, Pakistan and Sri Lanka with limited exceptions significantly increased with the increase in their exports to the region. So these countries would definitely be benefited from the regional trade expansion. The same may be true for India if the smuggled trend is prevented or reduced.

Sikdar (2005) evaluated the prospects of bilateral trade between India and Bangladesh during the period 1980 to 2004. The study measured trade intensity, revealed comparative advantage and trade complementarity indices of two countries. The study revealed that India has some potential to meet Bangladesh's import demand, as there has been a clear lack of such potential on the part of Bangladesh over the last two decades. This appears not only to goods in which the individual economy is endowed with revealed comparative advantage but to overall trade also, as reflected by trade complementarity indices. The study concluded that actual prospects of such a trading arrangement would seem to have a rather limited scope.

Boillot and Labbouz (2006) studied the trends in trade relations between India and China and their implications for the future configuration of world trade by using gravity model during the period 1981 to 2003. The study tested two scenarios. The continuation of the bilateral trade expansion between the two economies or the end of the catching up process and the emergence of a joint "India and China" upsurge at the world level. The latter hypothesis appeared more probable considering the models of specialisation and industrial transformation followed by the two countries at both the micro and macro-economic level. The study projected that as China is largely ahead of India therefore there would be a somewhat insignificant India–China bilateral flow at the world level.

Nag and Nandi (2006) explored India's trade dynamics in the SAARC region by using gravity model during 1990-2000. The study found that GDP and per capita GDP were positively related to India's exports. Exchange rate depreciation with respect to other countries gives a positive boost to its exports. India's relative export price with respect to world exports price negatively affected India's exports showing that India's exports are competitive. The study suggested that in spite of increasing trade complementarity between SAARC members, the members can be identified only moderately as natural trading partners. This validates the scope of simmering trade potentiality of SAFTA.

Verma (2006) examined the growth profile and economic outlook of India and Pakistan during the period 2000-05. The study revealed that volume of official trade in both the nations had been extremely low whereas the volume of unofficial trade between them had been 5-6 times the official trade during the study period. Pakistan benefited more by opening land route for Pak-India trade. Therefore, the study suggested that the opening of rail route would bring dividends only, if more rail wagons are permitted. Both the countries can benefit through bilateral trade.

Basu and Datta (2007) analyzed the reasons behind persistent bilateral trade deficit of Bangladesh with India. The study used different trade-related indices like RCA and cosine measures (Panchmukhi, 1995) to examine the extent of trade similarity and complementarity in inter-industry bilateral trade and Grubel Liyod (G-L) indices to examine intra-industry trade between the two countries during the period 1976-2001. The study revealed that Bangladesh had export similarity with India and hence faces high export competitiveness. The mismatch between Bangladesh export and Indian import generated a constraint of complementarity. The study also tried to identify the determinants of Bangladesh bilateral export and trade deficit by using an econometric time series analysis. The study found that export was to be of random nature and trade deficit had a perverse relation with exchange rate driven by flow of remittances. The study suggested that Bangladesh should pursue an appropriate exchange rate policy and aimed at increased diversification in its export structure in order to reduce bilateral trade deficit.

Chadha and Partap (2007) analysed the impact of South Asian free trade agreement during the period 2000-05 by using general equilibrium modeling package model. The study analysed the hypothetical welfare impact when more and more Asian countries joined the ASEAN FTA thus moving towards PAFTA (A Pan Asian Free Trade Agreement). The study revealed that the gains were larger under open regionalism as compared to preferential regionalism. Open trade liberalization had the impact on the economic welfare and real return to labour and capital in both industrialized and developing countries of the world. The study also revealed that welfare gains were considerably smaller than the ones resulting from multilateral trade liberalization.

Kannan and Mukherjee (2007) explored whether the East and South East Asian region including India is suitable to form an optimum currency area. The study examined the feasibility of the formation of an Asian common currency area (ACCA) in terms of some stylized facts during the period 1975-2004. The study revealed that there were variations in the size of the economy, stages of development, growth performance, inflation performance, degree of openness and other external sector factors among the ACCA group members. Therefore, the study concluded that the group has to go a long way towards the synchronization of their economies for a successful integration into an optimum currency area. The study suggested that India would gain from joining such union in terms of greater trade and financial integration with the rest of the Asia.

Sikdar (2008) analyzed the possibilities of bilateral trade between India and the EU during the period 1995-2003 by using linear programming approach and revealed comparative advantage index. The study revealed that India had consistently comparative advantage for goods like food, textile, non-metallic minerals and miscellaneous manufacturing over the entire study period while EU had comparative advantage in production of textiles and machines

II

Brada and Mendez (1985) examined six integration schemes and decomposed their ability to increase inter-member trade into environmental policy and system effects during the period 1960 to 1980. The study concluded that environmental factors and distance between the member countries were the most important factors. Central American Common Market (CACM) and The European Free Trade Area (EFTA) had followed more effective integration policies than the European Economic Community (EEC), (Latin American Free Trade Area) LAFTA and the Andean Pact.

Fayez (1986) examined Saudi Arabia's trade relationships with the European Economic Community during the period 1966-82 by using simple regression model. The study found that Saudi Arabia's total imports from the EEC countries increased at a faster rate during the period of the study than the rate of increase of the EEC imports. Saudi Arabia seemed to depend mainly on their industrial production and her imports from the EEC countries depended mainly on gross domestic product. The study suggested that trade between Saudi Arabia and the EEC countries could be encouraged through bilateral economic agreements.

Brada and Mendez (1988) examined two dynamic effects of regional economic integration viz. higher levels of investment and faster factor productivity growth of six integration schemes, i.e. European Economic Integration (EEC), The European Free Trade Area (EFTA), Latin American Free Trade Area (LAFTA), Central American Common Market (CACM), The East African

Common Market (EACM) and The Council of Mutual Economic Assistance (CMEA) for the period 1951-77. The study revealed that faster productivity effects were found only in LAFTA and CMEA; while investment levels increased in all regional groups except the CMEA, the cumulative impact of these dynamic effects was no more than 1% of members GNP. Consequently, the dynamic effects of integration could not explain rapid rates of growth experienced by members of some integration schemes nor could they serve as a rationale for integration.

Kreinin and Plummer (1992) measured the structural changes in East Asia by computing RCA and Spearman rank correlation coefficient for the year 1990. The study revealed that there were sizeable changes in the structural patterns of East Asian trade with the world. The manufacturing sector had been restructured at a faster pace than primary commodities. Intra-regional trade had been changing more rapidly than global trade. The study also highlighted the upgrading of these economies as they moved from strictly labour-intensive and material-based exports to more sophisticated and diverse products. An evaluation of dynamic changes in comparative advantage revealed a rapid movement toward the production of more sophisticated production in East Asia.

Braga et. al. (1994) quantified NAFTA's impact on non-members by using a partial equilibrium trade model and a gravity model during period 1970 to 1990. The study revealed that the NAFTA-induced trade diversion losses could range from $ 380 million to $ 700 million. Losses are concentrated in a few sectors such as textiles, clothing and ferrous metals—where high U.S. trade barriers existed. A larger share of Hong Kong and Macau China trade would be diverted than trade in other East Asian Economies because textile and clothing represented a larger share of their exports. Economies like Singapore specializing in products as machinery and equipment had relatively little trade diversion. East Asia's trade losses might be reduced by roughly half, once the results of the Uruguay Round were implemented because that would lower the preference margins which NAFTA members could extend to each other.

Jha (1996) analysed the trends in and prospectus for intra-regional trade in selected countries of Asia since 1980. Countries included were Japan, People's Republic of China (PRC); The NIEs (Newly Industrializing Economies); South East Asia (Indonesia, Malaysia, Philippines and Thailand) and South Asia (Bangladesh, India, Pakistan and Sri Lanka). Intra-Asian trade's share in total trade of Asia had been increasing steadily. By the early 1990's, Intra-Asian trade dominated in total trade of Asia. There was a great deal of variation among Asian countries in terms of integration within the region. While in absolute terms, Japan and NIEs dominated the intra-Asian trade and in relative terms, intra-Asian trade was more important to South East Asia, PRC and the NIEs than to Japan and South Asia. The study also explained the reasons for rapid intra-regional trade growth in Asia. The study pointed out the Intra-Asian trade was generated from the economic complementarity among the Asian Countries and was closely linked to the dynamism of real output growth in the region. The outward-looking trade liberalization policy adopted by Asian countries and the protectionist policies in the industrialized countries had played the most important role in stimulating trade in Asia. Moreover, intra-regional direct investment flows had complemented and reinforced the growth of intra-regional trade within Asia by building up export capability of the host countries on one hand and by directly increasing machinery imports from the capital exporting countries. It was noted that much of the expansion of intra-Asian trade had been an intra-industrial trade. Regional economic cooperation had also contributed to prosperity in the region and created large intra-regional trade and capital flows. The growth triangle type of sub-regional co-operation could be a strong stimulus for Asian trade in near future. Asian economies could not sustain their prevailing growth rates if protectionist policies were followed in the major world markets.

Vlachos (1996) examined the interaction between the Australian economy and economies of the individual members of the ASEAN (Indonesia, Malaysia, Philippines, Singapore and Thailand) during the period 1972-92. The study used the method of two stage least square for estimating the simultaneous equations. The study revealed that trade between Australia and ASEAN had grown significantly particularly over the past six years. Australian exports to members of the ASEAN were strongly influenced by the income of these members.

Australian relative prices were an important determinant of Australian exports to the ASEAN. This implies that Australia's trade relationship with members of the region would be improved if Australia achieved a better competitive position in international markets. ASEAN imports of Australian products were affected by a partial adjustment process with respect to income and prices. Therefore, changes in income and prices would likely to influence these imports for long periods of time. The income of Australia had a significant influence on Australian imports from each member of the alliance.

Francis and Yeats (1997) examined the East Asia's implications for regional cooperation and growth. The study revealed that East Asian intra-trade had a major positive influence on regional cooperation and growth. Since the mid-1980s, East Asian intra-trade has been growing at a rate roughly double than that of world trade and at a rate far higher than the intra-trade of NAFTA and the European Union. Similarly, evidence based on intra-industry trade ratios or statistics on international production sharing showed that economic linkages and the inter-dependence of East Asian economies have considerably been strengthened. Furthermore, the export and import profiles of East Asian countries had been changing in directions that increase complementarity which further increased the potential for intra-regional trade. China's emergence had a major positive influence on the region. Specifically China's internal counter cyclical policies and its maintenance of a stable exchange rate were generally viewed as important factors that helped to contain the effects of Asian financial crisis.

Goto (1997) analysed the economic impact of regional integration (EC) on agricultural trade by using a simple Krugman-type model with product differentiations during 1971-95. The study derived two propositions of regionalism about impact on trade flows. Firstly, the higher the degree of pre-integration protection, the greater the impact of regional integration and secondly, the lower the degree of product differentiation, greater the impact of regional integration. Taken together the two propositions predicted that regionalism had more impact on agricultural trade than on manufacturing because the initial level of protection is higher and the degree of product differentiation is lower for agricultural products. The study tested these propositions against actual data for two incidents of EC expansion: Greece's admission to the European Community in 1981 and that of Spain and Portugal in 1986. The data generally supported the theory. After the theoretical and *ex-post* analysis, Goto applied the model to examine the possible ex-ante impact of the APEC free trade agreement on Japanese rice imports. The results suggested that impact of partial liberalization of Japan's rice market would be relatively minor, but total liberalization would have a profound impact on Japanese rice production.

Pomfort (1997) discussed the prospects for regional integration within Economic Cooperation Organization (ECO). The study revealed that trade between the new land locked ECO members and three original members would increase due to improvement in transport links. There are practical difficulties of establishing preferential trading regime within ECO. Therefore, the study suggested that ECO members must continue their unilateral liberalization.

Venables (1997) examined benefits and costs of a free trade area among members' countries, based their analysis on member countries comparative advantage relative to all and to the rest of the world by applying generalized H-O model. The study revealed that free trade agreements between low income countries led to divergence in member country incomes, while agreements between high income countries led to convergence. Changes induced by comparative advantage might be amplified by the effect of agglomeration. The results suggested that developing countries may be better served by 'North-South' than by 'South-South' free trade agreements because 'North-South' agreements increased their prospects for convergence with high income members of the free trade area.

Yeats (1997) examined trade patterns in the MERCOSUR countries (Argentina, Brazil, Paraguay and Uruguay) over the period 1988-94 and also examined the static trade effects of RTAs by calculating RCA (revealed comparative advantage) index for MERCOSUR country's exports. The study revealed that most dynamic products in MERCOSUR's intra-trade generally were capital intensive goods in which members had not displayed a strong export performance in outside markets.

Neither the RCA indices nor statistics about factor proportions indicated that MERCOSUR had a comparative advantage in these products. The evidence suggested that MERCOSUR's own trade barriers were responsible for these trade changes. Most favoured nation tariffs on the fast growing products were above the average for all imports and provide MERCOSUR members with significant preferences. These evidences contributed towards the potential adverse effects of regional trade agreements on members and on third countries, as judged by the variance in their trade pattern from that current comparative advantage would predict.

Doganlar (1998) presented an empirical analysis of purchasing power parity for developing Asian countries namely, India, Indonesia, Pakistan, Philippines and Turkey using cointegration test during the period 1980 to 1995. The study could not find any supportive evidence for PPP for India, Indonesia, Pakistan and Philippines, but on the other hand, PPP has a better supportive power for Turkey.

Garnaut (1998) discussed the world-wide tendencies of ASEAN's life's three decades towards regionalization and globalization during the period 1965 to 1995. The study also compared the dynamics of trade expansion within ASEAN with those of the European Union and the North American Free Agreement territories. The present study argued that ASEAN is a successful example of economically efficient regional cooperation to achieve trade expansion. The ASEAN proved that trade discrimination within a custom union or free trade area is not necessary for powerful increases in intra-regional trade. Multilateral liberalization amongst neighbouring economies can generate large intra-regional trade expansion.

Gould (1998) and Krueger (1999) studied effects of NAFTA on bilateral trade flows by looking for evidence of trade diversion in the data. Gould used the estimated trade equations to predict bilateral trade flows in the absence of NAFTA. Comparing this prediction to actual trade data, he concluded that U.S. export growth rate to Mexico was 16.3 per cent higher and that U.S. import growth from Mexico was 16.2 percent higher due to NAFTA. Gould also examined North-American trade with non-NAFTA countries and found that it has increased. This suggested that the increase in NAFTA trade was net trade creating. The study concluded that there was no evidence of NAFTA trade diversion from non-NAFTA countries. Examining trade data at the three-digit SITC level, the study revealed that few sectors in which imports of any NAFTA country from the rest of the world fell while rising with in NAFTA. The study also used "Shift and Share Analysis" to determine the extent to which intra-NAFTA trade occurred at the expense of the shares of trade to Non-NAFTA countries. Focusing on Mexico, Mexico's increased exports to the United States did not come at the expenses of its exports to the rest of the world. The study also found that U.S. imports of textiles and apparel increased from Mexico and decreased from East Asia. However, Mexico's increase in sales to the United States did not come at the expense of its exports to the rest of the world. It was also revealed that for the US, the impact of NAFTA had been relatively small and that for Mexico, changes in trade flows to date do not give much support to the view that NAFTA might be seriously trade diverting.

Khan and Mahmood (1998) tried to review the impact of the major new developments in regional trade bloc (Economic Co-operation Organization) on Pakistan and also examined the current state of Intra-SAARC/Eco-trade relations during the period 1980-94. The study concluded that the recent development in the EU and NAFTA were likely to affect Pakistan adversely in many ways. Firstly, Pakistan was likely to face trade diversion, particularly in the areas of textiles and clothing and leather products. Secondly, the access conditions in these two markets had become more restrictive for Pakistan. Finally, the scope of using non-tariff measures including import quotas, VERs and the anti-dumping measures had increased in the EU and NAFTA. The large economic blocs like EU, NAFTA and APEC were likely to have far reaching impact on developing countries which were not members of any of these trading blocs. Thus, three trading blocs consisting of 33 members accounted for almost 87 percent of world trade in 1994. To survive in a new emerging trade environment, the left out countries including Pakistan have limited options. The study also recommended policy options for Pakistan. Pakistan and other South/Central Asian countries must liberalize their economies unilaterally but preferably in a coordinated and multilateral way and strengthen their regional associations—the SAARC and the ECO to enhance their bargaining power *vis-à-vis* the three large trading blocs (EU, NAFTA and APEC). The state of intra-SAARC and intra-ECO trade presented a dismal picture. The mutual trade in the regions had been stagnant over time ranging between 2 to 5 percent of the total trade of the regions. Both regional associations had signed PTAs which provided for tariff reduction on specified commodities. Since the current level of intra-regional trade was low. These PTAs had made very little impact on increasing intra-regional trade.

Fukao et. al. (1999) provided an econometric analysis of whether or not the tariff preferences were being extended to Canada and Mexico under NAFTA during the period 1992-98. The study revealed that trade diversion was found mainly for US imports of textile, apparel products and some footwear products but not for trade in motor cars, vehicles and television receivers. The study predicted that these commodities (motorcars, vehicles and television receivers) might have been more influenced by changes in FDI and outsourcing rather than tariff preferences.

Bhatt (2000) analysed the reasons for growth and determinants of FDI flows of the ASEAN region during 1987-94. The study revealed that FDI flows of ASEAN increased from an annual average of $ 8 billion during 1986-91 to 25.5 billion in 1997. The ASEAN adopted relatively free market, free trade, open capital account and liberalized policies to attract FDI. This success of ASEAN countries in attracting FDI may be attributed to a combination of factors including political, social, economic stability, buoyant economies with capacity, growing domestic markets, favourable factor endowments particularly natural resources and labour supply. The incentives given by ASEAN countries ranged from tax holidays, accelerated depreciation allowance, export incentives, import duty exemption and concession and low-cost credit facilities and subsidized infrastructure facilities such as industrial estate. The main vehicles of FDI inflows in ASEAN countries are through mergers and acquisitions (M & As). FDI inflows through M & As were 72 percent in 1994 and 66 percent in 1995. During these periods, the economies of the region showed higher level of development which had led to stronger M & As market structure and technology-based competition. The ratio of FDI in gross fixed capital formation ranged between 5 percent to 35 percent in the region. Though FDI has increased in ASEAN, but Intra-ASEAN investment accounted for only a small share of ASEAN's total inflow of FDI. However, Intra-ASEAN trade represented more than 50 percent of the total trade. The study also revealed that there was a strong positive influence of size of the economy (GNP) on FDI inflows. The investment-GNP ratio was significant for Malaysia and Thailand. However, exchange rate did not have any influence on FDI.

Matyas et. al. (2000) had used the gravity model for modeling and predicting trade flows of 11 APEC countries. The study revealed that APEC members need to pursue export-led expansionary policies. The study suggested there is a need to adopt policy in accordance not only with the correct response parameters but also that the various member states propensities to import and export are sufficiently and adequately taken into account.

Schiff (2000) combined two theories—one about how multilateral trade liberalization affected regional integration, the other about how it affected political disintegration by taping ratio of free trade areas to custom unions over time. Combining the two arguments, Schiff hypothesized that as multilateral trade liberalization proceeded and number of regional integration arrangements increased, the ratio of free trade areas to custom-unions also increased and this ratio would be larger for North-South than for South-South RIAs. The data showed an increase in that ratio in the 1990s and a higher ratio for North-South than for South-South RIAs and were thus consistent with both hypotheses.

Madani (2001) studied effect of regional arrangement (Andean pact) on developing country's industrial growth (Bolivia: 1973-94, Colombia: 1973-94 and Ecuador: 1974-95). The study explored two potential channels for industrial growth: scale effects and variety of imported intermediate inputs by taking data of 22 industries. By using 3-SLS (three stage least square) methodology on the countries industrial gross output, production, gross fixed capital, number of workers, wages and intermediate inputs, the study revealed that variety of intermediate inputs organizing from non-regional partners had a significant positive impact on growth in a handful of industries. The effect of regional variety is at best mixed, thus concluding the argument that unilateral liberalization can have a positive impact on output growth through the channel of imported intermediate inputs. There is significant heterogeneity in industry-level returns to scale. Moreover, in the three Andean countries studied, cross industry scale effects were small and negative. Therefore, three countries should not expect large or across the board gains through scale effects from their regional arrangement.

Sinha (2001) explored effects of openness and investment on GDP in Asian countries during the period 1950-92. The study considered following Asian countries, i.e. Bangladesh (1959-92), China (1960-92), Hong Kong (1960-92), India (1950-92), Indonesia (1960-92), Iran (1955-92), Iraq (1953-87), Israel (1953-92), Japan (1950-92), Jordan (1954-90), Malaysia (1955-92), Myanmar (1950-89), Pakistan (1950-92), Philippines (1950-92), Singapore (1960-92), Sri Lanka (1950-92), South Korea (1953-91), Taiwan (1951-92) and Thailand (1950-92). The study predicted that the growth rate of GDP should be positively related to the growth rates of openness, domestic investment and population and the results supported the prediction. For China, Hong Kong, Iran, Iraq, Israel, Myanmar, Pakistan and Singapore, the coefficients of the growth of openness was positive and significantly different from zero. For China, Hong Kong, Indonesia, Israel, Japan, Jordan, Philippines, Singapore and South Korea, the coefficient of the growth of domestic investment was positive and significantly different from zero. In some cases, Bangladesh, India, Iran, Iraq, Japan, Pakistan and Singapore, population growth rate had a negative coefficient. Thus study revealed that South Asian countries (Bangladesh and India) showed very small impact of either openness or investment growth and Pakistan showed a negative impact of investment growth. But the ASEAN Economies (Indonesia, Myanmar, Philippines and Singapore) had positive impact of openness and investment. For Pacific Rim countries like China, Hong Kong and South Korea, the result of higher investment and higher trade led to higher economic growth. Thus, generally, study revealed that growth rate of GDP was positively related to the growth rates of openness and domestic investment.

Egger and Faffermayr (2002) analyzed the effects of EU integration on intra EU trade volumes with a special focus on trade with in and between the developed (core) and developing countries (periphery) by using OLS regression model during the period 1964-98. The study revealed that in all phases of integration developed-developing and intra-developing the growth of trade had experienced stronger positive effects than intra-developed trade.

Geda and Kebret (2002) used the determinants for trade using Common Market for Eastern and Southern Africa (COMESA) as a case study. The study found that almost all the standard gravity model variables (except for proximity) had plausible and statistically significant coefficients. Good macro economic policies (such as financial deepening and infrastructure development) were important determinants of bilateral trade in Africa. The results also showed that all proxies used to measure political instability (exception) had the expected signs. But regional integration arrangement failed to positively affect intra-regional trade. COMESA intra-trade was found not to be significantly different from its trade with non-member countries.

Schiff et. al. (2002) examined the impact on total factor productivity of North-South and South-South trade related research and development (R and D) spill overs by regression technique during 1976-78. The study took sample of 16 manufacturing industries in 25 developing countries. The study revealed that North-South and South-South R and D flows had a positive impact on total factor productivity, though the North-South has larger R and D intensive industries benefited mainly from North-South R and D flows while low R and D intensive industries benefited mainly from South-South R and D flows.

Asher and Srivastava (2003) explored the contribution that India could benefit that it can derive as a member of JACIK during 1990s. The study revealed that while the political, social and economic constraints in progressing towards the Asian should not be underestimated, India was continuing to acquire capacities and capabilities which make it a valuable economic partner for other JACIK countries. There are indications of significant division of labour and complementarities in design, production, and distribution chain emerging in areas such as electronics, pharmaceuticals and biotechnology. India's largest market also made it an important trading partner, particularly for ASEAN. JACIK countries would also find economic opportunities in India's large pool of technical and professional man power and in cooperating with India's scientific research institutes.

Cernat (2003) assessed the economic impact of many RTAs (nine) among developing counties by using gravity model for the period 1995-2000. The results showed that with the exception of Andean Community and MERCOSUR, which seemed to have reduced trade with non-members, the other South RTAs examined are not only trade creating but also trade expanding thereby increasing overall trade, even with third countries.

Cernot (2003) investigated the potential impact of South-South RTAs on both intra as well as extra trade flows by using econometric OLS technique during the period 1994-98. The study also estimated the impact of nine RTAs on trade patterns among members. The study revealed that a large number of African RTAs were not trade diverting but trade creating both with regard to intra and extra RTA trade

Fillpini and Molini (2003) used a gravity equation model to analyze trade flows between East Asian Industrializing countries (including China) and some developed countries in order to show the surprising trade performance of East Asian countries. It was revealed that all signs of coefficients were consistent with model assumptions. High propensity of Asian countries (including China but excluding Japan) to exchange high tech manufactured products with Japan and USA. Another interesting result was that among the East Asian economies, China played a very important role as an exporter and as importer too during the study period.

Laurenceson (2003) analyzed the current level of economic integration between China and the ASEAN-5 during the period 1996-2002. The study revealed that China and the ASEAN-5 had strong linkages with respect to goods and service markets. (particularly Singapore and Malaysia). However, financial market integration remained significantly incomplete. The main implication of the study is that the impact of future liberalization would be felt most accurately in financial markets.

This made reforms complement to greater level of external finance aimed at improving the risk management practices of financial institutions, which are matters of urgency for both China and ASEAN-5.

Prabir and Ghosh (2003) reviewed trade and transport linkages in BIMST-EC (Bangladesh, India, Myanmar, Sri Lanka and Thailand-Economic Cooperation) with special emphasis on India. The study revealed that BIMST-EC economy is growing at a considerable pace, members of this regional grouping are moving at different levels of economic development because members are embodied with different levels of resource endowments. The study suggested that finding out of appropriate economic and social complementarities would help the policy-makers in carving an appropriate cooperation framework in BIMSTEC.

Yahya (2003) argued that Bay of Bengal Initiative for Multisectoral Technical and Economic Cooperation (BIMSTEC) balanced India's engagement with Southeast and South but it also countered China's growing influence among ASEAN members (in particular Myanmar). The study revealed that Thailand was the driving force behind BIMSTEC activities as this would enhance its trade hub status and engagement policy with Cambodia, Myanmar, Laos and Vietnam states. The main proponents for BIMSTEC are Thailand and India. BIMSTEC is important for India's energy needs and to counter the growing influence of China and India.

Zorzoso and Lehmann (2003) applied the gravity model of trade to assess Mercosur-European Union trade and trade potential during 1988-96. The study used panel data analysis to disentangle the time invariant country specific effects and to capture the relationships between the relevant variables over time. The study revealed that fixed effect model was to be preferred to the random effects gravity model. Further more, a number of variables namely infrastructure, income differences and exchange rates added to the standard gravity equation, are found to be important determinants of bilateral trade flows. The study also revealed that the potential for Mercosur exports exceeded the actual export value in 1996 for all EU countries studies and future trade liberalization arrangements between both blocs would have positive impact on the side of Mercosur.

Zorzoso (2003) applied the gravity model to annual bilateral exports between 19 countries. His results indicated that exporter and importer incomes, as expected, had positive influence on bilateral trade flows. Exporter population had a large and positive impact on imports indicated that bigger countries import more than small countries. Regarding transport infrastructure, the study revealed that export infrastructure fostered trade.

Heng and Gayathre (2004) explored and quantified the economic benefits and losses resulting from Vietnam's participation and involvement in regional trade agreements such as ASEAN Free Trade Area (AFTA) and planned ASEAN China Free Trade Agreement (ACFTA) by using general equilibrium model during 1986 to 2000. The study revealed that involvement in AFTA is a confirmation of Vietnam's continued commitment to develop a market-oriented economy. Her decision to participate actively in regional trade agreements through ASEAN would prove to be strategically very beneficial for its economy.

Nanda and Raikhy (2004) studied complementarities in production and trade among JACIK countries during the Pre-WTO period (1995) and Post-WTO period (2001). The study computed revealed comparative advantage index, trade intensity index and import share. The study revealed that there had been structural change in favour of service sector and against agriculture in 2001 as compared to 1995 in most of JACIK countries. Most of the items with highest revealed comparative advantage of these countries entered into machinery and transport section. India's RCA was highest in pearls, precious and semi-precious stones, textile and made up articles. The study suggested that formation of proposed Asian Economic community would facilitate fuller exploitations of the region's resources by increasing intra-regional trade. Intra-regional exports can be increased by expanding exports of India and other Asian countries to other JACIK countries through market and trade diversification.

Chand (2004) examined internal factors in case of Asian countries to go for regional integration in trade by taking the period 1980 to 2000 by using trend, growth and trade intensity measures. The results of the study demonstrated that

Developing Asian Countries (DAC) trade is becoming increasingly regionalized as revealed by the concentration ratios, trade shares and growth rates, etc. The trade pattern in DAC during the 1990s showed that neighbourhood factor had encouraged trade and a policy of trade liberalization had led to a growth in the share of intra-regional trade. The fast growth of intra-regional trade in Asia had not been followed by any regional integration in the form of trade blocs. Thus, there is a vast opportunity for trade creation and improvement in the welfare of Asian countries which in the long-run is likely to have a positive effect on the welfare of other countries also.

Abraham and Hove (2005) examined relevance of regional trade policy for China .The study estimated a gravity model for a set of 23 countries in Asia and the Pacific over a period of 9 years (1992-2000). The study revealed that ASEAN and APEC currently had small effects on Asia-Pacific exports which were mainly influenced by growth, trade barriers and common language. However, China's participation in regional agreements had large export potentials, not only with respect to ASEAN, but also in a broad agreement including South and East Asian Countries.

Badinger (2005) estimated the growth effects of 13 EU member states over 1950-2000 by OLS regression model. The study revealed that growth effects had only been of temporary nature. GDP per capita of EU would be approximately one-fifth lower than today if no integration had taken since 1950.

Ramos and Zarosos (2005) tested the gravity model of trade augmented with technological innovation and transport infrastructure variables for 62 country samples for the year 1999. The study revealed that there is a differential behaviour between the richest and the poorest economies in the gravity model framework. Geographical and cultural factors are more important for developing than for the developed economies and a good economic policy in developing countries is to invest in technological innovation and in transport infrastructure.

Hapsani and Mangunseng (2006) examined the importance of various determinants on intra and extra regional trade flows of ASEAN members. The study found that both reporting and partner country's GDP, distance, common language and common border were found to have significant effects on the bilateral exports of ASEAN members. The reduction of tariff was also found to have a significant effect in increasing the bilateral exports of ASEAN members. The econometric analysis is also suggested that AFTA may be causing some trade diversion and shifting trade from countries outside the bloc to possibly less efficient countries inside the bloc. The study also observed that since the export and import profiles of ASEAN members have become more complementary to each other over time, the potential for intra-regional trade is great for ASEAN members.

Karaman and Ozkale (2006) studied the Turkey's import demand function using an econometric panel data application during the period 1982-2004. The results showed that Turkey's import demand is income inelastic. The results also indicated that custom union agreement has trade creation effects among some sectors and trade diversion effects among some others, while no effects at all could be calculated for the remaining.

Simwaka (2006) examined Malawi's trade with her major trading partner using an econometrics gravity model during the period 1998 to 2004. The results indicated that Malawi's bilateral trade was positively determined by the size of the economies (GDP of the importing country) and similar membership to regional integration agreement. On the other hand, transportation cost, proxied by distance, was found to have a negative influence on Malawi's trade. Likewise, exchange rate volatility depresses regional economic groupings had non-significant effect on the flow of bilateral trade.

Zulkornain and Hook (2006) examined the China-ASEAN, bilateral trade relationship using the Gravity model during the period 1990-2005. The empirical results revealed that transportation cost and real GDP are statistically significant determinants of bilateral trade. The trade distance remains an important determinant to China-ASEAN trade and larger economy size of a country has positive and significant influence on bilateral trade flows. The significant positive sign of the per capita GDP difference variable suggested that Linder hypothesis does not hold for entire region.

Achay (2006) investigated the determinants of trade flows between various countries of the world by applying the gravity for the five year sub-periods between 1970 and 2000. His model also included variables like ratio of trade to GDP, distance and dummies of regional integration agreements. His findings showed that all estimated coefficient were statistically significant and their signs were in conformity with expectations. The adjustment quality of the model as measured by determination coefficient (adjusted R^2) was quite high, standing at 71%. The study found that GDP, GDP percaptia, common frontier, common official language, common currency or common colonial past had a positive impact on the volume of bilateral trade.

Nayak and Mandal (2007) examined the macro economic and commercial indicators of both the countries by regression technique during the period 1998-99 to 2004-05. The study revealed that size and economic development influence the bilateral trade between India and Thailand significantly. Real effective exchange rate and tariff rate do not significantly enhance the explanation of the Indo-Thai trade in textile and clothing. The study suggested that besides the exports, the countries are likely to benefit from more investment, intensified competition from service sectors and improvement in regulatory regimes.

Rault et al (2007) examined the evolution of trade flow configurations of countries belonging to last wave of joining the EU using panel data during 1987-2004. The study revealed that the trade flows developed between these countries is inter-industry trade and vertical intra-industry trade.

Santis and Vicarelli (2007) estimated the overall effect of the common commercial policy by including all the PTAs signed by European Union by using gravity model during the period 1960-2000. The study revealed that trade with in EU expanded in the study period relative to overall trade by European countries with the rest of the world. The results confirmed that the EU free trade area has been a very successful experiment in trade liberalization. On average, countries joining the EU internal market have increased their imports by 130%. The wider 'PTAs' had positive impacts on EU import flows. The positive and significant coefficient of PTAs signed by the EU with third countries may have some how limited the occurrence of trade diversion effects.

Thus from above studies, it is clear that SAARC countries do not possess a diversified trade structure. There is a low level of intra-regional trade of SAARC as compared to other regional blocs. Most of the studies have not tried to find out complementarities in production and trade, static and dynamic effects and the reasons for low level of intra-SAARC trade. Therefore, the present study has tried to find out complementarities in production and trade and quantified static and dynamic effects in case of SAARC region. By this, it is easy to examine whether further stages of regional integration can be easily implemented or not. Moreover, India's export potential with the help of gravity model has been worked out by taking into account economic and non-economic variables which has also not found out in various studies. The study has also tried to find out converging and diverging economies with regard to India's export potential.

4

Trade among SAARC Countries

Data Base and Methodology

The objective of this chapter is to discuss sources of data used in the study and methodology for analyzing data.

DATA BASE

The study mainly covers the period of 25 years, i.e. 1981-2005. Keeping in mind the nature of study, secondary data have been calculated from the following sources:

1. Data on structure of production and structure of trade of SAARC nations have been obtained from *UNCTAD Handbook of Statistics, UN.*
2. Data on direction of trade of India as well as SAARC countries have been obtained from *Directory of Trade Statistics Year Book, IMF* and *Key Indicators of Asia and Pacific Countries, UN.*
3. Data on commodity composition of India with SAARC nations and SAARC as a whole has been collected from

UN Comtrade Data, UN and *Foreign Trade and Balance of Payment Statistics, CMIE.*

4. Data on different variables like Gross Domestic Product, Population, Exchange Rate, Foreign Capital Inflows, Gross Capital Formation, Labour Employed and GDP Deflator have been collected from various issues of *World Development Indicators, World Bank.*

METHODOLOGY

Different indices have been used to find out *complementarities* in production and trade among SAARC countries. The indices are:

Commodity Diversification Index

Diversification Index measures the extent of difference between the structure of trade of a country and the world average. More is the value of index, more are the differences between the export structure of a country and the world export structure. Less is the value of the index, less is the difference between export structure of a country and the world export structure. This Index assigns a value of zero to the most diversified economies and a value of one to the least. This index value has been calculated for SAARC nations at three points of time 1985, 1995 and 2005 by measuring the absolute deviation of the country share from world structure as follows (Finger, J.M. and M.E. Kreinin, 1979):

$$S_j = \sum_{i=1}^{n} \frac{|h_{ij} - h_i|}{2}$$

h_{ij} = Share of commodity i in total exports (or imports) of country j.

h_i = Share of commodity i in total world exports (or imports).

Revealed Comparative Advantage

Revealed comparative advantage index (RCAI) is one of the most applied tools to measure the export competitiveness. It is defined as ratio of the share of a particular industry (or products) in a country's total exports, to the share of the industry's exports (or products) in world's total exports. This index for top 10 export items of SAARC nations has been calculated for recent years (2002 and 2005) with the help of following formula (Balassa, 1965):

$$RCA_{ij} = \frac{X_{ij} / X_i}{X_{jw} / X_w}$$

RCA_{ij} = Revealed comparative advantage of commodity j for country i
X_{ij} = Exports of commodity j in country i
X_i = Country i's total exports
X_{jw} = Exports of commodity j of the world
X_w = Total exports of the world

A country has a revealed comparative advantage only in those products for which its market share of world exports is above its average share of world exports. RCA_{ij} ranges from 0 to $+\infty$. A value of less than unity implies that the country has a revealed comparative disadvantage in the product. Similarly, if the index exceeds unity, the country is said to have revealed comparative advantage in the product (Mahmood, 2000).

Trade Competitiveness Index

Trade competitiveness is the ratio of net trade to total trade. Trade Competitiveness Index has been calculated for ten commodity sections under Standard International Trade Classification (SITC Rev 2) for SAARC nations at three points of time 1985, 1995 and 2005 (Balassa, 1965). Balassa Trade Competitiveness Index is given by the following formula:

$$B = \frac{X_{kt} - M_{kt}}{X_{kt} + M_{kt}}$$

where X_{kt} and M_{kt} denote exports and imports of commodity section k in time period t. The value of this index ranges between –1 to 1. A positive (negative) value of B indicates a trade surplus (deficit) indicating that a country has comparative advantage (disadvantage) in the trade of commodity k. An increasingly positive (negative) B value indicates increasing (decreasing) export penetration of the home country in foreign markets relative to the penetration of foreign suppliers in the domestic one (indicating an increase (reduction) in comparative advantage and a higher (lower) level of competitiveness for the domestic country).

Trade Intensity Index

The trade intensity index is used to determine whether the value of trade between two countries is greater or smaller than would be expected on the basis of their importance in world trade. It is defined as the share of one country's exports going to a partner dividing by the share of world exports going to the partner. Trade intensity of SAARC countries and SAARC as a whole has been calculated by divided the intra-country share by the share of country to total world trade at three points of time 1985, 1995 and 2005 in the following manner (Kojima, 1964):

$$I_{ij} = \frac{X_{ij} / X_i}{M_j / (M_w M_i)}$$

where I_{ij} = Trade Intensity Index of country i with j.

X_{ij}/X_j = Share of country j in i^{th} country's exports.

M_j, M_i and M_w = Imports of country j, i and world respectively.

It ranges between 0 to + ∞. Values greater than 1 indicate an intense trade relationship and *vice-versa*. In other words, an index of more (less) than one indicates a bilateral trade flow that is larger (smaller) than expected given the partner country's importance in world trade.

Market Concentration Index

Market Concentration Index for SAARC nations has been calculated at three points of time 1985, 1995 and 2005 with the help of Herfindahl-Hirschmann index (Hirschmann, 1940):

$$H_j = \frac{\sqrt{\sum_{i=1}^{n} (X_i / X)^2} - \sqrt{1/n}}{1 - \sqrt{(1/n)}}$$

H_j = Country concentration index
X_i = Value of exports (imports) of product i

$$X = \sum_{i=1}^{n} x$$

n = number of products at the three-digit Standard International Trade Classification (SITC), revision 3 level.

This index has been normalized to obtain values ranking from 0 to 1 (maximum concentration). Number of products exported/imported includes only those products whose value greater than $ 100,000 or which constitute more than 0.3 percent of the country's total exports (imports). The lower the index, the less concentrated are a country's exports/imports (United Nations, 2005).

Compound Growth Rate

The compound growth rates of India's exports and imports with SAARC, world and SAARC nations have been worked out during pre-WTO period (1985-94), post-WTO period (1995-2005) and entire period (1985-2005) and also for the different variables used in the study during 1981-2005 by the following formula:

$$Y = AB^t$$

where A and B are parameters, Y is dependent variable and t is time variable.

The compound growth rate is equal to $(\hat{B}-1) \times 100.\hat{B}$ is estimated value of B.

Coefficient of Variation

For calculating trade stability indices during pre-WTO period (1985-94), post-WTO period (1995-2005) and entire study period (1985-2005), the coefficient of variation of India's exports, imports and trade with SAARC, World and SAARC nations have been worked out with the help of following formula:

$$\text{Coefficient of variation} = \frac{\sigma}{\bar{X}} \times 100$$

Dynamic Effects of SAARC

To calculate dynamic effects of SAARC, two equations have been estimated. These are:

Effect on Investment

$$L_nC_{i,t} = a_0 + a_1L_nY_{i,t} + a_2L_nF_{1i,t} + D_{2i,t} + e_{it} \quad (1)$$

a_1, $a_2 > 0$ ($a_2 < 0$ for developing economies)

Effect on GDP

$$\Delta y / y_{i,t} = b_0 + b_1\Delta k / k_{i,t} + b_2\Delta L / L_{i,t} + D_{1i,t} + D_{2i,t} + e_{it} \quad (2)$$

b_1, $b_2 > 0$ ($b_2 < 0$ for developing economies)

$C_{i,t}$ = real gross capital formation of country *i* in year *t*;
$Y_{i,t}$ = real gross domestic product in country *i* in year *t*; and
$F_{i,t}$ = real foreign capital inflows (foreign direct investment (FDI) + official development assistance and official aid (ODA)) in country *i* in year *t*.
$D_{1\,i,t}$ = 1 if *t* belongs to 1985-94 (from SAARC to SAPTA),
= 0 otherwise.
$D_{2\,i,t}$ = 1 if $t \geq 1995$ (from SAPTA onwards),
= 0 otherwise.
L_n = natural logs

Foreign capital inflows can be divided into three categories:

1. Foreign Direct Investment (FDI)
2. Foreign Portfolio Investment (FPI)
3. Official Development Assistance and Official Aid (ODA)

Since limited data was available in foreign portfolio investment, the study has used two variables representing foreign capital inflows that are foreign direct investment (FDI) and official development assistance and official aid (ODA).

$\Delta y/y_{i,t}$ = growth rate of real GDP in country i in year t.
$\Delta k/k_{i,t}$ = growth rate of capital stock in country i in year t.
$\Delta L/L_{i,t}$ = growth rate of labour in country i year t.

Capital stock has been calculated by perpetual inventory method which is given as follows:

$$K_t = K_{t-1} + C_t - \delta K_{t-1}$$

K_t = Capital stock in time period t
K_{t-1} = Capital stock in time period $t-1$
C_t = Gross capital formation in time period t

Initial level of capital stock has been calculated with the help of following formula:

$$K_0 = \frac{C_0}{\delta + \psi}$$

K_0 = Initial level of capital stock
C_o = Gross capital formation at initial level
d = rate of deprecation = 0.05 (assumed to be constant)
y = rate of growth of gross capital formation in first 10 years

To convert above variables into real terms, suitable deflators have been used.

To find out the effects of SAARC as a whole, these two equations have been estimated by panel data model as well as restricted model which has been explained further. These two equations have also been estimated with the help of multiple regression analysis to find out the effects country by country.

Determinants of India's Exports

To know about impact of different variables on India's exports, a gravity model of international trade is empirically tested by analyzing India's exports with six SAARC members.

Gravity Model

The gravity model applies Newton's universal law of gravitation in physics, which states that gravitational attraction between the two objects is proportional of their masses and inversely relate to square to their distance (Zhang and Kristensen (1995) and Chritie (2002)). The gravity model is expressed as follows:

F_{ij} is the gravitational attraction.
M_i and M_j are mass of two objects.
D_{ij} is the distance.

Later on an astronomer, Stewart, and a sociologist, Zipf transferred his law to the social sciences and attempted to apply it to spatial interactions, such as trips among cities :

$$I_{ij} = G\,(Pop_i, Pop_j)/D_{ij}$$

where I_{ij} is the number of trips between cities i and city j.
$Pop_{i(j)}$ is population in city $i(j)$.
D_{ij} is distance between city i and city j.
G is coefficient.

The gravity model for trade is analogous to this law. The analogy is as follows, "The trade flows between two countries is proportional to the product of each country's economic mass generally measured by GDP, and each to the power of quantities to be determined divided by the distance between the countries respective economic centers of gravity, generally their capitals, raised to the power of another quantity to be determined." (Christie, 2002).

The study has used the following gravity model specification:

$$L_n E_{ijt} = \alpha + \beta_1 L_n Y_{it} + \beta_2 L_n Y_{jt} + \beta_3 L_n Pop_{it} + \beta_4 L_n Pop_{jt} + \beta_5 Rer_{it} + \beta_6 Rer_{jt} + \beta_7 L_n Pci_{ijt} + \beta_8 L_n Dis_{ij} + \beta_9\, \beta or_{ij} + \beta_{10}\, Lan_{ij} + e_{ijt} \quad (3)$$

E_{ijt} = Export flows in year t from country i (India) to country j (SAARC countries);
Y_{it} = Country i's GDP in year t (measured in US \$ millions);

Y_{jt} = Country j's GDP in year t (measured in US \$ millions);

Pop_{it} = Country i's population in year t (measured in thousands);

Pop_{jt} = Country j's population in year t (measured in thousands);

Pci_{ijt} = Absolute difference in per capita GDP (measured in US \$ millions);

Rer_{it} = Real exchange rate between the exporter's currency and the US \$ in period t;

Rer_{j} = Real exchange rate between the importer's currency and the US \$ in period t;

Dis_{ij} = Distance between country i and j (Kms);

Bor_{ij} = Border is a dummy variable for pair of countries sharing common border;

Lan_{ij} = This is also a dummy variable for a pair of countries sharing common language; and

L_n = Natural logs.

It is hypothesized that $\beta_{1,}\ \beta_{2,}\beta_{5,}\beta_{9,}\beta_{10} > 0$; $\beta_{3,}\ \beta_{4,}\ \beta_7 < 0$ *or* > 0 *and* $\beta_{6,}\ \beta_8 < 0$.

In data set of bilateral exports, some flows are recorded as zero or missing. However, omitting zero flows can bias the empirical results. Omitting zero entries observation implies losing information on the causes of (very) low trade. On the other side, a logarithmic formulation of the gravity model cannot include zero trade because logarithm of zero is undefined. Zero values may be substituted by a small constant. This approach has been followed by Linneman (1966), van Bergeijk and Oldersma (1990), Wang and Winters (1991) and Raballand (2003). Substituting small values prevents omission of observations from the sample, but is essentially adhoc. The inserted value is arbitrary and does not reflect the underlying expected value (Linders and Groot, 2006 and Shepherd, 2008). The study has also used this approach.

A panel framework is designed to estimate the above three equations during a period of 1981-2005. Panel estimation reveals several advantages over cross-section data and time series data as it controls for individuals heterogeneity (whereas time and cross-section studies do not control for this heterogeneity and it may give biased estimated results). Furthermore, more degree of freedom reduces the collinearity among explanatory variables, therefore improving the efficiency of econometric estimates. More importantly, panel data can measure effects that are not detectable in cross-sections and time series data (Baltagi, 1995).

Some early studies usually investigate the gravity model with single year cross sectional data or time series data. These methods are probably affected by problem of misspecification and yield biased estimation of volume of bilateral trade because there is no controlling for heterogeneity (Cheng and Wall, 2005). Matyas *et. al.* (1997), Egger (2000) etc. suggest applying panel data in gravity model because panel data is a general case of cross-sectional data and time series data.

Panel estimation can be done using pool estimation, fixed effect and random effect (Gujrati, 2003). Pool estimation is the simplest approach. Its function is as follows:

$$Y_{it} = \beta_1 + \beta_2 X_{2it} + \beta_3 X_{3it} + e_{it}$$

where i stands for cross sectional unit, t stands for time period and error term is normally distributed with mean zero and constant variance. Pooled estimation assumes there is one single set of slope coefficients and one overall intercept. It disregards the time and space dimension of panel data; the error term captures the differences overtime and individuals. The pooled estimation however, may provide inefficient and biased estimated results because it assumes there are no individual effects and time effects.

The fixed effects takes into account the individuals and time effects by letting the intercept varies for each individual and time period, but the slope coefficients are constant. The model is :

$$Y_{it} = \beta_{1i} + \beta_2 X_{2i,t} + \beta_3 X_{3i,t} + e_{it}$$

where it is usually assumed that e_{it} is independent and identically distributed over individuals and time with mean zero and variance σ^2 and all X_{it} are independent of all error terms. By introducing different intercept dummies one can allow for intercept to vary according to individuals and time.

One of the shortcomings of fixed effect model is that it may not be able to identify the impact of time invariant such as distance, and this variable will be excluded from fixed effects estimation. Cheng and Wall (2005) has suggested a method to estimate the time invariant variables by using the individual effects. In the fixed effect model the country pair individual effects cover all factors that remain constant over time such as: location, language, culture, and other trade barriers. Therefore, one can indirectly calculate the effect of time invariant variables like history and distance from the individual effects. The study has estimated the model using the fixed effect estimator, then follow Cheng and Wall (2005). They estimated an additional regression of the estimated country pair effects on the time invariant variables in order to find out the importance of these variables in the fixed effects. The regression is as follows:

$$\alpha_{ij} = a_1 + a_2 L_n Dis_{ij} + a_3 Bor_{ij} + a_4\ Lan_{ij} + e_{ij}$$

where:

α_{ij} is country individual effects
a_2, a_3, a_4 are coefficients.

It is expected that $a_2<0$ but a_3 and $a_4>0$

Another approach applies to estimate panel data is random effect estimation. The random effect treats the intercept as a random variable and the individuals included in the sample are drawn from a larger population. The model is written as follows:

$$Y_{it} = \beta_1 + \beta_2 X_{2it} + \beta_3\ X_{3it} + W_{it}$$

where $W_{it} = \varepsilon_i + U_{it}$

The composite error term W_{it} consists of two components, $e_{i,}$ which is the cross section or individual specific, error component and U_{it}, which is combined time series and cross-section error component. It is assumed that the individual error components are not correlated with each other and are not auto-correlated across sections and time series units.

$$\varepsilon_i \simeq N\ (0,\ \sigma^2_\varepsilon)$$
$$U_{it} \simeq N\ (0,\ \sigma^2_u)$$
$$E(\varepsilon_i\, u_{it}) = 0,\ E(\varepsilon_i \varepsilon_j) = 0(i \neq j)$$
$$E\ (u_{it}\, u_{is}) = 0,\ E\ (u_{it}\, u_{jt}) = E\ (u_{it}\, u_{js}) = 0\ (i \neq j;\ t \neq s)$$

Equations 1, 2 and 3 have been estimated by all three methods (restricted model, one-way fixed effect model (only cross section vary) and one-way random effect model (only cross section vary). And then F statistic test and Hausman test (Verbeek, 2004) have been run to select the most efficient method for interpreting the estimate results.

Restricted F-test

$H_0: u_i = \ldots\ldots\ldots\ldots\ldots\ u_{n-1} = 0$

$H_1 : not\ H_0$

If null hypothesis is rejected, fixed effect model is better than the pooled OLS model.

Hausman Test (Verbeek, 2004)

H_0: Explained variables are uncorrelated with individual effects

H_1: Explained variables are correlated with individual effects

$$H = \left(\hat{\beta}_{FE} - \hat{\beta}_{RE}\right)' \left[\hat{V}\left(\hat{\beta}_{FE}\right) - \hat{V}\left(\hat{\beta}_{RE}\right)\right]^{-1} \left(\hat{\beta}_{FE} - \hat{\beta}_{RE}\right)$$

where $\hat{\beta}_{FE}$, $\hat{\beta}_{RF}$ are estimated coefficients from the fixed and random effect estimators. $\hat{V}$'s are the covariance matrices of fixed and random effect. If the computed statistic H is larger than a chi-squared distribution with *k* degrees of freedom (*k* is the number of elements in β) then we reject the null hypothesis and conclude that random effect is not appropriate and it is better to use fixed effect.

Export Potentials

Calculating exports potential is a line of research that has been used intensively with the gravity model. Most of the studies apply the point estimated coefficient to data on the explanatory variables to calculate trade potential predicted by gravity model. The study has calculated export potentials with the help of three formulas:

1. *Predicted Export Flows—Actual Export Flows (P-A)*

Predicted export flows are based on gravity model of exports. Positive value of P-A shows that there is future possibility of export expansion while negative values shows that India has exceeded its export potential with the particular SAARC country (Batra, 2004).

2. *Predicted Export Flows/Actual Export Flows (P/A)*

If this ratio exceeds one, there is an implication in terms of potential expansion of India's exports with the respective country and vice versa (Batra, 2004).

There is uncertainty of calculating export potential based on above point estimates. There is another method (speed of convergence) which avoids this uncertainty.

3. *Speed of Convergence*

Jakob *et. al.* (2000) has proposed the concept of speed of convergence to replace the old method to calculate potential trade. Speed of convergence is defined as the average growth rate of potential trade divided by average growth rate of actual trade between the years of observations.

Speed of Convergence

$$= \left(\frac{Average\ growth\ rate\ of\ potential\ exports}{Average\ growth\ rate\ of\ actual\ exports} \right) \times 100 - 100$$

There is a convergence if growth rate of potential exports is lower than that of actual exports and the computed speed of convergence is negative. There is a divergence in the opposite case.

To estimate the convergence of the actual India's exports towards the estimated equilibrium, the study has estimated following simple regression model:

$$\Delta E_{ij,\,t} = \alpha + \beta \left(E_{ij,\,t-1} - Pot_{ij,\,t-1} \right)$$

DE_{ij} = Change in actual export value in time period t; and

$(E_{ij,t-1} - Pot_{ij,t-1})$ = difference between actual and potential exports in the previous period (t-1).

Certainly for convergence, the b should be negative and significant.

5

Production and Trade Structure among SAARC Nations

This chapter studies complementarities in production and trade among SAARC countries by estimating export and import shares of different commodities, trade intensity indices and revealed comparative advantage indices. The chapter has been divided into two sections. Sections I deals with complementarities in production and trade at commodity level while section II deals with complementarities at country level.

I

PERFORMANCE OF SAARC COUNTRIES

Table 5.1 shows the selected indicators of SAARC region in comparison to World in 2006. Table depicts that the SAARC countries accounted for about 22 percent of world population but their share in GDP was merely 2.77 percent, in world exports was about 1.32 percent and in imports share was about 1.87 percent. With in SAARC, India had the highest population and GDP whereas Maldives had the least population and GDP. The inward flows of FDI were also highest in India followed by

TABLE 5.1

Share of SAARC Region in World in Selected Indicators (2006)

	Population (Thousand)	GDP (millions of dollars)	GDP Per Capita (millions of dollars)	FDI Inward Flow (millions of dollars)	Exports (millions of dollars)	Imports (millions of dollars)	Trade Balance (millions of dollars) (2004-06)	Openness Ratio
(1)	(2)	(3)	(4)	(5)	(6)	(7)	(8)	(9)
World	6592900	40960425	6411	916277	11982932	12203386	-257134	—
Share of SAARC in world (percent)	22.17	2.77	12.40	1.07	1.32	1.87	—	—
SAARC	1461571	1133914	775.82	9765	157715	228641	—	—
Bangladesh	144345	6196.1	429.26	692	12277	16017	-3835	45.66
Bhutan	647	927	1423.49	1	304	500	-173	86.73
India	1109811	906268	816.60	6598	120887	169835	-25536	32.08
Maldives	337	915	2715	14	225	927	-454	125.90
Nepal	27658	8052	291	5	87	2604	-1079	42.49
Pakistan	159002	128830	810.24	2183	16470	28405	-4994	34.83
Sri Lanka	19771	26967	1363.96	272	6735	10353	-2083	63.36

Source : Worked out from the data given in *World Development Indicators*, 2006.

Pakistan and Bangladesh. Similarly, export earnings were also highest in India. All SAARC countries had deficit trade account balance in 2006. Openness ratio (trade to GDP ratio) ranged from 32.08 percent in India to 125.90 percent in Maldives.

Production Structure

Structure of production measured in terms of inter-sectoral composition of output given in Table 5.2 shows that in 1985, GDP of all SAARC countries except Bhutan and Nepal had been dominated by service sector. In Bhutan and Nepal, GDP had been dominated by agriculture sector (the share being 52.6 percent and 51.7 percent). The share of service sector in GDP was maximum in Pakistan (49 percent) followed by Sri Lanka (48.8 percent) and Bangladesh (47.0 percent). In 1995, in all SAARC countries, share of agriculture in GDP had decreased and share of manufacturing (industry) and service sector in GDP had increased. The rapid decline in share of agriculture in GDP was in case of Bhutan and Nepal (share declined from 52.6 percent and 51.7 percent in 1985 to 34.0 percent and 40.8 percent in 1995 respectively) and the rapid increase in share of service sector in GDP was in case of India (share increased from 38.8 percent in 1985 to 43.6 percent in 1995). In 2005, GDP of all SAARC countries (except Bhutan) again had been dominated by service sector .In Bhutan, share of industry in GDP was maximum (48.8 percent). Share of service sector in GDP was maximum in Maldives (73.7 percent) followed by Sri Lanka (54.7 percent), Pakistan (53.3 percent) and Bangladesh (51.6 percent). As compared to pre-WTO period (1985), share of all SAARC members had decreased in agriculture sector while in industry sector, it had increased (except India) in post-WTO period. Similar production structure of SAARC nations indicated lack of complementarities in production at sectoral level.

Growth of Exports and Imports of SAARC Countries

Regarding export performance Table 5.3 depicts that exports of SAARC increased at compound annual rate of 14.45 per cent per annum during 1985-90. SAARC countries, namely,

TABLE 5.2

Production Structure of SAARC Countries

(Percent)

Country	*Agriculture*			*Industry (Total)*			*Manufacturing*			*Services*		
	1985	1995	2005	1985	1995	2005	1985	1995	2005	1985	1995	2005
(1)	(2)	(3)	(4)	(5)	(6)	(7)	(8)	(9)	(10)	(11)	(12)	(13)
Bangladesh	32.0	25.7	21.9	20.9	24.9	26.5	13.82	15.4	16.0	47.0	49.5	51.6
Bhutan	52.6	34.0	22.3	19.0	34.8	48.8	5.46	10.9	6.3	30.6	31.2	28.9
India	33.0	28.2	19.0	28.2	28.1	27.4	17.9	18.1	15.9	38.8	43.6	53.6
Maldives	—	11.0	9.1	—	13.0	17.2	—	7.6	7.3	—	76.0	73.7
Nepal	51.7	40.8	38.3	15.1	22.2	21.3	5.70	9.3	7.8	34.1	37.0	40.4
Pakistan	28.5	26.7	21.6	22.5	23.7	25.1	15.9	16.3	18.2	49.0	49.6	53.3
Sri Lanka	24.4	20.6	15.5	26.8	29.7	29.8	16.6	18.5	18.4	48.8	49.7	54.7

Source : *UNCTAD Handbook of Statistics*, 2007.

TABLE 5.3

Average Annual Growth Rate of Merchandise Trade

(Percent)

Country	Exports						Imports					
	1985-90	1990-95	1985-95	1995-2000	2000-05	1995-2005	1985-90	1990-95	1985-95	1995-2000	2000-05	1995-2005
(1)	(2)	(3)	(4)	(5)	(6)	(7)	(8)	(9)	(10)	(11)	(12)	(13)
Bangladesh	11.94	11.1	11.52	17.2	8.60	12.9	8.82	11.8	10.31	5.0	9.85	7.43
Bhutan	27.64	0.9	14.27	-11.4	20.56	4.58	0.39	4.6	2.50	12.1	17.86	14.98
India	15.72	11.5	13.61	5.3	19.13	12.22	8.82	8.1	8.46	7.9	23.04	15.47
Maldives	27.68	0.5	14.09	4.9	10.87	7.89	24.32	13.1	18.71	8.1	15.04	11.57
Nepal	5.30	11.2	8.25	17.8	1.13	9.47	8.47	15.1	11.79	1.7	5.17	3.44
Pakistan	14.17	6.1	10.14	0.8	12.66	6.73	6.19	7.0	6.60	-2.8	18.99	8.10
Sri Lanka	7.65	15.4	11.53	6.4	4.09	5.25	7.30	14.6	10.95	3.5	7.90	5.7
SAARC	14.45	11.0	12.73	5.3	16.13	10.72	8.18	8.9	8.54	5.3	19.87	12.59

Source : *UNCTAD Handbook of Statistics*, 2007.

Bhutan, India and Maldives experienced higher growth rate of exports as compared to SAARC as a whole. However, during 1990-95, exports of SAARC increased at a lower rate of only 11.0 percent per annum as compared to 1985-90. The low growth in exports of SAARC was mainly due to decrease in export growth of countries namely, Bhutan, Maldives and Pakistan. The growth rate of exports of SAARC as a whole experienced further a rapid decline from 11.0 percent per annum during 1990-95 to 5.3 percent during 1995-00 again due to low growth rate of exports of SAARC countries namely, Bhutan, India, Maldives and Pakistan. However, during 2000-05, exports of SAARC increased at a higher rate of 16.13 percent per annum as compared to 1985-90, 1990-95 and 1995-00. Higher increase in growth rate of exports was mainly due to rapid increase in exports of Bhutan, India, Maldives and Pakistan. As compared to pre-WTO period (1985-95), Bangladesh and Nepal experienced an increase in growth rate of exports during 1995-2005.

Regarding the import performance of SAARC countries, Table 5.3 depicts that imports of SAARC increased at a rate of 8.18 percent per annum during 1985-90. SAARC countries namely, Bangladesh, India, Maldives and Nepal experienced higher growth rate of imports as compared to SAARC as a whole. During 1990-95, imports of SAARC increased at a little higher rate of 8.9 percent per annum as compared to 1985-90. However, the growth rate of imports of SAARC as a whole experienced a decline from 8.9 percent per annum in 1990-95 to 5.30 percent per annum in 1995-00 due to low growth rate of imports of SAARC countries namely, Bangladesh, Maldives, Nepal, Pakistan and Sri Lanka. But during 2000-05, imports of SAARC increased at a rapid rate of 19.87 percent per annum as compared to 1985-90, 1990-95 and 1995-00. This increase in imports of SAARC was due to higher growth rate of imports of all SAARC countries. As compared to pre-WTO period (1985-95), Bhutan, India and Pakistan experienced an increase in growth rate of imports in post-WTO period (1995-2005).

Complementarities in Trade

Complementarities in trade measured in terms of trade structure of SAARC countries given in Table 5.4 shows that in

1990, export basket for all SAARC countries had been dominated by manufactured goods. In Nepal, manufacturers accounted for 83 percent of total exports, 79 percent in Pakistan and 78 percent in Bangladesh. In manufacturers, other manufactured goods played an important role in these countries. Other manufactured goods accounted for 83 percent, 78 percent and 76 per cent of total exports in Nepal, Pakistan and Bangladesh, respectively. Fuels accounted for minimum share in export basket for all of the SAARC countries. In 1995, the situation remained same. The maximum share of manufactures in total exports was of Bangladesh (85.2 percent) followed by Nepal (83.7 percent) and Pakistan (83 percent). Again, other manufactured goods accounted for 82.4 percent, 81.8 percent and 80.5 percent of total exports in Nepal, Pakistan and Bangladesh, respectively. In 2005, export basket of the SAARC countries except Maldives had been dominated by manufactured goods. Among SAARC nations, again Bangladesh constituted major share in manufactures, i.e. 89.6 percent in total exports. In Maldives, all food items accounted for 66.7 percent share in total exports. As compared to pre-WTO period (1990), share of exports of manufactures of all SAARC nations (except India, Maldives, and Nepal) had increased in post-WTO period (2005).

Import basket for all SAARC nations had been dominated by manufactured goods in 1990. In imports, maximum share was of Sri Lanka (64.8 percent) followed by Bangladesh (55.8 percent) and Pakistan (54.1 percent). In imports of manufactured goods, other manufactured goods played an important role in all SAARC nations except Nepal and Pakistan. In 1995, all SAARC nations' share of manufactured goods in import basket had increased. However, the rapid increase was found in Bangladesh (share increased from 55.8 percent in 1990 to 69.1 percent in 1995). Imports of other manufactured goods witnessed decline or remained stable in all SAARC nations except Bangladesh. The share of machinery and transport in imports of all SAARC nations (except Bangladesh) had increased or remained stable. In 2005, import basket for all of the SAARC countries again had been dominated by manufactured goods. The maximum share was of Sri Lanka

(68.9 percent) followed by Maldives (63.0 percent) and Bangladesh (62.0 percent). Again in it, other manufactured goods played an important role by contributing in Bangladesh (29.7 percent), Nepal (32.4 percent) and Sri Lanka (38.7 percent) while for other SAARC nations, machinery and transport played an important role by contributing in India (22.8 percent), Maldives (30.8 percent) and Pakistan (29.4 percent). Thus the huge complementarities in trade had been found lacking at section level.

Commodity Diversification Index

This index reveals the extent of the difference between the structure of trade of the country and the world average. This index closer to 1 indicates a bigger difference from the world average. Table 5.5 depicts the diversification index of SAARC countries in 1985, 1995 and 2005. The export diversification index of Pakistan, India and Sri Lanka was 0.63 percent, 0.61 percent and 0.59 percent respectively in 1985 showing that a big difference between the structure of export of these countries and world average. In 1995, only two SAARC nations namely India and Nepal's export diversification Index had decreased while for other SAARC nations, it had increased depicting the increasing difference of the structure of the export from world average. As compared to pre-WTO period (1985), this index had increased for all SAARC nations except India in post-WTO period (2005). In the case of import diversification index, all SAARC nations had less than 0.50 percent in 1985. In 1995, only Bhutan's index had decreased, i.e. from 0.42 percent in 1985 to 0.37 percent in 1995. While for other SAARC nations, it has increased. In 2005, the picture was something different. This index had increased for all SAARC nations in 2005, as compared to 1985 indicating that increasing difference of the structure of import from world average.

Competitiveness in Trade

Trade competitiveness is defined as ability of domestic producers to maintain and increasing existing comparative advantages and develops new ones. Increasing competitiveness implies that domestic firms would maintain an increase in their market shares in home and foreign markets, achieve export

TABLE 5.4
Trade Structure of SAARC Countries

(Percent)

Country	All food items		Agricultural raw-materials		Fuels		Ores and metals	
	Manufactured goods		Chemical products		Other manufactured goods		Machinery and transport	
	Exports	Imports	Exports	Imports	Exports	Imports	Exports	Imports
(1)	(2)	(3)	(4)	(5)	(6)	(7)	(8)	(9)
Bangladesh								
1990	14.3	19.0	6.8	5.4	1.3	16.6	0.0	3.1
1995	10.4	17.3	2.7	3.4	0.4	7.8	0.0	2.3
2005	7.4	18.9	1.9	8.8	0.4	7.8	0.1	2.5
Bhutan								
1999	13.3	17.9	1.7	1.3	1.9	10.4	3.1	0.8
India								
1990	15.6	3.2	4.1	4.0	2.9	27.3	5.8	8.1
1995	18.7	4.2	1.3	3.9	1.7	23.7	3.6	6.8
2005	8.9	3.1	1.5	1.9	11.5	33.7	7.2	4.7
Maldives								
1990	—	—	—	—	—	—	—	—
1995	73.8	24.0	0.7	2.1	0.0	11.4	0.2	1.9

2005	66.7	15.6	0	3.6	24.2	15.5	0.7	2.3
Nepal								
1990	13.2	9.8	3.0	2.3	0.0	9.5	0.3	2.7
1995	7.8	9.8	1.1	2.3	0.0	9.5	0.1	2.6
2005	20.6	17.3	1.1	4.6	0.0	15.6	4.3	3.9
Pakistan								
1990	9.3	17.4	10.2	4.0	1.3	20.9	0.3	3.6
1995	11.7	17.5	3.8	5.5	1.0	16.2	0.2	2.6
2005	12.0	10.4	1.5	4.2	4.2	21.1	0.4	3.3
Sri Lanka								
1990	34.3	19.1	5.8	1.8	1.5	12.7	1.6	1.5
1995	33.9	19.1	5.7	1.8	1.5	12.7	1.6	1.5
2005	22.2	12.4	2.1	1.2	0	13.4	3.6	3.5

(Contd.)

TABLE 5.4 (Contd.)

(Percent)

Country	Manufactured Goods		Chemical Products		Other Manufactured Goods		Machinery and Transport	
	Exports	Imports	Exports	Imports	Exports	Imports	Exports	Imports
(1)	(2)	(3)	(4)	(5)	(6)	(7)	(8)	(9)
Bangladesh								
1990	77.5	55.8	1.1	8.2	75.5	29.1	0.9	18.6
1995	85.2	69.1	3.0	10.1	80.5	44.4	1.6	14.7
2005	89.6	62.0	0.3	11.2	88.9	29.7	0.4	21.0
Bhutan								
1999	40.0	69.6	11.4	5.8	28.3	22.0	0.3	41.7
India								
1990	70.1	51.2	7.4	12.9	55.3	20.8	7.4	17.6
1995	73.2	52.8	8.1	15.3	57.6	17.3	7.5	20.2
2005	69.8	48.4	11.6	9.3	47.3	16.4	10.9	22.8
Maldives								
1990	—	—	—	—	—	—	-	—
1995	25.3	60.7	0.0	5.9	25.3	28.8	0.0	26.5
2005	8.4	63.0	0.1	5.3	5.0	27.0	3.4	30.8
Nepal								
1990	83.3	36.9	0.5	8.6	82.8	13.3	0.0	15.0

1995	83.7	36.9	1.2	8.6	82.4	13.3	0.1	15.0
2005	74.0	58.6	6.8	10.2	66.0	32.4	0.4	16.0
Pakistan								
1990	78.7	54.1	0.4	16.3	78.0	12.3	0.3	25.6
1995	83.0	56.6	0.7	16.8	81.8	10.9	0.5	28.9
2005	81.8	59.0	3.0	16.0	77.0	13.0	1.8	29.4
Sri Lanka								
1990	52.7	64.8	1.0	11.7	49.8	33.9	1.9	19.2
1995	53.2	64.8	1.0	11.8	49.3	33.9	2.8	19.2
2005	70.2	68.9	1.3	10.0	70.2	38.7	4.5	20.2

Source : *UNCTAD Handbook of Statistics*, 2007.

TABLE 5.5
Commodity Diversification Index of SAARC Countries

(*Percent*)

Country	*1985*		*1995*		*2005*	
	Export	*Import*	*Export*	*Import*	*Export*	*Import*
Bangladesh	0.5 (49)	0.43 (170)	0.56 (74)	0.55 (204)	0.74 (112)	0.6 (232)
Bhutan	0.46 (25)	0.42 (58)	0.48 (22)	0.37 (119)	0.69 (39)	0.61 (117)
India	0.61 (201)	0.42 (193)	0.58 (221)	0.46 (213)	0.55 (258)	0.5 (256)
Maldives	0.45 (24)	0.36 (85)	0.48 (11)	0.43 (141)	0.76 (24)	0.49 (168)
Nepal	0.47 (42)	0.39 (167)	0.46 (38)	0.45 (124)	0.54 (101)	0.52 (215)
Pakistan	0.63 (137)	0.4 (199)	0.7 (1)	0.48 (208)	0.77 (207)	0.47 (247)
Sri Lanka	0.59 (114)	0.4 (199)	0.69 (160)	0.45 (218)	0.7 (167)	0.46 (215)

Figures in parentheses are the number of commodities covered in export/import.
Source : *UNCTAD Handbook of Statistics*, 2007.

penetration in foreign markets higher than the import penetration (Arghyrou and Bazina, 2003). The results of this index of SAARC countries have been reported in Table 5.6. Table depicts that India had competitive gain in food and live animals, beverage and tobacco, and miscellaneous manufactured articles, Bangladesh and Nepal in miscellaneous manufactured articles, Bhutan in crude materials, inedible except fuels; mineral fuels, lubricants and related materials and chemicals-related products, Sri Lanka in food and live animals and Pakistan in machinery and transport equipment in 1985, 1995 as well as in 2005. Maldives had modest competitive losses for all commodities sections during the study period. For crude materials, inedible except fuels, Nepal, Pakistan, and Sri Lanka had comparative loss in 1995 and 2005. This situation was also seen for food and live animals in Nepal and for unclassified goods in Bangladesh. For commodity sections like

TABLE 5.6

Section-wise Balassa Index in SAARC Countries

Country	*Year*	*Commodity Sections*									
		0	*1*	*2*	*3*	*4*	*5*	*6*	*7*	*8*	*9*
Bangladesh	1985	-0.55	-0.15	-0.01	-0.90	-0.99	-0.98	0.0004	-0.95	0.48	0.12
	1995	-0.28	-1	0.15	-1	-1	-0.68	-0.52	-0.81	0.72	-0.52
	2005	-0.31	-0.13	-0.82	-0.42	-0.99	-0.80	-0.48	-0.92	0.82	-0.68
Bhutan	1985	-0.15	-0.73	0.63	0.22	-1	0.44	-0.07	-1	-0.9	-1
	1995	-0.17	0.52	0.61	0.24	-1	0.28	-0.13	-1	-0.82	-1
	2005	-0.31	-0.17	0.24	0.44	-1	0.11	-0.01	-1	-0.66	-1
India	1985	0.48	0.96	-0.15	-0.77	-0.88	-0.76	-0.09	-0.70	0.50	-0.51
	1995	0.75	1.00	-0.27	-0.93	-0.49	-0.37	0.33	-0.51	0.64	-0.72
	2005	0.45	0.59	-0.15	-0.53	-0.75	-0.07	0.24	-0.49	0.48	-0.84
Maldives	1985	-1	-1	-1	-1	-1	-1	-1	-1	-1	-1
	1995	-0.16	-1	-1	-1	-1	-1	-1	-1	-0.38	—
	2005	0.04	-1	-0.94	-1	-0.99	-0.99	-0.99	-0.97	-0.99	-1
Nepal	1985	0.12	-0.89	0.06	-0.99	-0.36	-0.99	-0.57	-0.96	0.07	-0.75
	1995	-0.48	-0.95	-0.74	-1	-0.81	-0.92	-0.46	-0.99	0.31	-1
	2005	-0.15	-0.90	-0.87	-0.99	-.043	-0.62	-0.21	-0.95	0.50	-0.99

(*Contd.*)

TABLE 5.6 (*Contd.*)

		0	*1*	*2*	*3*	*4*	*5*	*6*	*7*	*8*	*9*
Pakistan	1985	-0.13	0.70	0.04	-0.95	-1	-0.74	0.26	-0.96	0.45	0.58
	1995	0.05	-0.21	-0.55	-0.91	-0.99	-0.93	0.65	-0.99	0.80	-0.57
	2005	0.04	0.38	-0.73	-0.79	-0.77	-0.81	0.41	0.74	-0.98	0.85
Sri Lanka	1985	0.23	-1	0.52	-0.48	0.50	-0.89	-0.84	-0.84	0.06	-1
	1995	0.22	-0.43	-0.42	-0.93	-0.85	-0.78	-0.44	-0.77	-0.56	0.78
	2005	0.16	-0.03	-0.93	-0.87	-0.61	-0.40	-0.69	-0.72	0.83	0.10

Note : 0 : Food and live animals; 1 : Beverage and tobacco; 2 : Crude minerals inedible except fuels; 3 : Mineral fuels lubricants and related products; 4 : Animals and vegetable oils and fats; 5 : Chemicals products; 6 : Manufactured goods; 7 : Machinery and transport; 8 : Miscellaneous manufactured articles; and 9 : Commodities and transactions not classified.

Source : Worked out from the data given in UN COMTRADE Statistics: Various Issues.

miscellaneous manufactured articles, food and live animals and unclassified goods, India, Pakistan and Sri Lanka recorded comparative gain in 1985 and 2005. The picture of the competitive gain/loss of SAARC countries remained more or less stable. But the one thing is certain that most of SAARC countries had competitive gain in manufactured articles section.

The summary of the Balassa's index is also depicted in Table 5.7. Table points out that Pakistan had competitive gain in maximum number of commodity sections (5) followed by Sri Lanka (4) in 1985. But in 1995 and in 2005 the situation had changed. Pakistan again had maximum number of commodity sections with competitive gains (5) followed by India (4) and Bhutan and Sri Lanka (3).

TABLE 5.7
Number of Commodities Sections with Competitive Gains

Country	*Year*		
	1985	*1995*	*2005*
Bangladesh	3	1	1
Bhutan	3	4	3
India	3	4	4
Maldives	0	0	1
Nepal	3	1	1
Pakistan	5	3	5
Sri Lanka	4	2	3

Source : Worked out from the data given in UN COMTRADE Statistics: Various Issues.

Trade Potential

Table 5.8 also summarizes the Balassa's index in form of trade potential. Table depicts that for food and live animals and miscellaneous manufactured articles, maximum number of SAARC countries were the potential exporters in 1985, 1995 and 2005.

Revealed Comparative Advantage

Besides the trade competitiveness of different sections of the commodities, RCA indices of ten top export items had also

TABLE 5.8
Trade Potential between SAARC Countries

Country	*Year*	*Commodity Sections*									
		0	*1*	*2*	*3*	*4*	*5*	*6*	*7*	*8*	*9*
Bangladesh	1985	P.I.	P.I.	P.I.	P.I.	P.I.	P.I.	P.E.	P.I.	P.E.	P.E.
	1995	P.I.	P.I.	P.E.	P.I.	P.I.	P.I.	P.I.	P.I.	P.E.	P.I.
	2005	P.I.	P.I.	P.I.	P.I.	P.I.	P.I.	P.I.	P.I.	P.E.	P.I.
Bhutan	1985	P.I.	P.I.	P.E.	P.E.	P.I.	P.E.	P.I.	P.I.	P.I.	P.I.
	1995	P.I.	P.E.	P.E.	P.E.	P.I.	P.E.	P.I.	P.I.	P.I.	P.I.
	2005	P.I.	P.I.	P.E.	P.E.	P.I.	P.E.	P.I.	P.I.	P.I.	P.I.
India	1985	P.E.	P.E.	P.I.	P.I.	P.I.	P.I.	P.I.	P.I.	P.E.	P.I.
	1995	P.E.	P.E.	P.I.	P.I.	P.I.	P.I.	P.E.	P.I.	P.E.	P.I.
	2005	P.E.	P.E.	P.I.	P.I.	P.I.	P.I.	P.E.	P.I.	P.E.	P.I.
Maldives	1985	P.T.	P.I.	P.I.	P.I.	P.I.	P.I.	P.I.	P.I.	P.I.	P.I.
	1995	P.I.	P.I.	P.I.	P.I.	P.I.	P.I.	P.I.	P.I.	P.I.	P.I.
	2005	P.E.	P.I.	P.I.	P.I.	P.I.	P.I.	P.I.	P.I.	P.I.	P.I.
Nepal	1985	P.E.	P.I.	P.E.	P.I.	P.I.	P.I.	P.I.	P.I.	P.E.	P.I.
	1995	P.I.	P.I.	P.I.	P.I.	P.I.	P.I.	P.I.	P.I.	P.E.	P.I.
	2005	P.I.	P.I.	P.I.	P.I.	P.I.	P.I.	P.I.	P.I.	P.E.	P.I.

Pakistan	1985	P.I.	P.E.	P.E.	P.I.	P.I.	P.I.	P.E.	P.I.	P.E.	P.E.
	1995	P.E.	P.I.	P.I.	P.I.	P.I.	P.I.	P.E.	P.I.	P.E.	P.I.
	2005	P.E.	P.E.	P.I.	P.I.	P.I.	P.I.	P.E.	P.E.	P.I.	P.E.
Sri Lanka	1985	P.E.	P.I.	P.E.	P.I.	P.E.	P.I.	P.I.	P.I.	P.E.	P.I.
	1995	P.E.	P.I.	P.I.	P.I.	P.I.	P.I.	P.I.	P.I.	P.I.	P.E.
	2005	P.E.	P.I.	P.I.	P.I.	P.I.	P.I.	P.I.	P.I.	P.E.	P.E.

Source : Worked out from the data given in UN COMTRADE *Statistics*: Various Issues.
P.I. = Potential importer. P.E. = Potential exporter.

been measured for the latest years (2002 and 2005). Table 5.9 shows that in 2002, of the 32 export commodities with highest revealed comparative advantage, Sri Lanka, India and Maldives had revealed comparative advantage in narrow range of commodities (4 or 5 out of 10 top exported items). Countries namely, Bangladesh, Nepal and Pakistan had revealed comparative advantage in 6 (out of 10) range of commodities. Most of items with highest revealed comparative advantage entered under manufactured goods section (11 out of 32) followed by food and live animals (8 items).

In food and live animals, Sri Lanka had highest revealed comparative advantage in tea and mate, Maldives in fish salted, dried as smoked, Pakistan in rice and Bangladesh in shell fish, fresh and frozen. In miscellaneous manufactured goods, RCA of Bangladesh was highest in under garment non-knit men's outwear knit and Nepal in textile clothing accessories. In manufactured goods, Nepal had highest revealed comparative advantage in floor coverings, Pakistan in textile articles, cotton fabrics, woven and textile yarn and India in pearl prec, stones indicating extent of complementarities in export structure in 2002.

Table 5.11 depicts that in 2005, of 46 export commodities with highest revealed comparative advantage, Sri Lanka had revealed comparative advantage in 9 (out of 10) range of commodities while number was 4 in 2002. Other SAARC country's condition also improved because all countries had revealed comparative advantage in at least 7 (out of 10) range of commodities. Most of the items with highest revealed comparative advantage entered under miscellaneous manufactured goods (23 out of 46) followed by machinery and transport (11) and food and live animals (7) (Table 5.12).

In food and live animals, Sri Lanka again had highest revealed comparative advantage again in tea and mate (333.0), Maldives in Fish, dried salted or smoked (190.25) and Pakistan in rice (67.33) (same position as in 2002). In miscellaneous manufactured articles, Bangladesh had highest comparative advantage in male clothing, knitted crocheted (64.71), Pakistan in male clothing knitted crocheted (37.5), Maldives and Sri Lanka in female clothing in knitted crocheted (36.32) and (25.08)

TABLE 5.9

Revealed Comparative Advantage Indices (2002)

Country	*Commodities*	*Number of Commodities*
Bangladesh	Under garments non-knit (80.59), men's outwear knit (38.43), shell fish, fresh, frozen (20.68), outer garments knit non-elastic (16.25), leather (12.92), other woven textile fabric (8.46)	6
India	Pearl, Prec. semi-precious stones (16.11), gold silver-ware, jewellery (7.83), petroleum products (2.19), iron, steel univ, plate sheet (2.13), pharmaceutical products (1.22)	5
Maldives	Fish salted, dried, smoked (293.75), fish etc. Prept, preservedness knitted (74.93), under garments knitted (45.14), fish, fresh chilled frozen (10.5), feeding stuff for animals (2.92)	5
Nepal	Floor coverings (92.71), processed animal and vegetable oil (59.71), textile clothing accessories ness (29.07), perfumery cosmetic (9.96), butter (6.4), special transaction (4.71)	6
Pakistan	Textile articles (58.52), rice (48.5), cotton fabrics, woven (35.27), textile yarn (18.49), head gear on textile clothing (15.29), woven man made fabric (9.23)	6
Sri Lanka	Tea and mate (344.75), women's out wear non-knit (20.79), rubber tyres tubes, etc. (5.17), copper (4.36)	4
Total		32

Source : Worked out from the data given in UNCTAD Handbook of Statistics, 2004.

respectively indicating existence of complementarities in export structure at commodity level in 2005.

Import Share

Table 5.13 and Table 5.14 shows that in import of 47 items considered, Bhutan, Maldives and India had sizeable imports in large range of commodities (9 or 8) in 2002. Machinery and transport accounted for large share in imports (12 items) followed by manufactured goods (11 items). Bhutan had high import share in most of items of machinery and transport,

TABLE 5.10

Section-wise Revealed Comparative Advantage in 2002

Country	*Food and live animals*	*Crude minerals inedible except fuels*	*Mineral fuels lubricants and related materials*	*Animals and vegetable oils and fats*	*Chemicals*	*Manu-factured goods*	*Machinery and transport*	*Misc. Manu. goods*	*Commo-dities transaction*	*Number of commo-dities*
(1)	(2)	(3)	(4)	(5)	(6)	(7)	(8)	(9)	(10)	(11)
Bangladesh	1	—	—	—	—	2	—	3	—	6
India	—	—	1	—	1	2	—	1	—	5
Maldives	4	—	—	—	—	—	—	1	—	5
Nepal	1	—	—	1	1	1	—	1	1	6
Pakistan	1	—	—	—	—	4	—	1	—	6
Sri Lanka	1	—	—	—	—	2	—	1	—	4
Number of commodities	8	0	1	1	2	11	0	8	1	32

Source : Worked out from the data given in UNCTAD Handbook of Statistics, 2004.

TABLE 5.11

Revealed Comparative Advantage in SAARC Countries (2005)

Country	*Commodities*	*Number of Commodities*
Bangladesh	Male clothing, knitted crocheted (64.71), male clothing, woven (43.42), articles of appearances (36.03), crustacean molluse aquat invertebra (32.21), leather (18.1), female clothing knitted crocheted (17.08), female clothing women (13.12), made up textile articlesness (8.71)	6
India	Pearls, prec. semi-prec. stones (13.93), irenore and concentrates (13.92), jewelleryness (10.46), made up textile articleness (7.38), other organic chemical (7.37), textiles yarn (5.7), female clothing women (4.71)	7
Maldives	Fish, dried, salted smoked (190.25), fish, fresh live chilled frozen (120.39), fish, shell fish, prepare and preserved (71.71), female clothing, knitted, crocheted (36.32), printed matter (10.42), crustacean morlluse aquat invertebra (6.89), heavy petroleum and bituminous oil (6.20)	7
Nepal	Processed animal and vegetable fats and oils (156.2), clothing accessories (18.05), female clothing woven (16.42), floor coverings etc. (11.64), perfume toilet cosmetics (10.90), flat platted iron non-alloy steel (9.06), articles of apparelness (6.91)	7
Pakistan	Rice (67.33), made up textile articleness (59.29), woven cotton fabrics (46.82) male clothing knitted crocheted (37.5), textile yarn (20.15), head gear non-textile clothing (17.75), male clothing woven (8.82), articles of apparelness (4.83)	8
Sri Lanka	Tea and mate (333), female clothing, knitted, crocheted (25.08), female clothing woven (24.35), male clothing knitted (20.30), male clothing woven (17.64), articles of apparealness (12.70), head gear non-textile clothing (10.6), rubber for wheels incl. inner tube (8.60), pearls prec. semi-prec. stones (5.15)	9
Total		46

Source : Worked out from the data given in UNCTAD Handbook of Statistics, 2007.

TABLE 5.12

Section-wise Revealed Comparative Advantage in 2005

Country	*Food and live animals*	*Crude minerals inedible except fuels*	*Mineral fuels lubricants and related materials*	*Animals and vegetable oils and fats*	*Chemicals*	*Manu-factured goods*	*Machinery and transport*	*Misc. Manu. goods*	*Commo-dities transaction*	*Number of commo-dities*
(1)	(2)	(3)	(4)	(5)	(6)	(7)	(8)	(9)	(10)	(11)
Bangladesh	1	—	—	—	—	—	2	5	—	8
India	—	—	1	—	—	1	3	2	—	7
Maldives	4	—	—	1	—	—	—	2	—	7
Nepal	—	—	—	—	1	1	1	4	—	7
Pakistan	1	—	—	—	—	—	3	4	—	8
Sri Lanka	1	—	—	—	—	—	2	6	—	9
Number of commodities	7	0	1	1	1	2	11	23	0	46

Source : Worked out from the data given in UNCTAD Handbook of Statistics, 2007.

TABLE 5.13
Import Share of SAARC Countries (2002)

Country	*Commodities*	*Number of Commodities*
(1)	*(2)*	*(3)*
Bangladesh	Cotton fabrics, woven (6.97), fabrics, woven of man made fibres (6.35), textiles yarn (5.86), universals, plates and sheets of iron or steel (4.76), lime, cemęnt and fabricated construction materials (3.45), cotton (3.38), ships, boats and floating structures (3.91)	7
Bhutan	Parts of and accessories suitable for office machines (10.86), rice (4.65), motor vehicles for transport of goods/material (4.40), passenger motor cars for transport of passenger and goods (3.89), civil engineering and contractors plants and parts (3.68), structure parts of structures, iron, steel, aluminum (2.96), household type, electrical and non-electrical equipment (2.72), other power generating machinery and parts (2.70), iron and steel bars, rods, angles, shapes and sects (2.42)	9
India	Petrol, oils, crude and oils obtained from bituminous minerals (18.52), pearls, precious and semi-precious stones (10.93), gold, non-monotony (8.71), inorganic chemical elements, oxides and naligen salts (2.49), fertilizer manufactures (2.17), cool, lignite and peat (1.65), fixed vegetable oil, soft, crude, refined (1.30), silver, platinum and other metals (1.21)	8
Maldives	Vegetables, fresh, chilled, frozen/preserved roots, tubers (2.89), internal combustion piston engines and parts (2.73), aircraft and associated equipment and parts (2.26), fruit and nuts, fresh or dried (2.17), furniture and parts (2.15), milk and cream (1.98), meat, edible meat offals, fresh, chilled or frozen (1.94), telecommunication equipment and parts (1.87), articles of material (1.83)	9

(Contd.)

TABLE 5.13 (*Contd.*)

(1)	*(2)*	*(3)*
Nepal	Special transactions and commodities not classified according to kind (13.92), medicinal and pharmaceutical products (3.19), machinery and equipment specialized for particular industry (2.56), other organic chemicals (2.00)	4
Pakistan	Petroleum products, refined (21.00), textile and leather machinery and parts (3.02), other fixed vegetable oils fluid or solid crude (2.95), polymerization and coop. products (2.52), sugar and honey (2.09), tea and mate (2.01), misc. manufacture goods (1.90)	7
Sri Lanka	Knitted or crocheted fabrics (5.17), special textile fabrics and related products (2.48), telecommunication and parts (2.30)	3
Total		47

Source : Worked out from the data given in UNCTAD Handbook of Statistics, 2004.

TABLE 5.14

Section-wise Import Share (2002)

Country	Food and live animals	Beverages and tobacco	Crude minerals inedible except fuels	Mineral fuels lubricants and related materials	Animals and vegetable oils and fats	Chemicals	Manu-factured goods	Machinery and transport	Misc. Manu. goods	Commo-dities tran-sactions	Number of commo-dities
(1)	(2)	(3)	(4)	(5)	(6)	(7)	(8)	(9)	(10)	(11)	(12)
Bangladesh	1	—	1	—	—	—	5	1	—	—	7
Bhutan	1	—	—	—	—	—	2	6	—	—	9
India	—	—	—	2	1	2	2	—	—	1	8
Maldives	4	—	—	—	—	—	—	3	2	—	9
Nepal	—	—	—	—	—	2	—	1	—	—	7
Pakistan	2	—	—	1	—	3	—	—	1	—	3
Sri Lanka	—	—	—	—	—	—	2	1	—	—	3
Number of commodities	7	0	1	3	1	7	11	12	3	2	47

Source : Worked out from the data given in UNCTAD Handbook of Statistics, 2004.

Pakistan in petroleum products, India in petrol, oils and crude oils, pearl and semi-precious stones, Nepal in special transactions and commodities, Sri Lanka in knitted or crocheted fabrics, Bangladesh in cotton fabric and woven and Maldives in vegetables fresh chilled frozen/preserved.

II

MARKET CONCENTRATION INDEX

This index is a measure of the degree of market concentration. It has been normalized to obtain values ranking from 0 to 1 (maximum concentration). Table 5.15 depicts the concentration index for exports as well as concentration index for imports of SAARC countries during the study period. In 1985, its value was less than 0.50 in all SAARC nations indicating that exports are geographically diversified. It was 0.22, 0.25 and 0.28 for Pakistan, Nepal and Bangladesh, respectively. In 1995, export market concentration index of SAARC countries namely, Bangladesh, Bhutan, India and Sri Lanka had decreased depicting the market diversification of their exports. While in case of Maldives, Nepal and Pakistan, it had increased. As compared to 1985, export market concentration index of all SAARC countries except Bangladesh and Maldives had decreased in 2005 depicting the geographic diversification of their exports. In case of import market concentration index, all SAARC nations had value less than 0.25 in 1985. The import market concentration of Maldives (0.14 per cent) followed by Bangladesh (0.13 per cent) and Nepal was 0.11 per cent. In 1995, all SAARC nations except Bangladesh and Nepal experienced a decrease in index. But as compared to 1985, only Bhutan, India and Nepal experienced an increase in import concentration index in 2005 indicating the increasing geographic concentration of import items of these countries.

Direction of Intra-SAARC Trade

Regarding the direction of intra-SAARC countries, Table 5.16 shows that maximum share's was of Nepal (31.88 percent) followed by Maldives (17.39 percent) and Bangladesh (7.66 percent) in 1985. In 1995, all SAARC countries except India and Bhutan experienced decline in exports to SAARC countries.

TABLE 5.15
Market Concentration Index of SAARC Countries

(Percent)

Country	*1985*		*1995*		*2005*	
	Export	*Import*	*Export*	*Import*	*Export*	*Import*
Bangladesh	0.28 (49)	0.13 (170)	0.26 (74)	0.14 (204)	0.3 (112)	0.1 (2)
Bhutan	0.47 (25)	0.23 (58)	0.33 (22)	0.1 (119)	0.29 (39)	0.39 (117)
India	0.31 (201)	0.18 (193)	0.14 (221)	0.14 (213)	0.13 (258)	0.24 (256)
Maldives	0.38 (24)	0.14 (85)	0.4 (11)	0.1 (141)	0.42 (24)	0.11 (168)
Nepal	0.25 (42)	0.11 (167)	0.44 (38)	0.25 (124)	0.17 (101)	0.12 (215)
Pakistan	0.22 (137)	0.15 (199)	0.24 (139)	0.11 (208)	0.21 (207)	0.13 (240)
Sri Lanka	0.34 (114)	0.17 (199)	0.22 (160)	0.09 (218)	0.21 (247)	0.1 (234)

Figures in parentheses are the number of commodities covered in export/import.
Source : *UNCTAD Handbook of Statistics* : Various Issues.

Nepal witnessed a rapid decline in exports to SAARC (as share decreased from 31.88 percent in 1985 to 9.23 percent in 1995). In 2005 the maximum share was of Nepal (41.42 percent) followed by Bhutan (37.38 percent) and Maldives (12.61 percent) indicating the increasing intra-regional exports of small SAARC countries. As compared to pre-WTO period, countries namely, Bangladesh, Maldives and Pakistan had experienced decrease in export share to SAARC exports during post–WTO period (share decreased from 7.66 percent, 17.39 percent and 5.29 percent to 2.00 percent, 12.61 percent and 4.56 percent, respectively), while other SAARC nations namely, Bhutan, India, Nepal ad Sri Lanka experienced an increase in share (as share increased from negligible to 37.38 percent, from 2.95 percent to 5.06 percent, from 31.88 percent to 41.42 percent and from 3.99 percent to 12.42 percent in 2005).

TABLE 5.16

Direction of Export of SAARC Countries

(*Percent*)

Country	*Year*	*Bangladesh*	*Bhutan*	*India*	*Maldives*	*Nepal*	*Pakistan*	*Sri Lanka*	*SAARC*
Bangladesh	1985	—	—	3.00	0.01	0.50	4.20	0.02	7.66
	1995	—	0.01	1.14	—	0.31	0.85	0.37	2.68
	2005	—	0.03	1.28	0	0.04	0.56	0.09	2.00
Bhutan	1985	—	—	—	—	—	—	—	—
	1995	6.00	—	15.53	—	0.59	1.74	0.0	23.5
	2005	3.43	—	27.76	—	.. —	0.19	0.0	37.38
India	1985	1.14	—	—	0.01	0.90	0.13	0.78	2.95
	1995	3.14	0.04	—	0.04	0.35	0.23	1.26	5.06
	2005	1.64	0.10	—	0.06	0.83	0.64	1.88	5.06
Maldives	1985	—	—	—	—	—	—	17.39	17.39
	1995	—	—	0.13	—	—	—	13.12	13.25
	2005	—	—	1.01	—	—	—	11.60	12.61
Nepal	1985	—	—	28.12	—	—	1.25	2.50	31.88
	1995	1.09	—	7.71	—	—	0.14	0.20	9.23
	2005	0.32	—	40.68	0.01	—	0.39	0.01	41.42

Pakistan	1985	2.37	—	1.39	0.01	0.00	—	1.54	5.29
	1995	1.92	0.01	0.49	0.02	0.04	—	0.69	3.16
	2005	1.46	0.02	2.10	0.02	0.02	—	0.96	4.56
Sri Lanka	1985	1.09	—	0.45	0.39	0.01	2.05	—	3.99
	1995	0.32	—	0.84	0.37	0.00	1.13	—	2.66
	2005	0.30	—	10.78	0.51	0.00	0.82	—	12.42

Source : Worked out from the data given in UNCTAD Handbook of Statistics: Various Issues.

TABLE 5.17
Trade Intensity Index of SAARC Countries

(Percent)

Country	Year	Bangladesh	Bhutan	India	Maldives	Nepal	Pakistan	Sri Lanka	SAARC
Bangladesh	1985	—	—	1.32	3.80	2.66	24.69	6.87	6.82
	1995	—	4.67	1.71	0.0	12.14	3.87	3.72	2.35
	2005	—	6.42	0.98	0.0	2.30	2.36	1.09	1.15
Bhutan	1985	—	—	—	—	—	—	—	—
	1995	47.96	—	23.26	—	23.01	7.87	0	20.55
	2005	26.45	—	21.33	—	24.70	0.80	0	18.12
India	1985	8.95	—	—	3.77	39.67	0.44	8.45	2.20
	1995	25.06	18.69	—	7.75	13.63	1.05	12.69	4.43
	2005	12.48	21.11	—	8.52	47.18	2.67	22.50	2.88
Maldives	1985	—	—	—	—	—	—	189.85	13.05
	1995	—	—	0.19	—	—	—	225.86	19.83
	2005	—	—	0.78	—	—	—	140.66	7.38
Nepal	1985	—	—	35.5	—	—	4.27	27.28	23.93
	1995	8.76	—	11.54	—	—	0.65	2.82	8.09
	2005	2.46	—	31.25	0.14	—	1.64	0.15	23.90

Pakistan	1985	18.70	—	1.75	3.79	0.13	—	16.76	3.96
	1995	15.40	4.67	0.74	3.90	1.56	—	6.94	2.77
	2005	11.23	0.32	1.61	2.87	1.15	—	11.61	2.62
Sri Lanka	1985	8.62	—	0.57	148.29	0.44	6.97	—	2.91
	1995	2.67	—	1.26	72.12	0.0	5.15	—	2.33
	2005	2.31	—	8.28	73.28	0.05	3.46	—	7.16

Source : Worked out from the data given in UNCTAD Handbook of Statistics: Various Issues.

Intra-SAARC exports show that for Bangladesh and Sri Lanka, Pakistan constituted main export market with share being 4 percent and 2 percent while for India and Pakistan, Bangladesh constituted main export market with share being 1.14 percent and 2.37 per cent respectively and for Nepal, India constituted main market with share being 28.12 percent in 1985. In 1995, all SAARC countries main export market remained same except Bangladesh and India. The share of Bangladesh in India's exports had increased from 1.14 percent in 1985 to 3.14 percent in 1995. In 2005, for most of the countries namely, Bangladesh, Bhutan, Nepal, Pakistan and Sri Lanka, India constituted main market with share being 1.28 percent, 27.76 percent, 40.68 percent, 2.10 percent and 10.78 percent respectively. For Maldives and India, Sri Lanka constituted main market with share being 11.60 percent and 1.88 percent respectively in 2005 indicating lack of market diversification of exports of SAARC countries.

Trade Intensity Index

Trade intensity indices highlight the importance of secular changes in bilateral trade flows. If it takes a value above (below) unity, the countries have greater (smaller) bilateral trade than world. Trade intensity indices of different SAARC countries have been shown in Table 5.17. Table depicts that in 1985, trade intensity index of Nepal with SAARC was maximum, i.e. 23.93 percent followed by Maldives (13.05 percent) and Bangladesh (6.82 percent). Country-wise analysis shows that Bangladesh's trade was most intense with Pakistan (24.69 percent), India with Nepal (39.67 percent), of Maldives with Sri Lanka (189.85 percent), of Nepal with India (35.5 percent), of Pakistan with Bangladesh (18.70 percent), and of Sri Lanka with Maldives (148.29 percent). As compared to 1985, intensity index of Bangladesh, Nepal, Pakistan and Sri Lanka with SAARC experienced decline in 1995. Nepal witnessed a rapid decline from 23.93 percent in 1985 to 8.09 percent in 1995. In 2005, index of Nepal with SAARC was maximum, i.e. 23.93 percent followed by Bhutan (18.12 percent) and Sri Lanka (7.16 percent). Country-wise analysis shows that Bangladesh's trade was most intense with Bhutan (6.42 percent), of Bhutan with Bangladesh (26.45 percent), of India with Nepal (47.18 percent), of Maldives with Sri Lanka (140.66 percent), of Nepal with India (31.25 percent), of Pakistan with Sri Lanka (11.61 percent) and of Sri Lanka with Maldives (73.28 percent). Heavy dependence on either one or two markets lead to reduction in intra-SAARC exports of countries like Bhutan, Maldives and Nepal.

Thus, the chapter analyses that there is a lack of complementarities in production and trade among SAARC countries. Therefore, there is a lack of intra-regional trade in SAARC. Heavy dependence on either one or two markets lead to reduction in intra-SAARC exports of countries. On the other side, trade of SAARC nations is geographically diversified.

6

Indo-SAARC Trade

Trends and Growth

This chapter examines India's trade performance with SAARC countries. For this, the chapter has been divided into two sections. Section I deals with trade performance at aggregate level, while section II deals with trade performance at disaggregated level.

I

PERFORMANCE OF INDIA IN SAARC

Table 6.1 depicts that India alone represented 76 percent of the SAARC region's population and 80 percent of its gross domestic product of the region in 2006. Not only India was a strong country in terms of GDP and population but also in terms of FDI inward flows, exports and imports (having share of 68 percent, 77 percent and 74 percent respectively of the region). Pakistan and Bangladesh were having the second position and third position respectively in terms of population, FDI inward flows, exports and imports. Bhutan and Maldives were poorest

TABLE 6.1

Selected Indicators of SAARC Nations (2006)

Country	*Population (thousand)*	*GDP (millions of dollars)*	*GDP Per Capita (millions of dollars)*	*FDI Inward Flows (millions of dollars)*	*Exports (millions of dollars)*	*Imports (millions of dollars)*
(1)	(2)	(3)	(4)	(5)	(6)	(7)
Bangladesh	144345 (9.9)	6196.1 (0.6)	429.26	692 (7.1)	12277 (7.8)	16017 (7.0)
Bhutan	647 (0.0)	927 (0.1)	1423.5	1 (0.0)	304 (0.2)	500 (0.2)
India	1109811 (75.9)	906268 (79.9)	816.6	6598 (67.6)	120887 (76.7)	169835 (74.3)
Maldives	337 (0.0)	915 (0.1)	2715	14 (0.1)	22.5 (0.1)	927 (0.4)
Nepal	27658 (1.9)	8052 (0.7)	291	5 (0.1)	87 (0.1)	2604 (1.1)
Pakistan	159002 (10.9)	128830 (11.4)	810.24	21.38 (22.4)	16470 (10.4)	28405 (12.4)
Sri Lanka	19771 (1.4)	26967 (2.4)	136396	272 (2.8)	6735 (4.3)	10353 (4.5)
SAARC	1461571	1133914	775.82	9765	157715	22864

Note : Figures in parentheses are percentage shares.
Source : Worked out from the data given in *World Development Indicators*, 2007.

countries in terms of GDP and Nepal was poorest country in terms of exports. There are huge differences in demographic as well as in economic factors among SAARC nations.

India's Trade Performance with SAARC Region and World

Table 6.2 shows the trade trends of India to SAARC as well as to the world during 1985-2005. Table depicts that India's *exports to SAARC* had been continuously increasing since 1995. During pre-WTO period, India's exports to SAARC increased from US $ 270 millions in 1985 to US $1022 millions in 1994, i.e. increased by 278.52 percentage points and during post-WTO period, it increased from US $ 1544 millions in 1995 to US $ 5129 millions in 2005, i.e. increased by 232.19 percentage points. India's *imports from SAARC* fluctuated but having tendency to increase during pre-WTO period. During post-WTO period, it showed continuous an upward trend and thus imports reached a level to US $ 1353 millions in 2005 from US $ 199 millions in 1995, i.e. imports increased by 579.90 percentage points. The growth rate of India's exports with SAARC was 15.35 percent during the entire study period. India's exports experienced a higher growth rate (16.61 percent) in pre-WTO period than in post-WTO period (13.07 percent). While for imports, India experienced a growth rate of 14.13 percent during the entire study period (1985-05). India's imports witnessed a higher growth rate, i.e. 19.00 percent in post-WTO period than in pre-WTO period (5.00 percent only). Thus the case was reversed for imports.

Table also depicts that India's *exports to world* had continuously increased during the entire study period. India's exports to world had increased from US $ 8265 millions in 1985 to US $ 24196 millions in 1994 during pre-WTO period and during post-WTO period; it reached a level of US $ 99474 millions in 2005 from US $ 30537 millions in 1995, i.e. increased by 225.75 points. Similar trends occurred for imports. India's imports to world showed an upward trend in pre-WTO period as well as in post-WTO period. The growth rate of India's exports to world was 11.35 percent during the entire study period. India's exports experienced a marginal higher growth rate of (12.33 percent) during post WTO period than in pre-WTO period (12.18 percent). During 1985-2005, the growth rate

TABLE 6.2
India's Trade with SAARC Region and World

(US $ Millions)

Year	India's Trade with SAARC				India's Trade with World				
	Exports	Imports	Total trade	Index 1995 = 100	Exports	Imports	Total trade	Index 1995=100	Share of SAARC in India's Trade
(1)	(2)	(3)	(4)	(5)	(6)	(7)	(8)	(9)	(10)
1985	270	112	382	21.92	8265	16329	24594	37.82	1.55
1986	277 (2.59)	73 (-34.82)	350 (-8.36)	20.08	9135 (10.53)	15051 (-7.83)	24186 (-1.66)	37.2	1.45
1987	306 (10.47)	84 (15.07)	390 (11.43)	22.38	10798 (18.20)	16841 (11.89)	27639 (14.27)	42.51	1.41
1988	364 (18.95)	96 (14.29)	460 (17.95)	26.39	13193 (22.18)	19035 (13.02)	32228 (16.60)	49.57	1.41
1989	550 (51.10)	62 (-35.42)	612 (33.04)	35.11	15839 (20.05)	19297 (1.38)	35136 (9.02)	54.04	1.23
1990	487 (-11.45)	97 (53.45)	584 (-4.58)	33.5	17813 (12.46)	23990 (24.32)	41803 (18.97)	64.29	1.4
1991	623 (27.42)	95 (-2.06)	718 (22.95)	41.19	17873 (0.34)	19509 (-18.68)	37382 (-10.57)	57.49	1.92

(Contd.)

TABLE 6.2 (Contd.)

(1)	(2)	(3)	(4)	(5)	(6)	(7)	(8)	(9)	(10)
1992	719	194	913	52.38	18500	23227	41727	64.17	2.19
	(15.40)	(104.21)	(27.16)		(3.51)	(19.05)	(11.62)		
1993	821	99	920	52.78	20259	21225	414814	63.8	2.22
	(14.18)	(-48.97)	(0.77)		(9.51)	(-8.62)	(-0.58)		
1994	1022	129	1151	66.03	24196	25477	49673	76.39	2.32
	(24.48)	(30.30)	(25.10)		(19.43)	(20.03)	(19.74)		
1995	1544	199	1743	100	30537	34484	65021	100	2.68
	(51.08)	(54.26)	(51.43)		(26.21)	(35.35)	(30.90)		
1996	1650	197	1847	107.82	32325	36055	68380	105.16	2.7
	(6.87)	(-1.00)	(5.97)		(5.86)	(4.56)	(5.17)		
1997	1633.6	236	1869.7	107.27	33289	38911	72200	111.04	2.59
	(-0.99)	(19.80)	(5.97)		(2.98)	(7.92)	(5.59)		
1998	1662.1	40.78	2069.9	118.76	33437	46979	82646	144.19	2.27
	(1.74)	(72.46)	(10.71)		(0.44)	(9.30)	(8.15)		
1999	1465.8	414.6	1880.4	107.88	35667	51523	93902	127.11	2.39
	(-11.81)	(1.72)	(-9.15)		(0.60)	(9.67)	(13.61)		
2000	1795	448.8	2243.8	128.69	42379	50392	93753	144.42	2.73
	(22.46)	(8.41)	(19.32)		(-18.82)	(-2.20)	(-0.15)		
2001	2051	50.38	2554.8	146.57	43361	50392	93753	144.42	2.73
	(13.45)	(12.25)	(13.86)		(2.32)	(-2.20)	(-0.15)		

2002	2549 (25.17)	526 (4.41)	3075 (20.37)	176.42	49250 (13.58)	56517 (14.14)	105767 (12.81)	162.67	2.91
2003	3794 (48.84)	629 (19.59)	4423 (43.83)	253.76	57085 (15.91)	72558 (23.86)	129643 (21.33)	199.38	3.41
2004	4262 (12.34)	847 (34.66)	5109 (15.51)	293.11	76649 (34.27)	99775 (40.06)	176424 (37.48)	71.33	2.9
2005	5129 (20.34)	1353 (64.36)	6522 (27.64)	374.18	99474 (29.78)	136360 (39.67)	238834 (35.38)	367.32	2.73
Compound Growth Rate (percent)									
1985-94	16.61	5.00	14.42	—	12.18	5.16	8.05	—	—
1995-05	13.07	19.00	13.95	—	12.33	22.50	7.38	—	—
1985-05	15.35	14.13	14.91	—	11.35	10.12	10.60	—	—

Note : Figures in parentheses are annual growth rates. *India's Share in SAARC Trade.*
Source : Worked out from the data given in *Key Indicators of Asia and Pacific Countries:* Various Issues.

of India imports from world was 10.12 percent while during post-WTO period, growth rate of imports was (22.50 percent) which was higher than the growth rate of imports during pre-WTO period (5.16 percent).

The comparative analysis of India's trade with SAARC and world depicts that India's growth rate of trade with SAARC was higher than her growth with world during pre-WTO period, post-WTO period and entire study period. Share of SAARC in India's trade had increased from 1.55 percent in 1985 to 2.32 percent in 1994 and reached a level of 2.73 percent in 2005 exhibiting increased role of SAARC in India's trade.

India's Share in SAARC Trade

Table 6.3 shows India's share in SAARC trade during 1985-2005. India's share in SAARC exports ranged between 45 percent (1985) to 71.3 percent (1994) during pre-WTO period and between 67.2 percent (1999) to 85 percent (2002) during post-WTO period. However, its share in imports ranged

TABLE 6.3
India's Share in SAARC Trade

(Percent)

Year	Exports	Imports	Total Trade	SAARC
1985	45.0	22.1	34.3	100
1986	50.0	14.2	32.8	100
1987	49.9	16.1	34.4	100
1988	45.8	13.8	31.2	100
1989	54.8	10.1	35.4	100
1990	56.5	13.4	36.9	100
1991	61.9	10.6	37.7	100
1992	58.4	15.5	63.8	100
1993	68.9	7.8	37.6	100
1994	71.3	8.6	40.0	100
1995	76.2	8.9	42.3	100
1996	77.0	7.1	37.5	100
1997	75.1	9.5	40.0	100
1998	67.4	13.3	37.2	100

1999	67.2	15.8	39.1	100
2000	69.2	16.5	42.2	100
2001	72.6	16.3	43.2	100
2002	85.0	16.0	49.0	100
2003	79.5	21.3	51.4	100
2004	72.0	15.0	44.2	100
2005	72.6	19.6	46.0	100
Average (1985-94)	56.25	13.22	35.71	—
Average (1995-05)	81.38	15.93	47.21	—
Average (1985-2005)	62.19	16.35	39.11	—

Source : Worked out from the data given in *Key Indicators of Asia and Pacific Countries:* Various Issues.

between 7.8 percent (1993) to 22.1 (1985) during pre-WTO period and between 7.1 percent (1996) to 21.3 percent (2003) during post-WTO period. On an average, India's share in SAARC exports and imports was 56.25 percent and 13.22 percent during pre-WTO period, 81.38 percent and 15.93 percent during post-WTO period and 62.19 percent and 16.35 percent during the entire study period. Thus in SAARC trade, India was the major exporter and minor importer during pre-WTO period, post-WTO period and entire study period.

India's Trade Performance with SAARC Countries

Exports

Country-wise analysis given in Table 6.4 shows that *during pre-WTO period* India's exports to Bangladesh increased from US $ 104 millions in 1985 to US $ 521 millions in 1994 (exhibiting growth rate of 20.50 percent). Her exports to Bhutan increased from negligible to US $ 7 millions in 1994. Her exports to Maldives and Nepal had been fluctuating but tendency to increase during pre-WTO period (exports to Maldives and Nepal increased from US $ 1 millions and US $ 82 millions in 1985 to US $ 16 millions and US $ 85 millions in 1994) there by

TABLE 6.4
Destination of India's Exports to SAARC Countries and SAARC

(*US $ Millions*)

Year	*Bangladesh*	*Bhutan*	*Maldives*	*Nepal*	*Pakistan*	*Sri Lanka*	*SAARC*
(1)	(2)	(3)	(4)	(5)	(6)	(7)	(8)
1985	104	0	1	82	12	71	270
1986	113	0	2	82	13	67	277
	(8.65)	0.00	(100.00)	0.00	(8.33)	(-5.63)	(2.59)
1987	145	0	2	73	12	74	30.6
	(28.31)	0.00	0.00	(-10.98)	(-7.69)	(10.44)	(10.47)
1988	170	0	3	82	19	90	364
	(17.24)	0.00	(50.00)	(12.33)	(58.33)	(21.62)	(18.95)
1989	176	0	0	215	42	117	550
	(3.53)	0.00	(-66.67)	(162.20)	(121.05)	(30.00)	(51.10)
1990	297	0	5	40	43	102	487
	(68.75)	0.00	(400.00)	(-81.40)	(2.38)	(-12.82)	(-11.45)
1991	325	1	5	77	40	175	623
	(9.43)	(100.00)	0.00	(92.50)	(-6.98)	(71.57)	(27.42)
1992	353	2	8	73	52	231	719
	(8.62)	(100.00)	(60.00)	(-5.19)	(30.00)	(32.00)	(15.40)
1993	430	5	6	75	58	247	821
	(21.81)	(1590.00)	(-25)	(2.74)	(11.54)	(6.93)	(14.18)
1994	521	7	16	85	59	334	1002
	(21.16)	(40.00)	(166.67)	(13.33)	(1.72)	(35.22)	(24.48)

1995	960	12	12	107	70	383	1544
	(84.26)	(71.43)	(-25)	(25.88)	(18.64)	(14.67)	(51.08)
1996	832	10	51	158	141	458	1650
	(-13.33)	(-16.67)	-325	-47.66	-101.43	-19.58	-6.87
1997	807	15.5	9.1	168.9	14.67	468	1615.2
	(-3.00)	(55.00)	(-82.16	(6.90)	(4.04)	(2.18)	(-0.99)
1998	943	10.5	8.5	134.3	115.4	450.1	1662.1
	(16.85)	(-32.26)	(-6.59)	(-20.48)	(-21.34)	(-3.82)	(1.74)
1999	726	8.1	7.6	144	96.2	483.8	1465.8
	(-23.00)	(-22.86)	(-10.59)	(722.00)	(-16.64)	(7.49)	(-11.81)
2000	860	2.7	20.3	143.4	163.3	604.9	1795
	(18.45)	(-66.67)	(167.10)	(-0.42)	(69.75)	(25.03)	(22.46)
2001	1087	3	37 .0	158.3	219.7	546.8	2051.8
	(26.27)	(11.11)	(82.27)	(10.39)	(34.17)	(-9.60)	(13.45)
2002	1133	31	30 .0	31.6	191	848	2549
	(4.33)	(933.33)	(-18.92)	(99.62)	(-12.83)	(55.08)	(25.17)
2003	1600	77	40 .0	590	267	1220	3794
	(41.21)	(148.39)	(33.33)	(86.71)	(39.79)	(43.86)	(48.84)
2004	16.25	85	42 .0	714	451	1345	4262
	(1.56)	(10.39)	(5.00)	(21.02)	(68.91)	(10.25)	(12.34)
2005	1632	96	62 .0	830	642	1867	5129
	(0.44)	(12.35)	(48.36)	(16.30)	(42.27)	(38.31)	(20.34)
Compound Growth Rate (percent)							
1985-94	20.50	—	29.42	—1.33	23.17	20.29	16.61
1995-05	7.69	25.41	15.67	21.96	19.23	16.18	13.07
1985-05	15.08	25.41	20.15	10.94	19.61	17.42	15.35

Source : Worked out from the data given in *IMF Direction of Trade Statistics Year Book*: Various Issues.

witnessing growth rate of 29.42 percent and -1.33 percent respectively. India's exports to Pakistan and Sri Lanka had continuously increased during pre-WTO period and thus witnessed growth rate of 23.17 percent and 20.29 percent respectively, India's exports to SAARC region as a whole continuously increased thereby witnessed growth rate of 16.61 percent. Among SAARC nations, India's exports to Maldives increased at highest rate (29.42 percent) followed by Pakistan (23.17 percent) and Bangladesh (20.50 percent) during pre-WTO period. India's exports to all SAARC nations increased at higher rate than SAARC as a whole (except Bhutan and Nepal).

During Post-WTO Period, India's exports to Bangladesh continuously increased (except 1996, 1997 and 1999) and exhibiting growth rate of 7.69 percent. Her exports to Bhutan and Maldives had been fluctuating but having tendency to increase during post-WTO period (exports to Bhutan and Maldives increased from US $ 12 millions in 1995 to US $ 96 millions and from US $ 12 millions to US $ 62 millions in 2005) and thereby witnessing growth rate of 25.41 percent and 15.67 percent. Her exports with Nepal and Sri Lanka also continuously increased (except 1998 and 2000 for Nepal and 1998 and 2001 for Sri Lanka). Exports with these nations increased from US $ 107 millions and US $ 383 millions in 1995 to US $ 830 millions and US $ 1867 millions, respectively in 2005, thereby exhibiting growth rate of 21.96 percent and 16.18 percent, respectively. Her exports to Pakistan fluctuated but increased during post-WTO period thereby experiencing growth rate of 19.23 percent. For SAARC region as a whole, India's exports had continuously increased and exhibited growth rate of 13.07 percent during post-WTO period which was less as compared to pre-WTO period. Among SAARC nations, India's exports to Bhutan increased at highest rate (25.41 percent) followed by Nepal (21.96 per cent) and Pakistan (19.23 percent) in post-WTO period. India's exports to all SAARC nations (except Bangladesh) increased at a higher rate than SAARC as a whole. During the entire study period (1985-2005), India's exports to SAARC increased at a rate of 15.35 percent. Among SAARC nations, India's exports to Bhutan increased at highest rate (25.41 percent) followed by Maldives (20.15 percent) and

Pakistan (19.61 percent), respectively. India's exports to all SAARC nations except Nepal increased at a higher rate than SAARC as a whole.

Thus table depicts that among SAARC nations, Maldives was the major export partner of India and Nepal was the minor export partner of India during pre-WTO period. In post-WTO period, Bhutan was the major export partner of India while Nepal and Bangladesh were the minor export partners of India. During the entire study period, Bhutan was the major export partner and Nepal was the minor export partner of India.

Imports

Country-wise analysis given in Table 6.5 shows that *during pre-WTO period* India's imports from Bangladesh fluctuated but decreased and reached a level of US $ 34 millions in 1994 from US $ 29 millions in 1985 (exhibiting growth rate of only 0.69 percent). Her imports from Bhutan was nil during the initial years of pre-WTO period and in 1994, it reached a level of US $ 3 millions. Her imports from Maldives were very low, fluctuated but increased and reached a level of only US $ 0.498 millions in 1994 from US $ 0.024 millions in 1985. Imports exhibited growth rate of 31.52 percent. Her imports from Nepal fluctuated but decreased (imports from Nepal reached a level of US $ 14 millions in 1994 from US $ 50 millions in 1985) and thus exhibiting growth rate of -12.75 percent. Her imports from Pakistan and Sri Lanka fluctuated but increased thus exhibiting growth rate of 15.27 percent and 16.59 percent, respectively. Thus, India's imports from SAARC as a whole had been continuously increasing thereby witnessing growth rate of 5.00 percent. During pre-WTO period, among SAARC nations, India's imports from Maldives increased at a highest rate (31.52 percent) followed by Sri Lanka (16.59 percent) and Pakistan (15.27 percent). India's imports from SAARC nations except Bangladesh and Nepal increased at a higher rate than SAARC as a whole.

Country-wise analysis shows that *during post-WTO period,* India's imports from Bangladesh fluctuated but increased from US $ 79 millions in 1995 to US $ 104 millions in 2005 and exhibited growth rate of 2.28 percent only. India's imports from Bhutan and Maldives also fluctuated having tendency to

TABLE 6.5
Sources of India's Imports from SAARC Countries and SAARC

(*US $ Millions*)

Year	*Bangladesh*	*Bhutan*	*Maldives*	*Nepal*	*Pakistan*	*Sri Lanka*	*SAARC*
(1)	*(2)*	*(3)*	*(4)*	*(5)*	*(6)*	*(7)*	*(8)*
1985	29	0	0.024	50	28	5	112.024
1986	8	0	0.024	40	15	10	73.024
	(-72.41)	0.00	0.00	(-20)	(-46.43)	(100.00)	(-34.81)
1987	14	0	0.015	41	23	6	84.015
	(75.00)	0.00	(-37.5)	(2.50)	(53.33)	(-40)	(15.05)
1988	12	0	0.012	35	38	11	96.012
	(-14.29)	0.00	(-20)	(14.63)	(65.22)	(83.33)	(14.28)
1989	14	0	0.029	3	34	11	62.029
	(16.67)	0.00	(141.67)	(-91.43)	(-10.53)	0.00	(-35.39)
1990	15	0	0.03	15	45	22	97.03
	(7.14)	0.00	(3.45)	(400.00)	(32.35)	(100.00)	(56.43)
1991	6	0	0.025	19	58	12	95.025
	(-60)	0.00	(-16.67)	(26.67)	(28.29)	(-45.45)	(-2.06)
1992	10	1	0.089	23	146	14	194.089
	(33.37)	(100.00)	(256.00)	(21.05)	(151.72)	(16.67)	(104.25)
1993	13	3	0.063	19	47	17	99.063
	(30.00)	(200.00)	(-29.21)	(-17.39)	(-67.81)	(21.43)	(-48.97)
1994	34	3	0.498	14	47	31	129.498
	(161.54)	0.00	(690.47)	(-26.32)	0.00	(82.35)	(30.72)

1995	79	16	0.13	27	37	39	198.13
	(132.25)	(433.33)	(-7390)	(92.86)	(-21.28)	(25.81)	(53.00)
1996	58	16.5	0.176	49.3	39	35	197.976
	(-26.58)	(31.25)	(35.38)	(82.59)	(5.41)	(-10.26)	(-0.08)
1997	53.7	18.5	0.2	87.4	42	34	235.8
	(-7.41)	(12.12)	(13.64)	(77.28)	(7.69)	(-2.86)	(19.10)
1998	59.5	7.9	0.125	132.5	171.9	35.8	407.725
	(10.80)	(-57.29)	(-37.5)	(51.60)	(309.29)	(5.29)	(72.91)
1999	74.3	15	0.325	177.7	104.8	42.6	414.725
	(24.87)	(89.80)	(160.00)	(34.11)	(39.03)	(19.00)	(1.72)
2000	79.9	20.3	0.25	238.5	65.1	44.8	448.85
	(7.54)	(35.33)	(-23.08)	(34.21)	(-37.88)	(5.16)	(8.22)
2001	66.9	22.4	1.332	262.3	72.8	79.2	504.932
	(-16.27)	(10.34)	(432.80)	(9.98)	(11.83)	(76.79)	(12.49)
2002	61	30	0.349	300	50	8.5	526.349
	(-8.82)	(33.93)	(-73.80)	(14.37)	(-31.32)	(7.32)	(4.24)
2003	74	47	0.364	285	54	169	629.364
	(21.31)	(56.67)	(4.30)	(-5.00)	(80.00)	(98.82)	(19.57)
2004	61	51	0.528	327	86	322	847.528
	(-17.56)	(8.51)	(45.05)	(14.73)	(59.26)	(90.53)	(34.66)
2005	104	84	2	523	157	523	1393
	(70.34)	(65.47)	(210.23)	(60.05)	(82.38)	(62.53)	(64.36)
Compound Growth Rate (percent)							
1985-94	0.69	—	31.52	—12.75	15.27	16.59	5.00
1995-05	2.28	18.53	22.38	28.82	20.44	14.15	19.00
1985-05	12.73	18.53	23.94	18.71	6.78	20.49	14.43

Source : Worked out from the data given in *IMF Direction of Trade Statistics Yearbook:* Various Issues.

increase and witnessed growth rate of 18.53 percent and 22.38 percent respectively. Imports from Nepal had been continuously increasing during post-WTO period (except 2003) and reached a level of US $ 523 millions in 2005 and exhibited growth rate of 28.82 percent. Her imports from Pakistan had been continuously increasing (imports increased from US $ 37 millions in 1995 to US $ 171.9 millions in 1998) and after that fluctuated and reached a level of US $ 157 millions in 2005 and witnessed growth rate of 20.44 percent. Her imports from Sri Lanka also fluctuated but increased and reached a level of US $ 523 millions in 2005 from US $ 39 millions in 1995 and witnessed growth rate of 14.15 percent.

During post-WTO period, India's imports from SAARC as a whole had continuously increased and witnessed growth rate of 19.00 percent. Among SAARC nations, in post-WTO period, India's imports from Nepal increased at a highest rate (28.82 percent), followed by Maldives (22.38 percent), Pakistan (20.44 percent) and Bhutan (18.53 percent). During post-WTO period, her imports from SAARC nations (except Bangladesh, Bhutan and Sri Lanka) increased at higher rate than SAARC as a whole. During the entire study period (1985-2005), India's imports from SAARC increased at a rate of 14.43 percent. Among SAARC nations, India's imports from Maldives increased at a highest rate (23.94 percent) followed by Sri Lanka (20.49 percent) and Nepal (18.71 percent). India's imports from SAARC nations except Bangladesh and Pakistan increased at a higher rate than SAARC as a whole. Table also depicts that Maldives was the major import partner of India and Bhutan was the minor import partner of India during pre-WTO period. While during post-WTO period, Nepal was the major import partner of India while Bangladesh was the minoı import partner of India.

Trade Performance at Constant Prices

Exports

Table 6.6 shows that India's exports to SAARC had increased at higher rate (13.03 percent, 10.80 percent and 12.68 percent) than World (8.74 percent, 9.20 percent and 8.77 percent) during pre-WTO period, post-WTO period and entire study

TABLE 6.6

Trade Performance with SAARC and World at Constant Prices

Item	Bangladesh	Bhutan	Maldives	Nepal	Pakistan	Sri Lanka	SAARC	World
(1)	(2)	(3)	(4)	(5)	(6)	(7)	(8)	(9)
Exports								
1985-94	16.81	—	25.58	-4.52	19.31	16.70	13.03	8.74
1995-2005	5.50	22.87	13.31	19.48	16.82	13.82	10.80	9.20
1985-2005	12.42	22.87	17.36	8.37	16.84	14.70	12.68	8.77
Imports								
1985-94	-2.45	—	27.35	-16.31	11.74	13.02	1.75	1.94
1995-2005	1.00	16.11	20.01	26.18	5.65	27.64	17.99	10.77
1985-2005	10.12	16.11	21.03	15.97	4.31	17.71	12.55	7.57
Trade								
1985-94	15.11	—	25.61	-7.80	15.18	16.38	10.92	4.74
1995-2005	5.20	19.90	13.37	21.46	13.34	15.46	11.83	10.06
1985-2005	12.11	19.90	17.41	10.48	11.64	15.07	12.58	8.04

Source : Based on data given in Tables 6.4 and 6.5.

period, respectively. However, as compared to pre-WTO period, India's exports to SAARC increased at lower rate in post-WTO period.

County-wise analysis shows that during entire period, Bhutan experienced highest growth rate, i.e. 22.87 percent followed by Maldives (17.36 per cent) and Sri Lanka (14.70 percent). All countries (except Bangladesh and Nepal) experienced higher growth than SAARC during the entire study period. During the pre-WTO period, India's exports to Maldives increased at highest rate (25.58 percent) followed by Pakistan (19.31 percent) and Sri Lanka (16.70 percent). Nepal witnessed negative growth rate. During post-WTO period, India's exports to Bhutan increased at highest rate (22.87 percent) followed by Nepal (19.48 percent) while exports to Bangladesh increased at lowest rate (5.50 percent).

Imports

Regarding India's imports from SAARC and world, Table 6.6 depicts that India's imports from SAARC had increased at higher rate (17.99 percent and 12.55 percent) than world (10.77 percent and 7.57 percent) during post-WTO period and entire study period but during pre-WTO period, the case was reversed. India's imports from SAARC had increased at higher rate during post-WTO period as compared to pre-WTO period (witnessed growth rate of 17.99 percent as compared to 1.75 percent) Country-wise analysis shows that during entire period, Maldives experienced highest growth rate in imports (21.03 percent) followed by Sri Lanka (17.71 percent) and Bhutan (16.11 percent). All SAARC countries (except Bangladesh and Pakistan) experienced higher growth than SAARC during entire study period. During the pre-WTO period, India's imports from Maldives increased at highest rate (27.35 percent) followed by Sri Lanka (13.02 percent) and Pakistan (11.74 percent). Bangladesh and Nepal witnessed negative growth rate. During post-WTO period, India's imports from Sri Lanka increased at highest rate (27.64 percent) followed by Nepal (26.18 percent) and Maldives (20.01 percent) while imports from Bangladesh increased at lowest rate, i.e. 1.00 percent.

Trade

Regarding the India's trade (exports + imports) with SAARC and world, Table 6.6 also depicts that India's trade with SAARC had increased at higher rate (10.92 percent, 11.83 percent and 12.58 percent) than world (4.74 percent, 10.06 percent and 8.04 percent). However, India's trade with SAARC had increased at higher rate in post-WTO period as compared to pre-WTO period (witnessed growth rate of 11.83 percent as compared to 10.92 percent).

Country-wise analysis shows that during entire period, Bhutan experienced highest growth rate of 19.90 percent followed by Maldives (17.41 percent) and Sri Lanka (15.07 percent). SAARC countries namely, Bangladesh, Nepal and Pakistan experienced lower growth than SAARC as a whole. Period-wise analysis shows that during pre-WTO period, India's trade with Maldives increased at highest rate (25.61 percent) followed by Sri Lanka (16.38 percent) and Pakistan (15.18 percent). Nepal experienced a negative growth rate (-7.80 percent). During post-WTO period, India's trade with Nepal increased at highest rate (21.46 percent) followed by Bhutan (19.90 percent) and Sri Lanka (15.46 percent).

India's Balance of Trade with SAARC and World

Table 6.7 depicts the India's balance of trade with world had been unfavorable while for SAARC, it had been favourable in pre-WTO period as well as in post-WTO period. On an average, India's trade balance with SAARC as a whole was US $ 1243.32 millions during the entire study period and it had increased from US $ 439.72 millions during pre-WTO period to US $ 1973.88 millions during post-WTO period.

Country-wise analysis shows that India's surplus in trade balance with Bangladesh had been continuously increasing during the entire study period (except 1996, 1997, 1999 and 2005) and on an average, it increased from US $ 247.9 millions during pre-WTO period to US $ 1039.32 millions during post-WTO period. India's trade balance with Bhutan had been fluctuating Maximum surplus in trade balance was US $ 34 millions in 2004 and on an average, trade balance increased from US $ -0.8 millions during pre-WTO period to US $ 1.93 millions during post-WTO period. India's trade balance with

Table 6.7
India's Balance of Trade with SAARC and World

(US $ Millions)

Item	Bangladesh	Bhutan	Maldives	Nepal	Pakistan	Sri Lanka	SAARC	World
(1)	(2)	(3)	(4)	(5)	(6)	(7)	(8)	(9)
1985	75	0	0.976	32	-16	66	157.97	-8064
1986	105	0	1.976	42	-2	57	203.97	-5916
1987	131	0	1.985	32	-11	68	221.98	-6043
1988	158	0	2.988	47	-19	79	267.98	-5842
1989	162	0	-0.029	212	8	106	487.97	-3458
1990	282	0	4.97	25	-2	163	389.97	-6177
1991	319	0	4.975	58	-18	217	527.97	-1636
1992	343	1	7.911	50	-94	230	524.91	-4727
1993	417	2	5.937	56	11	303	721.94	-966
1994	487	4	15.502	80	33	423	892.50	-1281
1995	881	-4	11.87	80	33	423	1345.87	-3947
1996	774	-6.5	50.824	108.7	102	434	1452.02	-3730
1997	753.3	-3	8.9	81.5	105	414.3	1379.4	-5622
1998	883.5	2.6	8.375	1.8	-56.5	441.2	1253.97	-13542

1999	651.7	-6.9	7.275	-33	-8.6	560.1	1050.97	-15856
2000	780.1	-17.6	14.05	-95.1	98.2	467.6	1345.75	-9144
2001	1019.1	-19.4	35.67	-104	146.7	763	1546.86	-7031
2002	1072.0	1.0	29.651	16	141	1051	2022.65	-7267
2003	1526	30	39.636	305	213	1023	3164.64	-15473
2004	1564	34	41.477	387	365	1344	3414.47	-23126
2005	1528	11.11	60	307	484.8	1300	3736	-36886
Average								
1985-94	247.9 (56.38)	-0.8 (0.18)	4.72 (1.07)	62.5 14.21)	-13.1 (-2.98)	136.9 (31.13)	439.72	-4411
1995-05	1039.32 (52.66)	1.93 (0.09)	27.97 (1.44)	95.83 (4.86)	147.6 (7.48)	660.46 (33.46)	1973.88	-12874.9
1985-05	662.51 (53.28)	1.44 (0.12)	17.19 (1.38)	79.96 (6.43)	71.08 (5.72)	411.15 (33.06)	1243.32	-8844.48

Source : Worked out from the data given in *IMF Direction of Trade Statistics Yearbook*: Various Issues.

Maldives had been facing surplus during the entire study period (except 1989). Trade surplus had drastically increased from US $ 0.976 millions in 1985 to US $ 60 millions in 2005 and on an average, trade surplus had increased from US $ 4.72 millions during pre-WTO period to US $ 27.97 mullions during post-WTO period. India's trade balance with Nepal had been continuously fluctuating but increased. On an average, it increased from US $ 62.5 millions during pre-WTO period to US $ 95.83 millions during post-WTO period. India's trade balance with Nepal was surplus (except for some years 1999, 2000 and 2001). India's trade balance with Pakistan had been continuously facing deficit during 1985-92 (except 1989) and then started having surplus (except 1998 and 1999). On an average, it increased from US $ -13.1 millions (during pre-WTO period) to US $ 147.60 millions (during post-WTO period). India's trade balance with Sri Lanka had been facing surplus during the entire study period. On an average, it increased from US $ 136.9 millions during pre-WTO period to US $ 660.6 millions during post-WTO period.

Country-wise analysis shows that during pre-WTO period, India's trade balance was almost favourable with all SAARC nations except Pakistan. It might be due to political constraints. During post-WTO period, it was favourable with Bangladesh, Maldives and Sri Lanka but it was having deficit with Bhutan, Nepal and Pakistan. Inter-country analysis also shows that contribution of Bangladesh was most in India's trade surplus (53 percent) followed by Sri Lanka (33 percent) and Pakistan (6 percent) during the entire study period. During pre-WTO period, Bangladesh contribution was most in India's trade surplus (56 percent) followed by Sri Lanka (31 percent) and Nepal (14 percent) and during post-WTO period, the position of these countries remained same and having contribution of 53 percent, 33 percent and 5 percent respectively.

Trade Instability Indices

Export Variations

Table 6.8 shows that the variations in India's exports with SAARC were higher (46.70 percent, 51.44 percent and 86.92 percent) than world (33.13 percent, 44.87 percent and 70.29

TABLE 6.8

Trade Instability Indices of India with SAARC Nations and World

(US $ Millions)

Item	*Bangladesh*	*Bhutan*	*Maldives*	*Nepal*	*Pakistan*	*Sri Lanka*	*SAARC*	*World*
(1)	(2)	(3)	(4)	(5)	(6)	(7)	(8)	(9)
Exports								
1985-94	54.50	166.94	92.50	52.37	54.96	61.08	46.70	33.13
1995-2005	31.33	112.15	65.14	84.34	75.78	61.32	51.44	44.87
1985-2005	71.77	170.70	105.24	107.65	115.77	98.32	86.92	70.29
Imports								
1985-94	57.89	178.72	183.50	57.25	76.31	55.98	35.27	17.28
1995-2005	20.44	75.24	103.43	66.08	58.43	122.87	62.13	52.75
1985-2005	68.77	136.55	144.60	112.26	68.39	170.68	106.16	74.74
Trade								
1985-94	52.36	169.72	93.73	36.85	60.02	59.60	42.07	23.66
1995-2005	29.96	92.59	65.18	73.68	64.00	69.40	55.42	49.25
1985-2005	71.06	151.80	105.32	105.53	91.45	106.64	85.07	72.61

Source : Based on data given in Tables 6.4 and 6.5.

percent) during pre-WTO period, post-WTO period and entire study period India's export variations with SAARC were higher than world due to large variations in India's exports with Bhutan, Pakistan and Nepal during post-WTO period and entire study period, while with Bhutan, Maldives and Sri Lanka during pre-WTO period. As compared to pre-WTO period, trade instability index with SAARC increased during post -WTO period due to increase in index witnessed by Nepal and Pakistan.

Country-wise analysis shows that India's exports variations were found to be maximum in Bhutan (170.70 percent) followed by Pakistan (115.77 percent) and Nepal (107.65 percent) during entire period. Period-wise analysis shows that during pre-WTO period, Indian exports were most variable with Bhutan (166.94 percent) followed by Maldives (92.50 percent); while during post-WTO period, variations were maximum again with Bhutan (112.15 though value decreased) followed by Nepal (84.34 percent). As compared to pre-WTO period, India's export variations decreased with Bangladesh, Bhutan and Maldives in post-WTO period.

Import Variations

Table 6.8 also depicts that during pre-WTO period, post-WTO period and entire study period, the variations in India's imports with SAARC were higher (35.27 percent, 62.13 percent and 106.16 percent) than world (17.28 percent, 52.75 percent and 74.74 percent). During pre-WTO period, India's import variations with SAARC were higher than world due to large variations in India's imports with Maldives, Bhutan and Pakistan. While during post-WTO period it was due to large variations in India's imports with Sri Lanka, Maldives and Bhutan and during entire study period, it was due to variations with Sri Lanka, Maldives and Bhutan.

Table also highlights that India's import variations with SAARC as well as with world were less than her export variations with SAARC as a whole, Sri Lanka and with world in pre-WTO period. In post-WTO period, her import variations with SAARC as a whole as well as with two member countries namely, Maldives and Sri Lanka and world were more than the export variations indicating the existence of less stability in India's exports to SAARC countries in post-WTO period.

Trade Variations

Table 6.8 shows that during pre-WTO period, post-WTO period and entire study period, variations in India's trade with SAARC was higher (42.07 percent, 55.42 percent and 85.07 percent) than the variations with world (23.66 percent, 49.25 percent and 72.61 percent).

These higher trade variations were due to large variations in India's trade with Bhutan, Pakistan, Maldives, Nepal and Sri Lanka during entire study period, with Bhutan, Maldives and Pakistan during pre-WTO period and with Bhutan, Nepal and Sri Lanka during post-WTO period. As compared to pre-WTO period, trade instability index with SAARC increased during post-WTO period due to large trade variations by Bhutan, Nepal, Sri Lanka and Maldives.

Country-wise analysis shows that India's trade variations were found to be maximum in Bhutan (151.80 percent) followed by Sri Lanka (106.64 percent), Nepal (105.53 percent) and Maldives (105.32 percent) during entire study period. Period-wise analysis shows that during pre-WTO period, Indian trade was most variable with Bhutan (169.72 percent) followed by Maldives (93.73 percent) and Pakistan (60.02 percent) while during post-WTO period, variations were maximum again with Bhutan (92.59 percent) followed by Nepal (73.68 percent). As compared to pre-WTO period, India's trade variations with Bangladesh, Bhutan and Maldives decreased during post–WTO period, while with remaining SAARC nations, it increased.

II

COMMODITY COMPOSITION OF INDIA'S EXPORTS TO SAARC NATIONS

An analysis of direction structure in exports of all commodity sections (SITC Rev. 2) has been given in Table 6.9. Table depicts that among the different commodities sections, machinery and transport equipment occupied the highest share in India's exports to SAARC, i.e. 14.29 per cent followed by chemical and related products (6.52 percent) and commodities and transactions not classified (3.99 percent) in 1985. In 1995, the share of machinery and transport, chemical and related

TABLE 6.9

Section-wise Commodity Composition of India's Exports to SAARC Countries and SAARC

(Percent)

Commodity Sections	*Bangladesh*			*Bhutan*			*Maldives*			*Nepal*		
	1985	*1995*	*2004*	*1985*	*1995*	*2004*	*1985*	*1995*	*2004*	*1985*	*1995*	*2004*
(1)	*(2)*	*(3)*	*(4)*	*(5)*	*(6)*	*(7)*	*(8)*	*(9)*	*(10)*	*(11)*	*(12)*	*(13)*
Food and live animals	0.36	6.48	9.5	—	0.07	1.92	0.04	0.09	0.16	0.49	0.3	1.07
	(17.73)	(73.30)	(58.21)	(0.79)	(11.76)	(1.97)	(1.02)	(0.98)	(24.13)	(3.39)	(6..56)	
Beverage and tobacco	0.003	5.97	1.5	—	0.89	1.6	0.03	0.15	0.14	3.79	4.36	2.6
	(10.08)	(45.85)	(19.33)	(6.84)	(20.62)	(0.77)	(1.15)	(1.80)	(96.68)	(33.49)	(33.51)	
Crude minerals	0.87	1.6	0.75	—	0.01	0.07	0.02	0.06	0.08	0.24	0.15	0.38
inedible except fuels	(48.60)	(49.84)	(30.73)	(0.31)	(2.87)	(1.11)	(1.87)	(3.28)	(13.41)	(4.67)	(15.57)	
Mineral fuels lubricants	0.92	4.49	1.2	—	0.22	0.04	—	—	0.0002	0.4	0.96	3.7
and related products	(69.70)	(77.95)	(10.82)	(3.82)	(0.36)	(0.00)	(30.30)	(16.67)	(33.36)			
Animals and vegetable	—	1.95	0.59	—	0.27	0.28	—	0.51	0.002	—	0.12	0.43
oils and fats	(65.00)	(36.42)	(9.00)	(17.28)	(17.00)	(0.12)	(0.04)	(26.50)				
Chemical products	1..34	2.56	1.59	—	0.03	0.03	0.07	0.04	0.05	2.23	1.18	1.01
	(20.55)	(40.18)	(22.52)	(0.47)	(0.42)	(1.07)	(0.63)	(0.71)	(34.20)	(18.52)	(14.31)	
Manufactured goods	1.24	3.3	1.64	—	0.01	0.08	0.01	0.47	0.03	0.86	0.36	0.52
	(47..33)	(61.57)	(45.81)	(0.19)	(2.23)	(0.38)	(8.76)	(0.84)	(32.82)	(6.72)	(14.53)	
Machinery and	6..98	6.57	1.98	—	0.04	—	0.01	0.04	0.37	4.41	2.19	1.34
transport	(48.85)	(49.77)	(25.48)	(0.30)	(0.07)	(0.30)	(4.76)	(30.86)	(16.59)	(17.25)		
Miscellaneous	0.22	0.14	0.27	—	0.001	0.004	0.01	0.02	0.04	0.12	0.05	0.18
manufactured articles	(57.89)	(33.33)	(28.72)	(0.24)	(0.43)	(2.63)	(4.76)	(30.86)	(31.58)	(11.90)	(19.15)	
Commodities and	1.76	0.48	0.18	—	1.45	0.19	0.05	0.04	0.04	2	0.03	0.71
transactions not classified	(44.11)	(18.05)	(11.61)	(54.51)	(12.26)	(1.25)	(1.50)	(2.58)	(50.13)	(1.13)	(45.81)	

(Contd.)

TABLE 6.9 (*Contd.*)

Commodity Sections	*Pakistan*			*Sri Lanka*			*SAARC*		
	1985	*1995*	*2004*	*1985*	*1995*	*2004*	*1985*	*1995*	*2004*
(1)	*(14)*	*(15)*	*(16)*	*(17)*	*(18)*	*(19)*	*(20)*	*(21)*	*(22)*
Food and live animals	0.25 (12..32)	0.7 (7.92)	1.02 (6.25)	0.89 (43.84)	1.5 (16..97)	2.65 (16.24)	2.03	8.84	16.32
Beverage and tobacco	0.01 (0.26)	0.09 (0.69)	0.25 (3.22)	0.09 (2.30)	1.56 (11.98)	1.67 (21.52)	3.92	13.02	7.76
Crude minerals inedible except fuels	—	0.94 (29.98)	0.74 (30.33)	0.66 (36.87)	0.39 (12.15)	0.42 (17.21)	1.79	3.21	2.44
Mineral fuels lubricants and related products	—	0.08 (1.39)	0.85 (7.67)	—	0.01 (0.17)	5.3 (47.79)	1.32	5.76	11.09
Animals and vegetable oils and fats	—	0.01 (0.33)	0.09 (5.56)	—	0.14 (4.67)	0.23 (14.20)	—	3	1.62
Chemicals products	0.08 (1.23)	0.68 (10.67)	2.9 (41.08)	2.8 (42.94)	1.88 (29.51)	1.48 (20.96)	6.52	6.37	7.06
Manufactured goods	0.01 (0.38)	0.02 (0.37)	0.2 (5.59)	0.5 (19.08)	1.2 (22.39)	1.11 (31.00)	2.62	5.36	3.58
Machinery and transport	0.06 (0.42)	0.13 (0.98)	0.07 (0.90)	2.83 (19.80)	423 (32.05)	4.01 (51.61)	14.29	13.2	7.77
Miscellaneous manufactured articles	0.03 (7.89)	0.03 (7.14)	0.04 (4.26)	0.13 (34.21)	0.18 (42.85)	0.41 (43.62)	0.38	0.42	0.94
Commodities and transactions not classified	0.04 (1.00)	0.01 (1.00)	0.03 (1.94)	0.13 (3.26)	0.65 (24.43)	0.4 (25.81)	3.99	2.66	1.55

Note : Figures in parentheses are percentage shares in SAARC.
Source : Worked out from the data given in *UN COMTRADE Statistics*: Various Issues.

products and commodities and transactions not classified decreased to 13.20 percent, 6.37 percent and 2.66 percent respectively in 1995. In 2004, food and line animals had the major share, i.e. 16.32 percent followed by mineral fuel lubricants and related materials (11.09 percent) and machinery and transport equipment (7.77 percent). As compared to pre-WTO period, share of machinery and transport equipment and commodities and transactions not classified in India's exports to SAARC decreased during post-WTO period.

Section-wise and Country-wise Analysis

Food and Live Animals

In case of food and live animals exports, among SAARC nations, largest India's export market was of Sri Lanka (44 percent) followed by Nepal (24 percent), Bangladesh (18 percent) and Pakistan (12 percent) in 1985. Share of SAARC has rapidly increased due to increase share of Bangladesh (share of Bangladesh in exports increased rapidly from 18 percent in 1985 to 58 percent in 2004). During post-WTO period, Bangladesh, Sri Lanka and Bhutan emerged as important market for exports of food and live animals.

Thus, there was a shift in direction of exports in post-WTO period as compared to pre-WTO period.

Beverage and Tobacco

In case of Beverage and Tobacco, Nepal was main market which accounted for 97 percent of exports in 1985. The export share of SAARC in India's exports has increased due to rapid increase in share of Bangladesh (46 percent) and Nepal (33 percent). In 2004, share of SAARC nations has decreased due to decrease in share of Bangladesh (from 5.97 percent to 1.5 percent) and Nepal (from 4.36 per cent to 2.60 percent). During post-WTO period, Nepal, Sri Lanka, Bhutan and Bangladesh emerged as important markets for exports.

Crude Materials Inedible Except Fuels

In case of crude materials inedible except fuels, the largest contribution was of Bangladesh (49 percent) and Sri Lanka (37 percent) in 1985. The share of SAARC has increased due to increase in the share of Pakistan and Bangladesh. In 2004, share of SAARC has decreased due to decrease in share of Bangladesh and Pakistan. During pre-WTO period, Bangladesh and Sri Lanka were the main export markets for India while during post-WTO period, Bangladesh and Pakistan were the main markets.

Mineral Fuels, Lubricants and Related Materials

In case of mineral fuels, lubricants and related materials, Bangladesh was the main export market having share of 0.92 per cent (70 percent) in 1985. The share of SAARC has rapidly increased in 1995 (due to increase in share of Bangladesh) as well as in 2004 (due to increase in share of Sri Lanka and Nepal). As compared to pre-WTO period, share of all SAARC nations has increased for mineral fuels, lubricants and related materials in post-WTO period. During pre-WTO period, Bangladesh was the main export market of India while during post-WTO period, Sri Lanka (5.3 percent) and Nepal (3.7 percent) emerged as important markets.

Animal and Vegetable Oils, Fats and Waxes

In case of animal and vegetable oils, fats and waxes, the largest contribution was of Bangladesh 1.95 (65 percent) in 1995. Share of SAARC in India's exports has decreased in 2004 due to rapid decrease in share of Bangladesh from 65 percent in 1995 to 36 percent in 2004.

Chemical and Related Products

In case of chemical and related products, the main export market of India was of Sri Lanka 2.80 (43 percent) followed by Nepal 2.23 (34 percent) and Bangladesh 1.34 (21 percent) in 1985. Share of all SAARC nations except Bhutan and Pakistan has decreased in 2004. Thus, there was a shift in direction of exports in 2004 as compared to 1985 (with decrease in share of most of SAARC nations (4 out of 6)). Pakistan and Bangladesh emerged as important markets for its exports during post-WTO period.

Manufactured Goods Classified Chiefly by Materials

In case of manufactured goods classified chiefly by

materials, Bangladesh was the main export market having share of 1.24 per cent (47 percent) in 1985. In 1995, share of SAARC has rapidly increased due to increase in share of main export market, i.e. Bangladesh. But SAARC experienced decrease in share in 2004 due to decrease in share of Bangladesh market. But still, Bangladesh constituted main export market in post-WTO period.

Machinery and Transport Equipment

In case of machinery and transport equipment exports, main export market was Bangladesh (49 percent), followed by Nepal (31 percent) and Sri Lanka (20 percent) in 1985. The share of SAARC has rapidly decreased in 2004 (due to rapid decrease in share of Bangladesh and Nepal). Sri Lanka emerged as main market for exports during post-WTO period.

Miscellaneous Manufactured Articles

In case of miscellaneous manufactured articles exports, Bangladesh was the main export market having share of 58 percent in exports in 1985. Share of SAARC has marginally increased in 2004. Now, Sri Lanka was the main export market having share of 44 percent. Thus, there was a shift in direction of exports in 2004 as compared to 1985 (with increase in share of all SAARC nations, though this increase was marginal).

Commodities and Transactions not Classified

In case of commodities and transaction not classified, SAARC accounted for 3.99 percent share in 1985. The main export markets were Nepal (50 percent) and Bangladesh (44 percent). Share of SAARC had rapidly decreased in 2004 due to decrease in share of all SAARC nations except Sri Lanka. Sri Lanka emerged as main export market having share of (26 percent) in 2004.

The direction structure of India's exports of all commodity sections (SITC Rev. 2) to SAARC nations revealed that Bangladesh, Nepal and Sri Lanka were major destinations for most of the India's exports in pre-WTO period. In post -WTO period, these countries again remained as major destinations. Section-wise analysis showed that in India, Bangladesh became important market for *mineral fuel lubricants and related materials, crude materials inedible except fuels, manufactured goods classified chiefly by materials, machinery and transport equipment, miscellaneous manufactured articles* and *commodities and transaction not classified;* Nepal for *beverage and tobacco and commodities and transactions not classified* and Sri Lanka for *food and live animals and chemical and related products* in pre-WTO period. While in post-WTO period, Bangladesh became main export market for *food and live animals, crude materials, inedible except fuels, mineral fuel lubricants and related materials, animals and vegetable oils* and *manufactured goods classified chiefly by materials;* Nepal for *beverage and tobacco, mineral fuel lubricants and related materials* and *commodities and transactions not classified* and Sri Lanka for *mineral fuel lubricants and related materials, machinery and transport equipment* and *miscellaneous manufactured articles.* Thus, it is clear that though major export partners (Bangladesh, Nepal and Sri Lanka) among SAARC nations remained same in post-WTO period, but there was structural shift in direction of India's exports to SAARC

In pre-WTO period, *machinery and transport equipment, chemical and related products, commodities, transactions not classified and beverage and tobacco* were the main commodity groups of India's exports. But in post-WTO period, *food and live animals, mineral fuels, lubricants and related materials, machinery and transport equipment and beverage and tobacco* were the main commodity groups.

Commodity Composition of India's Imports from SAARC Nations

An analysis of direction structure in imports of all commodity sections (SITC Rev. 2) has been given in Table 6.10. Table 6.10 shows the percentage share of section-wise commodity composition of India's imports from SAARC as a whole and SAARC nations in 1985, 1995 and 2004.

Table depicts that among the different commodity sections, food and live animals occupied the highest share in India's imports from SAARC, i.e. 3.05 percent followed by crude materials inedible except fuels (1.41 percent) and commodities and transactions not classified (1.18 percent). In 1995, share of animals and vegetable oils, fats and waxes drastically increased from negligible in 1985 to 30.06 percent. Share of other

TABLE 6.10

Section–wise Commodity Composition of India's Imports from SAARC Countries and SAARC

(Percent)

Commodity Sections	*Bangladesh*			*Bhutan*			*Maldives*			*Nepal*		
	1985	*1995*	*2004*	*1985*	*1995*	*2004*	*1985*	*1995*	*2004*	*1985*	*1995*	*2004*
(1)	*(2)*	*(3)*	*(4)*	*(5)*	*(6)*	*(7)*	*(8)*	*(9)*	*(10)*	*(11)*	*(12)*	*(13)*
Food and live animals	— (16.41)	1.07 (6.64)	0.63	— (4.14)	0.27 (1.05)	0.1	—	— (0.01)	0.001 (3.93)	1.95 (27.91)	1.82 (26.87)	2.55
Beverage and tobacco	—	—	0.41 (4.78)	—	4.03 (99.73)	6.4 (74.68)	—	—	—	0.7 (100.00)	—	1.65 (19.25)
Crude minerals inedible except fuels	0.19 (13.48)	0.43 (26.88)	0.17 (16.50)	—	0.16 (10.00)	0.01 (0.97)	—	—	—	0.62 (43.97)	0.21 (13.13)	0.1 (9.71)
Mineral fuels lubricants and related products	—	—	—	—	0.01 (98.04)	—	—	—	—	—	0.0002 (1.96)	—
Animals and vegetable oils and fats	—	—	0.004 (0.28)	—	—	—	—	—	—	—	30.06 (100.0)	0.57 (0.89)
Chemical products	0.05 (14.70)	1.2 (65.21)	0.28 (21.37)	—	0.19 (10.33)	0.12 (9.16)	—	—	—	0.23 (67.65)	0.2 (10.88)	0.82 (62.60)
Manufactured goods	0.31 (43.66)	0.02 (3.45)	0.03 (1.30)	—	0.27 (46.55)	0.27 (11.74)	—	—	—	0.3 (42.25)	0.22 (37.93)	0.89 (38.70)
Machinery and transport	—	0.02 (47.62)	0.003 (1.12)	—	—	0.00004 (0.01)	—	—	0.00004 (0.01)	0.001 (2.94)	0.002 (4.76)	0.26 (97.38)
Miscellaneous manufactured articles	0.01 (27.78)	0.01 (20.00)	0.07 (5.79)	—	—	0.05 (4.13)	—	—	0.05 (4.13)	0.02 (55.55)	0.0002 (0.40)	0.6 (49.59)
Commodities and transactions not classified	0.01 (0.84)	0.01 (5.13)	0.01 (32.26)	—	0.004 (2.05)	0.008 (25.81)	—	0.004 (2.05)	0.008 (25.81)	1.13 (95.76)	0.06 (30.77)	0.002 (6.45)

TABLE 6.10 (*Contd.*)

Commodity Sections	*Pakistan*			*Sri Lanka*			*SAARC*		
	1985	*1995*	*2004*	*1985*	*1995*	*2004*	*1985*	*1995*	*2004*
(1)	*(14)*	*(15)*	*(16)*	*(17)*	*(18)*	*(19)*	*(20)*	*(21)*	*(22)*
Food and live animals	0.76 (24.92)	2.98 (45.70)	3.7 (38.99)	0.34 (11.15)	0.38 (5.83)	2.51 (26.44)	3.05	6.52	9.491
Beverage and tobacco	—	—	0.01 (0.12)	—	0.01 (0.25)	0.1 (0.17)	0.7	4.04	8.57
Crude minerals inedible except fuels	0.97 (68.79)	0.2 (12.50)	0.14 (13.59)	0.25 (17.73)	0.75 (46.88)	0.61 (59.22)	1.41	1.6	1.03
Mineral fuels lubricants and related products	—	—	0.003 (96.77)	0.0001 (100.00)	—	0.0001 (3.23)	0.0001	0.0102	0.0031
Animals and vegetable oils and fats	—	—	—	—	—	0.82 (58.23)	—	30.06	1.394
Chemical products	0.04 (11.76)	0.23 (12.50)	0.01 (0.76)	0.02 (5.88)	0.02 (1.09)	0.08 (2.71)	0.34	1.84	1.31
Manufactured goods	0.08 (11.27)	—	0.09 (3.91)	0.02 (2.82)	0.07 (12.07)	1.02 (44.35)	0.71	0.58	2.3
Machinery and transport	0.03 (88.24)	0.001 (2.10)	0.001 (0.37)	0.003 (8.82)	0.02 (47.62)	0.003 (1.12)	0.034	0.042	0.267
Miscellaneous manufactured articles	0.003 (8.33)	0.01 (20.00)	0.04 (3.31)	0.003 (8.33)	0.03 (60.00)	0.4 (33.06)	0.036	0.05	1.21
Commodities and transactions not classified	0.02 (1.69)	0.00 (0.51)	0.00 (3.23)	0.02	0.12 (61.54)	0.00 (9.68)	1.18	0.195	0.031

Note : Figures in parentheses are percentage shares in SAARC.
Source : Worked out from the data given in *UN COMTRADE Statistics*: Various Issues.

commodity sections except manufactured goods chiefly by materials also increased in the same year. In 2004, again the maximum share of food and live animals in India's imports from SAARC was 9.49 percent followed by beverage and tobacco (8.57 per cent) and manufactured goods chiefly by materials (1.31 percent). As compared to pre-WTO period, share of all commodities in India's imports from SAARC (except crude materials inedible except fuels and commodities and transactions not classified) increased in post-WTO period (2004).

Section-wise and Country-wise Analysis

Food and Live Animals

In case of food and live animals, among SAARC nations, largest import basket in India's imports was Nepal (64 percent), followed by Pakistan (25 percent) and Sri Lanka (11 percent) in 1985. Share of SAARC has rapidly increased in 2004. This was due to increase in share of all SAARC nations. The highest increase had been in case of Pakistan (share of Pakistan in imports increased rapidly from 25 percent in 1985 to 39 percent in 2004) and Sri Lanka (share of Sri Lanka in imports increased rapidly from 11 percent in 1985 to 26 percent in 2004). During pre-WTO period as well as post-WTO period, Nepal, Pakistan and Sri Lanka remained as important markets for food and live animals.

Beverage and Tobacco

In case of beverage and tobacco, largest contribution was only for one SAARC nation namely. Nepal in 1985. Share of SAARC increased in 1995 as well as in percent in 2004. This was due to the active contribution of Bhutan (100 percent in 1995 and 75 percent in 2004). Thus, there was a shift in direction of imports of beverage and tobacco in post-WTO period as compared to pre-WTO period. During post-WTO period, Bhutan came as important import market for it.

Crude Materials Inedible Except Fuels

In case of crude materials inedible except fuels, the main import markets of India were Pakistan (69 percent) and Nepal (44 percent) in 1985. The share of SAARC increased in 1995 (due to increase in share of Bangladesh, Bhutan and Sri Lanka) and then further declined in 2004 (due to decrease in share of all SAARC nations). During pre-WTO period, Pakistan and Nepal were the main import markets for its imports while during post-WTO period (2004), Sri Lanka and Bangladesh were the main markets.

Mineral Fuels, Lubricants and Related Materials

In case of mineral fuels, lubricants and related materials, Sri Lanka was the only import market having share of 0.0001 percent in 1985. Though share of SAARC increased to 0.0031 percent in 2004, yet it was very low. In post-WTO period (2004), Pakistan was the main import market.

Animal and Vegetable Oils, Fats and Waxes

In case of animals and vegetable oils, even a single SAARC member was not importing from India in 1985. But in 1995, share of SAARC sharply increased percent due to increasing share of Nepal and sharply decreased in 2004 due to decreasing share of Nepal. In 1995, Nepal was the major import partner while in 2004, Srilanka was the major import partner.

Chemical and Related Products

In case of chemical and related products, the main import market was Nepal consisting of 0.23 per cent (68 percent) in 1985. In 1995, share of SAARC has marginally increased due to increase in share of Bangladesh. While in 2004, it has marginally declined due to rapid decrease in share of Bangladesh from 65 percent in 1995 to 21 percent in 2004. During pre-WTO period as well as post-WTO period, Nepal was the main import market.

Manufactured Goods Classified Chiefly by Materials

In case of manufactured goods classified chiefly by materials imports, Bangladesh was the main import market having share of 44 percent in 1985. Share of SAARC rapidly increased in 2004 due to increase in share of Nepal and Sri Lanka. In post-WTO period, Sri Lanka was the main import market.

Machinery and Transport Equipment

In case of machinery and transport equipment, the main import market was Pakistan having share of 88 percent. In 1995, share of SAARC had marginally increased due to increase in share of Bangladesh and Sri Lanka and in 2004, due to increase in share of Nepal. Thus, there was a structural shift in structure of imports in 2004 as compared to 1985.

Miscellaneous Manufactured Articles

In case of miscellaneous manufactured articles, Nepal was having maximum share in India's imports, i.e. 56 percent in 1985. Share of SAARC had marginally increased in 1995 due to increase in share of Sri Lanka and in 2004, due to increase in share of Nepal and Sri Lanka. During pre-WTO period as well as post-WTO period, Nepal was the main import market.

Commodities and Transactions Not Classified

In case of commodities and transactions not classified, Nepal was the main import market having percentage share of 1.13 percent. Percentage share of SAARC declined in 1995 and •0.031 in 2004 due to rapid decrease in share of Nepal. There was a shift in structure of imports in 2004 as compared to 1985 (with decrease in share of almost all SAARC nations).

An Analysis of direction structure in import of commodity sections (SITC Rev. 2) revealed that Nepal, Pakistan and Bangladesh were major destinations for most of India's imports in pre-WTO period. In post-WTO period, these countries remained as major destinations but Sri Lanka also emerged as important import market for most of the commodities in India. Section-wise analysis showed that Nepal became important import market for *food and live animals, beverage and tobacco, chemical and related products, miscellaneous manufactured articles* and *commodities and transactions not classified*; Bangladesh *for manufactured goods classified chiefly* and Pakistan for *crude materials inedible except fuels* and *machinery and transport equipment* during pre-WTO period (1985). While in post-WTO period (2004), Nepal became important import market for *animals and vegetable oils, chemical and related products, machinery and transport equipment* and *miscellaneous manufactured articles,* Bangladesh for *commodities and transactions not classified,*

Pakistan for *food and live animals* and *mineral fuel lubricants and related materials* and Sri Lanka for *crude materials inedible except fuels* and *manufactured goods classified chiefly*. Thus, it is clear that, major import partners (Bangladesh, Nepal, and Pakistan) among SAARC nations remained same in post-WTO period and one more import partner namely, Sri Lanka also emerged as new import market for India in post-WTO period. With this change, there was also structural shift in direction of India's imports from SAARC.

Thus, in pre-WTO period, *food and live animals, crude materials inedible except fuels and commodities and transactions not classified* were the main commodity groups of India's imports but in post-WTO period, *food and live animals, beverage and tobacco, manufactured goods classified chiefly, animals and vegetable oils, chemical and related products and miscellaneous manufactured articles* were the main commodity groups.

Comparative Analysis of Commodity Composition of India's Exports and India's Imports

Table 6.9 and 6.10 shows that in pre-WTO period, commodities and transactions not classified was among the main export as well as import commodity group in India while in post-WTO period, food and live animals and beverage and tobacco were among the main export commodity group as well as main import commodity group. Both tables also depict that Bangladesh, Nepal and Sri Lanka were the main export markets as well as main import markets of India in post-WTO period.

Commodity Composition of India's Trade with SAARC

Exports

Table 6.11 shows that commodity composition of India's exports to SAARC region. In 1998-99, Table depicts that non-basmati rice constituted major share (32.16 percent) followed by cotton yarn fab, made ups (11.76 percent), transport equipment (6.92 percent), drugs, pharma and five chemicals (5.83 percent) and machinery and instruments (5.46 percent) in India's exports to SAARC. In 2000-01, the picture had totally changed. The share of non-basmati rice in India's exports to SAARC declined rapidly from 32.16 percent in 1998-99 to 3.88 percent in 2000-01

TABLE 6.11
Commodity Composition and Structural Changes in India's Exports to SAARC

(*Percent*)

Commodity	*Year*			
	1998-99	*2000-01*	*2004-05*	*2005-06*
Transport equipment	6.92	8.41	8.38	8.54
Cotton yarn Fab, made ups	11.76	13.90	7.15	7.11
Prime Semi-fin. iron steel	2.28	3.73	3.04	4.62
Drugs Pharma and five chemicals	5.83	6.34	5.01	4.37
Machinery and instruments	5.46	6.14	4.58	4.01
Dyes intermediates etc.	1.49	1.28	3.89	3.67
Non-Basmati rice	32.16	3.88	5.91	3.77
Manufactures of metals	2.75	4.12	3.84	2.87
Plastic and linoleum Products	1.48	2.75	3.08	2.87
Pulses	1.39	2.44	1.55	2.42
Manmade yarn fab. Made ups	1.85	2.90	2.00	2.34
Paper/wood products	1.73	3.10	2.21	2.06
Oil meals	2.10	2.72	3.08	2.03
Wheat	0.02	1.36	4.56	1.96
Glass/glassware/ceramics/cement	2.10	4.34	2.70	1.96
Fresh vegetables	0.94	1.70	2.13	1.89
Cotton raw incl. waste	—	—	—	1.79
Sugar	—	—	—	1.50
Inorg./org./agro-chemicals	1.26	3.27	2.16	1.49
Rubber manufactured products	1.77	1.50	1.30	1.43
Electronic goods	0.92	1.13	1.12	1.18
Other cereals	0.03	0.22	1.22	1.15
Coal	1.95	1.94	1.14	0.96
Spices	1.51	2.20	1.26	0.94
Non-ferrous metals	0.08	0.17	0.72	0.93
Other ores and metals	0.49	0.78	0.70	0.84
Fresh fruits	0.52	0.88	0.74	0.69
Cosmetics/toiletries	0.68	0.67	0.67	0.69
Dairy Products	—	0.43	0.65	0.65

Source : Worked out from the data given in Foreign Trade and Balance of Payments, 2006 (September).

and cotton yarn fab, madeup's share in India's exports to SAARC increased to 13.90 percent thus constituting major share in India's exports to SAARC. Transport equipment constituted 8.41 percent in India's exports to SAARC followed by drugs pharma and fine chemicals (6.34 percent) and machinery and instrument (6.14 percent) in 2000-01. In 2004-05, share of cotton yarn fab, madeups in India's exports to SAARC rapidly decreased from 13.90 percent in 2000-01 to 7.15 percent in 2004-05. The commodities having major share in previous years like transport equipment, drugs pharma and five chemicals and machinery and instrument's share in India's exports decreased as compared to 2000-01. In 2005-06, transport equipment occupied first position in India's exports by constructing major share, i.e. 8.54 percent followed by cotton yarn fab, madeups (7.11 percent), prime semi-fin., iron and steel (4.62 percent) and drugs pharma and five chemicals (4.37 percent). In 2005-06, two new commodities namely, cotton raw incl. waste and sugar came in composition of India's exports by constituting the share 1.79 percent and 1.50 percent, respectively .Of 29 commodities considered, 20 commodities experienced an increase in share in 2005-06 as compared to 1998-99 showing the existence potential of exports in these commodities.

Imports

Table 6.12 shows the overall commodity composition of India's imports during the post-WTO period. Table depicts that fruits and nuts constituted major share in imports from SAARC region (5.19 percent) in 1997-98 followed by jute raw (4.40 percent), spices (4.03 percent), essential oil and cosmetics (2.89 percent) and inorganic chemicals (2.44 percent) in 1998-99. In 2000-01, share of commodities like essential oil and cosmetic prepared inorganic chemicals, man made filament/spun and made up textile articles rapidly increased. In 2004-05, non-ferrous metals occupied first position by constituting the share, i.e. 7.27 percent, followed by iron and steel (6.65 percent) and spices (5.04 percent). In 2005-06, non-ferrous metals constituted major share in imports from SAARC region, i.e. 16.26 percent followed by iron and steel (4.61 percent), pulses (4.29 percent) and inorganic chemicals (4.16 percent). Of 29 commodities, 22

TABLE 6.12
Commodity Composition and Structural Changes in India's Imports from SAARC

(Percent)

Commodity	*Year*			
	1998-99	*2000-01*	*2004-05*	*2005-06*
Non ferrous metals	0.28	4.97	7.27	16.26
Iron and steel	0.65	2.25	6.65	4.61
Pulses	1.52	2.44	1.11	4.29
Inorganic chemicals	2.44	7.22	2.71	4.16
Spices	4.03	5.24	5.04	3.49
Manmade filament/spun	—	5.78	4.62	3.34
Other yarn/waste tent yarn, fab; made upwards	—	1.11	3.92	3.32
Organic chemicals	—	0.57	0.35	2.77
Cotton yarn and fabrics	—	0.51	1.43	2.40
Manufactures of metals	0.21	0.60	1.70	2.38
Fruits and nuts	5.19	6.14	3.42	2.28
Electrical machinery	0.13	0.57	3.41	2.19
Medical and Pharma Products	1.08	2.16	0.63	2.08
Artful resins, plastic materials etc.	0.28	0.45	3.68	2.03
Metal ferries ores and metal scrap	1.39	1.75	1.99	1.65
Essential oil and cosmetic preparation	2.89	7.86	3.61	1.39
Paper board and Manufacture	0.5	1.23	1.27	1.39
Jute raw	4.40	4.00	0.78	1.27
Madeup textile articles	—	5.65	0.67	1.22
Non-Metallic mineral mnfs.	0.07	0.15	1.54	1.15
Chemical material and products	0.16	0.13	0.67	0.86
Primary steel pig iron based items	0.09	1.69	1.06	0.79
Readymade garments (wov. and tool)	—	1.01	0.82	0.77
Wood and wood products	1.30	1.66	0.83	0.73
Pulp and waste paper	0.56	0.55	0.93	0.70
Non-electrical machinery	0.17	0.62	2.37	0.59
Electronic goods	0.21	0.34	0.96	0.53
Vegetable oils (edible)	1.08	2.16	0.63	0.52
Tea	—	0.79	0.61	0.50

Source : Worked out from the data given in Foreign Trade and Balance of Payments, 2006 (September).

commodities experienced an increase in share of imports from SAARC in 2005 as compared to 1985. The rapid increase was in case of ferrous metals, iron and steel, pulses and inorganic chemicals.

Thus, it is clear that India's growth rate of trade with SAARC is higher than the growth rate of trade with world. India's trade is not intense with all SAARC nations. The structure of exports and imports of India more or less remains same.

7

Static and Dynamic Effects of SAARC

Free trade regional integration leads to static effects (trade creation, trade diversion and trade expansion) as well as dynamic effects (economics of scale, external economies, technical change and increasing investment, etc.). This chapter quantifies some of these effects in case of SAARC region. Accordingly the chapter has been divided into two sections. Section I considers static effects while section II discusses dynamic effects of SAARC.

I

STATIC EFFECTS

For many years, the general opinion was that any economic integration that represents a movement towards free trade flows is beneficial and welfare enhancing. This opinion was being challenged in 1950 when Jacob Viner showed in his custom union issue that the net impact of a regional trade agreement on welfare is uncertain and depends on a number of economic circumstances. Thus, early theoretical and empirical literature that started in 1950s with Viner's seminar work opened up new ground advancing the idea that the net welfare effects stemming from the formation a regional trade integration (RTA) are ambiguous (Viner, 1950). In a simple partial equilibrium model under perfect competition, RTA will increase the level of trade between members at the expense of less efficient domestic producers and also of more efficient third countries (trade diversion). The net effect of an RTA on trade (as a proxy for welfare) depends thus on the relative size of these two effects. Thus, the issue of the net effect of RTAs on the welfare of the member countries and on the world economy is therefore an empirical issue.

Static Effects of SAARC

(i) Exports

Exports Expansion

Exports expansion (measured in terms of total exports of SAARC) given in Table 7.1 depicts that total exports of SAARC had been continuously increasing during period 1981-2005 except 1998. Exports increased from US $ 11615 millions in 1981 to US $ 129569 millions in 2005, thus experiencing average growth rate of 10.82 percent. The growth of total exports of SAARC ranged between 1.37 percent in 1985 to 19.19 percent in 1987 during pre-WTO period, while it ranged between -1.39 percent in 1998 to 30.81 percent in 2004 during post-WTO period. Exports increased at rate of 9.65 percent during pre-WTO period and 12.21 percent during post-WTO period depicting that in post-WTO period, the growth of total exports was greater than pre-WTO period.

Exports Creation

Exports creation (measured in terms of intra-SAARC exports) given in Table 7.1 shows that of total exports of SAARC, intra-regional exports of SAARC had been continuously increasing during period 1981-2005 except 1982, 1983, 1985, 1986, 1993 and 1999. Intra-regional exports increased from US $ 566 millions in 1981 to US $ 7062 millions in 2005 and thus experiencing average growth rate 12.32 percent. During the pre-WTO period, growth of intra-regional exports of SAARC was maximum in 1984, i.e. 33.70 percent. While it was maximum in 2003, i.e. 59.21 percent during post-WTO period. The average growth of intra-regional of SAARC was 8.37 in pre-WTO period and 16.99 percent in post-WTO period depicting that growth of intra-regional exports of SAARC was more rapid in post-WTO period than in pre-WTO period.

Exports Diversion

Exports diversion (measured in terms of exports of SAARC with rest of the world) given in Table 7.1 shows that exports of SAARC with rest of world had been continuously increasing during 1981-2005 (except 1998). Exports increased from US $ 11049 millions in 1981 to US $ 122507 millions in 2005, thus experiencing average growth rate of 10.80 percent. Exports diversion measured in terms of exports with the rest of world given in Table shows that the growth of SAARC exports with rest of the world was maximum in 1987, i.e. 19.51 percent during pre-WTO period, while it was maximum in 2004, i.e. 31.22 percent during post-WTO period. Its average growth rate was 9.75 percent in pre-WTO period and 12.03 percent in post-WTO period.

Thus, the average growth of exports expansion, exports creation and exports diversion in post-WTO period was more than in pre-WTO period. The comparative analysis also showed that the growth of exports creation was more rapid than the growth of exports expansion and growth of exports diversion in post-WTO period and entire study period while growth of exports diversion was more in pre-WTO period.

(ii) Imports

Imports Expansion

Imports expansion (measured in terms of total imports of SAARC) given in Table 7.2 depicts that total imports of SAARC had been continuously increasing during period 1981-2005 except 1983, 1986 and 1993. Imports increased from US $ 24988 millions in 1981 to US $ 185476 millions in 2005, thus experiencing average growth rate of 9.32 percent. The growth

TABLE 7.1

Intra-Exports of SAARC (1981-2005)

(US $ millions)

Year	Total Exports of SAARC	Intra-SAARC Exports	SAARC's Exports with Rest of the World	Total SAARC Exports	Share of Intra-SAARC Exports	Share of SAARC Exports with rest of the world
(1)	(2)	(3)	(4)	(5)	(6)	(7)
1981	11615	566	11049	100	5	95
1982	12521 (7.80)	527 (-6.89)	11994 (8.55)	100	4	96
1983	12801 (2.24)	460 (-12.71)	12342 (2.90)	100	4	96
1984	13253 (3.52)	615 (33.70)	12638 (2.40)	100	5	95
1985	13425 (1.37)	601 (-2.28)	12824 (1.55)	100	4	96
1986	14729 (9.63)	554 (-7.82)	14175 (10.44)	100	4	96
1987	17555 (19.19)	615 (11.01)	16941 (19.51)	100	4	96
1988	20721 (18.02)	787 (27.97)	19934 (17.67)	100	4	96

(Contd.)

TABLE 7.1 (*Contd.*)

(1)	(2)	(3)	(4)	(5)	(6)	(7)
1989	23572 (13.75)	862 (9.53)	22710 (13.93)	100	4	96
1990	27229 (15.51)	863 (0.12)	26366 (16.10)	100	3	97
1991	28353 (4.13)	1013 (17.38)	27340 (3.69)	100	4	96
1992	31697 (11.80)	1239 (22.31)	30459 (11.40)	100	4	96
1993	33229 (4.83)	1191 (-3.87)	32037 (5.18)	100	4	96
1994	37776 (13.69)	1434 (20.40)	36342 (13.43)	100	4	96
1995	45832 (21.33)	2024 (41.14)	43808 (20.54)	100	4	96
1996	49429 (7.85)	2144 (5.93)	47285 (7.94)	100	4	96
1997	51976 (5.15)	2174 (1.40)	49802 (5.32)	100	4	96
1998	51255 (-1.39)	2466 (13.43)	48789 (-2.03)	100	5	95

1999	54140 (5.63)	2180 (-11.60)	51960 (6.50)	100	4	96
2000	63295 (16.91)	2593 (18.94)	60701 (16.82)	100	4	96
2001	65598 (3.64)	2827 (9.02)	62771 (9.11)	100	4	96
2002	71490 (8.98)	2998 (6.05)	68492 (9.11)	100	4	96
2003	84767 (18.57)	4773 (59.21)	7994 (16.79)	100	6	94
2004	11088 (30.81)	5919 (24.01)	104965 (31.22)	100	5	95
2005	129569 (16.85)	7062 (19.31)	122507 (16.71)	100	5	95
Average (1981-94)	21320.57 (9.65)	809.07 (8.37)	20511.5 (9.75)	—	—	—
Average (1995-05)	70748.55 (12.21)	3378.18 (16.99)	67370.36 (12.03)	—	—	—
Average (1981-05)	43068.88 (10.82)	1939.48 (12.32)	41129.4 (10.80)	—	—	—

Figures in parentheses are annual growth rates.
Source : Worked out from the data given in *UNCTAD Handbook of Statistics* : Various Issues.

TABLE 7.2
Intra-Imports of SAARC (1981-2005)

(US $ millions)

Year	Total Exports of SAARC	Intra-SAARC Exports	SAARC's Exports with Rest of the World	Total SAARC Exports	Share of Intra-SAARC Exports	Share of SAARC Exports with rest of the world
(1)	(2)	(3)	(4)	(5)	(6)	(7)
1981	24988	610	24378	100	2	98
1982	25570 (2.33)	476 (-21.97)	25094 (2.94)	100	2	98
1983	23611 (-7.66)	462 (-2.94)	23149 (-7.75)	100	2	98
1984	25843 (9.46)	571 (23.59)	25273 (9.17)	100	2	98
1985	26941 (4.24)	514 (-9.98)	26427 (4.57)	100	2	98
1986	25191 (-6.68)	514 0.00	24627 (-6.81)	100	2	98
1987	28008 (11.40)	531 (3.31)	27477 (11.57)	100	2	98
1988	31592 (12.80)	671 (26.37)	30921 (12.53)	100	2	98

1989	32682 (3.45)	543 (-19.07)	32139 (3.94)	100	2	98
1990	38391 (17.47)	756 (39.23)	37636 (17.10)	100	2	98
1991	35085 (-8.61)	900 (19.05)	34185 (-9.17)	100	3	97
1992	40441 (15.26)	1248 (38.67)	39193 (14.65)	100	3	97
1993	39515 (-2.28)	1266 (1.44)	38249 (-2.41)	100	3	97
1994	44042 (11.45)	1502 (18.64)	42540 (11.22)	100	3	97
1995	58045 (31.80)	2242 (49.27)	55804 (31.18)	100	4	96
1996	61528 (6.00)	2785 (24.22)	58743 (5.27)	100	5	95
1997	66641 (8.31)	2495 (-10.41)	64147 (9.20)	100	4	96
1998	66890 (0.37)	3091 (23.89)	63799 (-0.54)	100	5	95
1999	74406 (11.24)	2626 (-15.04)	71780 (12.51)	100	4	96
2000	78193 (4.45)	2718 (3.50)	75746 (5.52)	100	3	97

(Contd.)

TABLE 7.2 (*Contd.*)

(1)	(2)	(3)	(4)	(5)	(6)	(7)
2001	85158 (8.53)	3083 (13.43)	82075 (8.36)	100	4	96
2002	92957 (9.16)	3275 (6.23)	89682 (9.27)	100	4	96
2003	101084 (8.74)	4464 (36.30)	96620 (7.74)	100	4	96
2004	145618 (44.05)	5638 (26.30)	139981 (44.88)	100	4	96
2005	185476 (27.37)	7104 (26.00)	178371 (27.42)	100	4	96
Average (1981-94)	31560.86 (4.82)	754.57 (8.95)	30806.29 (4.74)	—	—	—
Average (1995-05)	92388.09 (14.64)	3592.82 (16.70)	88795.27 (14.61)	—	—	—
Average (1981-05)	58324.8 (9.32)	2003.4 (12.50)	56321.44 (9.26)	—	—	—

Figures in parentheses are annual growth rates.
Source : Worked out from the data given in *UNCTAD Handbook of Statistics*: Various Issues.

rate of total imports of SAARC ranged between -8.61 percent in 1991 to 15.26 percent in 1992 during pre-WTO period, while it ranged between 0.37 percent in 1999 to 44.05 percent in 2003 during post-WTO period. On an average, growth rate was found to be 4.82 percent in pre-WTO period, 14.64 percent in post-WTO period and 9.32 percent during entire study period.

Imports Creation

Imports Creation (measured in terms of intra-SAARC imports) given in Table 7.2 shows that of total imports of SAARC, intra-SAARC imports had been continuously increasing during period 1981-2005 except seven years (1982, 1983, 1985, 1989, 1997 and 1999). Intra-SAARC imports increased from US $ 610 millions in 1981 to US $ 7104 millions in 2005, thus experiencing growth rate of 16.70 percent. Growth rate of intra-SAARC imports was maximum in 1990, i.e. 39.23 percent during pre-WTO period, while it was maximum in 1995, i.e. 49.27 percent during post-WTO period. The average growth rate of intra-SAARC imports was 8.95 percent in pre-WTO period and 16.70 percent in post-WTO period depicting that growth of intra-SAARC imports was more rapid in post-WTO period than in pre-WTO period. The average growth of intra-regional imports of SAARC was 12.50 percent during 1981-2005.

Imports Diversion

Imports diversion (measured in terms of imports of SAARC from rest of the world) given in Table 7.2 shows that imports of SAARC from rest of the world had been continuously increasing during 1981-2005 except for five years (1983, 1986, 1991, 1993 and 1998). Imports had increased from US $ 24378 millions in 1981 to US $ 178371 millions in 2005, thus experiencing growth rate of 14.61 percent. The growth rate of SAARC with rest of the world was maximum in 1990, i.e. 17.10 percent in pre-WTO period while it was maximum, i.e. 44.88 percent in 2004 in post-WTO period. The average growth rate of SAARC's imports with rest of the world was 4.74 per cent during pre-WTO period while it was 14.61 percent during post-WTO period which was much higher than pre-WTO period.

Thus, it has been observed that average growth of imports expansion, imports creation and imports diversion in post-WTO period was more than in pre-WTO period. The comparative analysis also showed that the growth of imports creation was more rapid than the growth of imports expansion and growth of imports diversion in pre-WTO period, post-WTO period and entire study period.

II

DYNAMIC EFFECTS

Regional integration has effects on trade, welfare, balance of payments and growth. At first, the benefits of integration were trade effects known as static effects brought about by elimination of trade barriers among member countries (Viner (1950), Lipsey (1960) and Meade (1968)). Effect other than trade effects are mainly dynamic effects like competitiveness, technological development, scale economies, resource allocation and investment. Various studies found that the static benefits were very small (Scotovsky (1958), Janssen and Wemelsfelder (1960)). Therefore, studies diverted towards dynamic effects of integration. Easten and Grubel (1982) argued that dynamic benefits are likely to be very large relative to the static effects. Kruger (1980, 85) argued that the growth enhancing effects of more liberal trade regimes were significant for developing countries.

The creation of a large multinational market reduces the risk or raises the expected return to an investment project by enabling firms to lower costs through economies of scale, by providing a large pool of customers with heterogeneous tastes and by enabling the firms to serve national markets with asynchronous business cycles and seasonal buying patterns. Risks of changes in trade policies are reduced by the formation of an integration scheme and investors may experience reduces volatility in share price due to integration of national capital markets. Firms will also benefit from factor mobility and from the ability to establish operations in other member countries. There effects will result in a higher level of investment. The reason behind is that there are some firms unable to compete and other competitive firms have excess capacity which means increasing investment outlays (Brada and Mendez, 1988).

Integration can increase the growth rate of inputs in some cases. The reason is that integration promotes a higher level of disembodied technical progress among member countries. This faster technical progress among member countries will increase the competition between firms in member countries. This will stimulate research and development, the adoption of new technology and better management. Finally, the resources will move now from stagnant to progressive sectors (Corden (1970) and Martin, (1978)). In this chapter, the dynamic effects of SAARC integration have been quantified in terms of investment and total factor productivity as suggested by Brada and Mendez (1988).

Factors Affecting Dynamic Effects in SAARC Nations

Table 7.3 depicts the selected variables of SAARC nations affecting dynamic effects. There are wide disparities among SAARC nations in terms of real gross capital formation, real gross domestic product, real foreign capital inflows, employed labour and real capital stock. India had 1st rank in terms of all these indicators in 2005. Pakistan had got second position in real

TABLE 7.3

Factors Affecting Dynamic Effects in SAARC Nations (2005)

Country	*Real Gross Domestic product (US $ millions)*	*Real Gross Capital Formation (US $ millions)*	*Real Foreign Capital Inflows (US $ millions)*	*Labour (thousand)*	*Real stock (US $ millions)*
Bangladesh	48484	17187	4092	63869	132492
Bhutan	670	280	379	249	2312
India	650730	171169	21228	435036	1241236
Maldives	595	209	267	117	1777.77
Nepal	6606	1631	651	10522	14397.72
Pakistan	89888	13586	12530	56532	152836.6
Sri Lanka	19010	5385	1660	8402	49070.02

Source : Worked out from the data given in *World Development Indicators*, 2006.

gross domestic product, real foreign capital inflows and real capital stock while Bangladesh had got second position in real capital formation and employed labour. Bhutan and Maldives were the poorest countries among SAARC nations in terms of these indicators.

Table 7.4 depicts the *growth rate of real GDP* among SAARC nations during 1981-2005. Table depicts that growth rate of real GDP ranged between -16.34 percent in 1982 to 12.88 percent in 1984 for Bangladesh; for Bhutan, between -20.02 percent in 1991 to 23.11 percent in 1987; for India, between -18.87 percent in 1991 to 16.45 percent in 2003; for Maldives, between -11.28 percent in 1987 to 86.05 percent in 1984; for Nepal between -16.19 percent in 1992 to 12.52 percent in 2004; for Pakistan between -11.98 percent in 1983 to 16.53 percent in 2004 and for Sri Lanka, between -5.64 percent in 2001 to 14.13 percent in 2005. The compound growth rate of GDP was maximum in Maldives, i.e. 6.72 percent followed by Sri Lanka (4.11 percent), Bhutan (3.66 percent), Pakistan (2.76 percent), India (2.56 percent), Bangladesh (2.49 percent) and Nepal (2.25 percent) during the period 1981-2005.

Table 7.5 depicts the *growth rate of real gross capital formation* among SAARC nations during 1981-2005. Growth rate of real gross capital formation ranged between 1.40 percent in 1991 to 12.06 percent in 1998 in Bangladesh; for Bhutan, between -20.88 percent in 2005 to 53.73 percent in 1983; for India, between -15.6 percent in 1991 to 21.99 percent in 1994; for Maldives, between -29.61 percent in 1993 to 288.79 percent in 1995; for Nepal, between -14.35 percent in 1991 to 45.13 percent in 1992; for Pakistan between -9.19 percent in 1999 to 18.54 percent in 1982 and for Sri Lanka, between -17.47 percent in 2001 to 15.95 percent in 2003. The compound growth rate of real gross capital formation was maximum in Bhutan, i.e. 7.91 percent followed by Bangladesh (7.81 percent), India (7.16 percent), Nepal (6.38 percent), Maldives (4.76 percent), Sri Lanka (3.84 percent) and Pakistan (3.16 percent) during period 1981-2005.

Table 7.6 depicts the *growth of foreign capital inflows* among SAARC nations during 1981-2005. The compound growth rate of foreign capital inflows was maximum in Maldives 7.98 percent followed by Bhutan (6.07 percent), India (5.02 percent),

TABLE 7.4
Growth of Real GDP among SAARC Nations

(US $ Millions)

Year	*Bangladesh*	*Bhutan*	*India*	*Maldives*	*Nepal*	*Pakistan*	*Sri Lanka*
(1)	(2)	(3)	(4)	(5)	(6)	(7)	(8)
1981	32350.17	243.74	311759.96	98.04	3725.16	45999.83	7229.26
1982	27065.11 (-16.34)	227.65 (-6.60)	295804.7 (-5.12)	99.79 (1.79)	3583.85 (-3.79)	45977.73 (-0.05)	7136.12 (-1.29)
1983	24197.67 (-10.59)	238.08 (4.58)	303490.44 (2.60)	118.25 (18.49)	3451.32 (-3.70)	40469.52 (-11.98)	7289.17 (2.14)
1984	27315.3 (12.88)	233.57 (-1.90)	284484.02 (-6.26)	220 (86.05)	3501.41 (1.45)	42131.95 (4.11)	8199.21 (12.48)
1985	28263.88 (3.47)	230.22 (-1.43)	300696.56 (5.70)	254 (15.45)	3425.77 (-2.16)	40728.77 (-3.33)	7818.01 (-4.65)
1986	26846.87 (-5.01)	260.46 (13.14)	312585.99 (3.95)	260.55 (2.58)	3617.44 (5.59)	40472.21 (-0.63)	8126.67 (3.95)
1987	29514.2 (9.94)	320.67 (23.11)	342548.34 (9.59)	231.15 (-11.28)	3669.78 (1.45)	41393.45 (2.28)	8293.18 (2.05)
1988	30965.46 (4.92)	342.8 (6.90)	354052.19 (3.36)	264.06 (14.24)	4211.4 (14.76)	46465.54 (12.25)	8427.66 (1.62)
1989	31323.5 (1.16)	325.9 (-4.93)	342038.86 (-3.39)	279.41 (5.81)	4115.84 (-2.27)	46907.85 (0.95)	8158.95 (-3.19)

(Contd.)

TABLE 7.4 (*Contd.*)

(1)	*(2)*	*(3)*	*(4)*	*(5)*	*(6)*	*(7)*	*(8)*
1990	33895.32 (8.21)	342.5 (5.09)	357153.54 (4.42)	302.82 (8.38)	4081.55 (-0.83)	45011.79 (-4.04)	9037.4 (10.77)
1991	33529.66 (-1.08)	273.93 (-20.02)	289759.63 (-18.87)	305 (0.72)	4246.71 (4.05)	49229.88 (9.37)	9748.42 (7.87)
1992	33184.45 (-1.03)	265.99 (-2.90)	256978.74 (-11.31)	313.19 (2.68)	3559.05 (-16.19)	50898.15 (3.39)	10154.73 (4.17)
1993	33928.94 (2.24)	243.53 (-8.44)	282378.86 (9.88)	322 (2.81)	3743.76 (5.19)	52660.63 (3.46)	10576.82 (4.16)
1994	33769 (-0.47)	275 (12.92)	323505.98 (14.56)	325.11 (0.97)	4067 (8.63)	51895 (-1.45)	11718 (10.79)
1995	37156.44 (10.03)	300.93 (9.43)	365061.48 (12.85)	341.03 (4.89)	4309.9 (5.97)	59383.4 (14.43)	12761.07 (8.90)
1996	39029.85 (5.04)	308.31 (2.45)	372722.1 (2.10)	365.85 (7.28)	4339.98 (0.70)	60772.94 (2.34)	13339.37 (4.53)
1997	39857.75 (2.12)	351.42 (13.98)	387017.27 (3.84)	390.77 (6.81)	4632.59 (6.74)	58802.26 (-3.24)	14214.41 (6.56)
1998	40845.34 (2.48)	355.88 (1.27)	385603.12 (-0.37)	412.21 (5.49)	4498.17 (-2.90)	57612.67 (-2.02)	14632.34 (2.94)
1999	41864 (2.49)	390.25 9.66	412721.5 (7.03)	486.78 (18.09)	4612.06 (2.53)	57696.16 (0.14)	14344 (-1.97)

2000	42534.96 (1.60)	404.8 (0.73)	415620.35 (0.70)	520 (6.83)	4961.85 (7.58)	66219.25 (14.77)	14749.42 (2.83)
2001	41500.25 (-2.43)	428.9 (5.95)	422747.52 (1.71)	508.13 (-2.28)	5309.25 (7.00)	63195.98 (-4.57)	13917.59 (-5.64)
2002	41007.42 (-1.19)	469.55 (9.48)	438375.33 (3.70)	510.76 (0.52)	5222.16 (-1.64)	61692.35 (-2.38)	14273.17 (2.55)
2003	43958.85 (7.20)	535.6 (14.07)	510492.47 (16.45)	560.32 (9.70)	5369 (2.81)	69846.52 (13.22)	15478.06 (8.44)
2004	47071.41 (7.08)	592.46 (10.62)	577924.84 (13.21)	641.32 (14.46)	6041.05 (12.52)	81388.78 (16.53)	16656.67 (7.61)
2005	48484.81 (3.00)	670.78 (13.22)	650730.64 (12.60)	595.28 (-7.18)	6606.16 (9.35)	89888.12 (10.44)	19010.06 (14.13)
Compound Growth Rate (percent)	2.49	3.66	2.56	6.72	2.25	2.76	4.11

Note : Figures in parentheses are annual growth rates.
Source : Worked out from the data given in *World Development Indicators:* Various Issues.

TABLE 7.5

Growth of Real Gross Capital Formation among SAARC Nations

(US $ Millions)

Year	Bangladesh	Bhutan	India	Maldives	Nepal	Pakistan	Sri Lanka
(1)	(2)	(3)	(4)	(5)	(6)	(7)	(8)
1981	2793.18	53.73	29501.25	56.64	340.29	5352.79	1924.35
1982	3019.57 (8.10)	59.19 (10.17)	29453.11 (0.16)	41.58 (-26.59)	378.03 (11.09)	6345.27 (18.54)	2028.34 (5.40)
1983	3172.62 (5.06)	59.19 (53.73)	30944.64 (5.06)	55.04 (32.38)	367.79 (-2.70)	6500.38 (2.44)	2298.16 (13.30)
1984	3475.54 (9.54)	53.73 (-9.23)	33404.06 (7.94)	56 (1.73)	446.8 (21.48)	6817.55 (4.87)	2340.32 (1.83)
1985	3684.92 (6.02)	72.85 (35.59)	36620.23 (9.62)	84 (50.00)	469.12 (4.99)	7509.42 (10.15)	2222.27 (-5.04)
1986	3930.44 (6.66)	66.48 (-8.75)	36821.24 (0.55)	93.57 (11.40)	452.7 (17.81)	7837.92 (4.37)	2428.39 (9.27)
1987	4250.36 (8.13)	57.37 (-13.7)	41985.86 (14.03)	117.83 (25.92)	530.04 (-4.10)	8149.005 (3.96)	2416.21 (-0.50)
1988	4508.63 (6.07)	68.3 (19.05)	47819.39 (13.89)	139.06 (18.01)	523.96 (-1.14)	8053.15 (-1.18)	2249.44 (-6.90)
1989	4825.37 (7.02)	71.03 (4.00)	51089.61 (6.83)	152.71 (9.81)	670.66 (27.99)	8655.26 (7.47)	2099.54 (-6.66)

1990	5130.41 (6.32)	76.49 (7.69)	59662.12 (16.78)	140.64 (-7.90)	664.13 (-0.97)	9100.53 (5.14)	2134.21 (1.65)
1991	5202.68 (1.40)	67.39 (-11.9)	50350.6 (-15.6)	40.02 (-71.54)	568.82 (-14.35)	9375.01 (3.01)	2297.22 (7.63)
1992	5434.38 (4.45)	90.15 (33.78)	55168.1 (9.56)	39.77 (-0.61)	825.55 (45.13)	10348.33 (10.38)	2393.72 (4.20)
1993	5951.99 (9.52)	101.99 (13.13)	58575.98 (6.17)	28 (-29.61)	826 (0.05)	10757 (3.94)	2642 (10.37)
1994	6507.87 (9.33)	127.49 (25.00)	71457.55 (21.99)	27.39 (-2.15)	890.14 (7.76)	1067.22 (-0.77)	2983.96 (12.94)
1995	7100.94 (9.11)	121.12 (-5.0)	76904.26 (7.62)	106.51 (288.79)	1034.25 (16.18)	11082.89 (3.82)	2977.4 (-0.22)
1996	7853.45 (10.60)	116.5696 (-3.76)	76519.13 (-0.5)	111.74 (4.90)	1176.07 (13.71)	11707.66 (5.63)	3071.09 (3.14)
1997	8723.93 (11.08)	101.0877 (13.28)	85801.93 (12.13)	129.5 (15.89)	1152.93 (-1.96)	11285.05 (-3.61)	3184.45 (3.69)
1998	9776.15 (12.06)	115.65 (14.41)	85905.81 (0.12)	123.19 (-4.87)	1163.51 (0.91)	11628.36 (3.04)	3668.82 (15.21)
1999	10743.36 (9.89)	148.44 (28.28)	101069.4 (17.65)	163.63 (32.82)	1002.68 (-13.82)	10560.07 (-9.19)	3902.1 (6.35)
2000	11525.62 (7.28)	193.06 (30.06)	96301.77 (-4.72)	136.66 (-16.48)	1263.17 (25.97)	11101.19 (5.12)	4289.97 (9.94)
2001	1218.91 (5.76)	203.08 (5.18)	98537.38 (2.32)	142.27 (4.10)	1225.76 (-2.96)	11576.08 (4.27)	3540.46 (-17.47)

(Contd.)

TABLE 7.5 (*Contd.*)

(1)	(2)	(3)	(4)	(5)	(6)	(7)	(8)
2002	13184.74 (8.16)	283.22 (39.46)	109585.4 (11.21)	130.67 (-8.15)	1112.09 (-9.27)	11547.33 (-0.25)	3746.58 (5.82)
2003	14222.09 (7.86)	305.99 (8.03)	123398.5 (12.60)	152.22 (16.49)	1222.44 (-9.92)	12280.15 (6.34)	4344.31 (15.95)
2004	15526.22 (9.16)	353.35 (15.48)	144024 (16.71)	224.79 (47.67)	1466 (19.92)	11644.92 (-5.17)	4852.09 (11.68)
2005	17187.46 (10.70)	279.58 (-20.88)	171168.9 (18.85)	208.66 (-7.17)	1630.83 (11.24)	13586.32 (16.67	5385.18 (10.99)
Compound Growth Rate (percent)	7.81	7.91	7.16	4.76	6.38	3.16	3.84

Note : Figures in parentheses are annual growth rates.
Source : Worked out from the data given in *World Development Indicators:* Various Issues.

TABLE 7.6

Growth of Real Foreign Capital Inflows among SAARC Nations

(US $ Millions)

Year	Bangladesh	Bhutan	India	Maldives	Nepal	Pakistan	Sri Lanka
(1)	(2)	(3)	(4)	(5)	(6)	(7)	(8)
1981	2993	52	9864	96.43	822.17	6281	796
1982	2600 (13.13)	59 (13.46)	8878 (-9.996)	41.11 (-57.368)	960.97 (16.88)	3609 (-37.81)	816 (2.51)
1983	3003 (15.50)	72 (22.03)	7253 (-18.3)	91.13 (121.67)	1009.68 (5.07)	4064 (4.045)	901 (10.42)
1984	1954 (-34.93)	80 (11.11)	7183 (-0.965)	41.25 (-54.735)	864.52 (-14.37)	3399 (-16.36)	1056 (17.20)
1985	2005 (2.61)	109 (36.25)	6462 (-10.04)	65.68 (59.467)	454.18 (-47.46)	2773 (-18.42)	887 (-16.00)
1986	2374 (18.40)	217 (99.08)	7000 (8.3256)	145.45 (121.12)	722.15 (59.00)	3532 (27.37)	1048 (18.15)
1987	3178 (33.86)	235 (8.29)	9507 (35.81)	139.03 (-4.4139)	960.21 (8.3256)	4010 (8.3256)	1200 (14.50)
1988	3947 (24.19)	215 (-8.51)	7109 (-25.22)	262.1 (88.52)	1015.64 (-11.77)	3538 (-11.77)	1089 (-9.25)

(Contd.)

TABLE 7.6 (*Contd.*)

(1)	*(2)*	*(3)*	*(4)*	*(5)*	*(6)*	*(7)*	*(8)*
1989	3269 (-17.17)	195 (-9.30)	7432 (4.5435)	267.72 (2.1442)	1163.44 (14.55)	5267 (14.55)	1230 (14.55)
1990	3383 (3.48)	213 (9.23)	6767 (-8.948)	207.54 (-22.479)	1000.69 (-13.96)	4719 (-10.40)	1200 (-2.44)
1991	4384 (29.58)	210 (-1.40)	3796 (-43.9)	345.56 (14.55)	820.44 (-18.01)	5628 (19.26)	1511 (25.92)
1992	4356 (-0.63)	198 (-5.71)	8973 (136.38)	376.31 (8.8986)	964.65 (8.8986)	4974 (-11.62)	1866 (8.8986)
1993	4537 (4.15)	203 (2.52)	7721 (-13.95)	330.63 (-12.139)	745.32 (-22.74)	4499 (-9.55)	1522 (-18.44)
1994	3679 (-18.91)	255 (25.61)	7474 (50.171)	342.54 (3.6022)	969.39 (3.6022)	7359 (3.6022)	1845 (3.6022)
1995	4648 (26.33)	238 (-6.66)	4977 (-35.54)	645.31 (88.372)	854.9 (-11.81)	5576 (-24.23)	1581 (-14.31)
1996	3248 (-30.12)	201 (-15.54)	12794 (71.18)	425.49 (-34.06)	820.89 (-3.98)	5924 (6.24)	1298 (-17.90)
1997	3122 (-3.87)	255 (26.86)	15363 (20.08)	388.6 (-8.67)	832.84 (1.46)	4474 (-24.48)	1262 (2.77)
1998	2844 (-8.90)	241 (-5.53)	17377 (13.11)	401.07 (3.209)	806.95 (-3.11)	5420 (7.45)	1654 (7.45)
1999	3260 (14.62)	268 (11.20)	14114 (-18.78)	430.95 (7.45)	641.3 (-20.53)	4115 (-24.08)	1287 (-22.19)

2000	3169 (-2.79)	196 (-26.87)	10986 (-22.16)	281.91 (-34.87)	732.12 (14.16)	2843 (-30.91)	821 (-36.21)
2001	2417 (-23.73)	230 (17.35)	16088 (46.44)	349.21 (23.87)	798.44 (9.06)	7973 (180.44)	833 (1.46)
2002	2150 (-11.04)	296 (29.00)	23759 (47.68)	362.57 (3.83)	726.41 (-9.02)	9717 (21.874)	970 (16.44)
2003	2961 (37.72)	295 (-0.34)	24521 (3.21)	347.09 (-4.27)	903.07 (24.32)	5384 (-44.59)	1031 (6.29)
2004	3726 (25.83)	329 (11.23)	19603 (-20.06)	331 (-4.64)	751.53 (-16.78)	8169 (51.727)	1622 (57.32)
2005	4092 (9.82)	379 (15.20)	21228 (8.29)	267.44 (-19.20)	651.25 (-13.34)	12530 (8.29)	1660 (2.34)
Compound Growth Rate (percent)	0.78	6.07	5.02	7.98	-0.69	2.99	1.37

Note : Figures in parentheses are annual growth rates.
Source : Worked out from the data given in *World Development Indicators*: Various Issues.

Pakistan (2.99 percent) and Sri Lanka (1.37 percent) during period 1981-2005. For Nepal, it was negative, i.e. (-0.69 percent).

Table 7.7 depicts the *growth of real gross capital stock* (calculated by perpetual inventory method) among SAARC nations. The compound growth rate real gross capital stock was maximum in Bangladesh (12.31 percent) followed by Bhutan (11.76 percent), Nepal (11.74 percent), Maldives (9.79 percent), Sri Lanka (8.61 percent) and Pakistan (7.64 percent) during period 1981-2005.

Table 7.8 depicts the *growth of employed labour* among SAARC nations during 1981-2005. Its compound growth rate was maximum in Maldives (3.79 percent), followed by Pakistan (2.80 percent), Nepal (2.40 percent), Bangladesh (2.18 percent), India (1.73 percent), Sri Lanka (1.51 percent) and Bhutan (0.93 percent) during 1981-2005.

Effect of Real Gross Domestic Product, Real Foreign Capital Inflows and Integration on Investment

Table 7.9 reports the effect of real gross domestic product, real foreign capital inflows and integration on investment for SAARC as a whole and SAARC nations during 1981-2005. For SAARC as a whole, regression equation has been estimated with the help of pooled (restricted) model and one-way fixed effects model (due to panel data). A restriction F-test has been carried out to check for the pool ability of the data. It value was 9.17 at (6,164) d.f., which was significant indicating OLS results are biased and suggesting to select a model with individual effects. Therefore, the equation has also been estimated with the help of one-way random effects model. In order to discriminate between two models, null hypothesis, i.e. explanatory variables and individual effects are uncorrelated has been tested using a Hausman test. Its value was 3.23 at 4 degrees of freedom suggesting fixed effect model was better than random effects model for the present data. Therefore, highlighted row of Table 7.9 reports the results of only fixed effect model. Real GDP had highly significantly and positively affected the real gross capital formation of SAARC during 1981-2005. The value of its coefficient was 1.01 percent depicting that an increase by one per cent in real GDP will go in increase in real gross capital formation by an average index of 1.01 per cent. Coefficient of

TABLE 7.7

Growth of Real Gross Capital Stock among SAARC Nations

(US $ Millions)

Year	Bangladesh	Bhutan	India	Maldives	Nepal	Pakistan	Sri Lanka
(1)	(2)	(3)	(4)	(5)	(6)	(7)	(8)
1981	5459	97	62438	120	741	11571	4499
1982	8206 (50.30)	151 (55.83)	88769 (42.17)	155 (29.69)	1082 (46.04)	17337 (49.84)	6302 (40.08)
1983	10968 (33.66)	203 (34.03)	115275 (29.86)	203 (30.41)	1395 (29.00)	22971 (32.49)	8285 (3146.00)
1984	13895 (26.69)	246 (21.46)	142916 (23.98)	249 (22.62)	1772 (27.01)	28640 (24.68)	10211 (23.24)
1985	16885 (21.52)	307 (24.52)	172390 (20.62)	320 (28.79)	2153 (21.47)	34717 (21.22)	11923 (16.96)
1986	19971 (18.28)	358 (16.63)	200592 (16.36)	397 (24.23)	2598 (20.67)	40819 (17.58)	13755 (15.37)
1987	23223 (16.28)	397 (11.00)	232548 (15.93)	496 (24.63)	2998 (15.40)	46927 (14.96)	15483 (12.57)
1988	26571 (14.41)	446 (12.17)	268740 (15.56)	610 (23.06)	3372 (12.47)	52634 (12.16)	16959 (9.53)

(Contd.)

TABLE 7.7 (*Contd.*)

(1)	*(2)*	*(3)*	*(4)*	*(5)*	*(6)*	*(7)*	*(8)*
1989	30067 (13.16)	495 (10.92)	306392 (14.01)	732 (20.03)	3874 (14.89)	58658 (11.44)	18210 (7.38)
1990	33694 (12.06)	547 (10.45)	350735 (14.47)	836 (14.21)	4345 (12.14)	64825 (10.51)	19434 (6.72)
1991	37212 (10.44)	587 (7.32)	383549 (9.36)	834 (-0.21)	4696 (8.96)	70959 (9.46)	20760 (6.82)
1992	40786 (9.66)	648 (10.36)	419540 (9.38)	832 (-0.23)	5287 (12.58)	77759 (9.58)	22115 (6.53)
1993	44699 (9.59)	717 (10.74)	457139 (8.96)	819 (-1.64)	5849 (10.62)	84629 (8.83)	23652 (6.95)
1994	48972 (9.56)	809 (12.77)	505739 (10.63)	805 (-1.65)	6446 (10.22)	91071 (7.61)	25453 (7.62)
1995	53624 (9.50)	890 (9.97)	557357 (10.21)	872 (8.23)	7158 (11.04)	97600 (7.17)	27158 (6.70)
1996	58796 (9.65)	962 (8.10)	606007 (8.73)	940 (7.82)	7976 (11.43)	104428 (7.00)	28871 (6.31)
1997	64580 (9.84)	1015 (5.51)	661509 (9.16)	1022 (8.78)	8731 (9.45)	110492 (5.81)	30612 (6.03)
1998	71127 (10.14)	1080 (6.40)	714339 (7.99)	1094 (7.05)	9458 (8.33)	116596 (5.52)	32750 (6.98)

1999	78314 (10.10)	1174 (8.75)	779692 (9.15)	1203 (9.95)	9987 (5.60)	121326 (4.06)	35015 (6.91)
2000	85924 (9.72)	1308 (11.44)	837009 (7.35)	1280 (6.36)	10751 (7.65)	126361 (4.15)	37554 (7.25)
2001	93818 (9.19)	1446 (10.52)	893697 (6.77)	1358 (6.12)	11439 (6.40)	131619 (4.16)	39217 (4.43)
2002	102312 (9.05)	1657 (14.59)	958597 (7.26)	1421 (4.62)	11980 (4.72)	136585 (3.77)	41003 (4.55)
2003	111418 (8.91)	1880 (13.47)	1034065 (7.87)	1502 (5.71)	12603 (5.20)	142036 (3.99)	43297 (5.59)
2004	121374 (8.94)	2140 (13.79)	1126386 (8.92)	1652 (9.97)	13439 (6.63)	146579 (3.20)	45984 (6.21)
2005	132492 (9.16)	2312 (8.07)	1241236 (10.20)	1777 (7.63)	14398 (7.13)	152837 (4.27)	49070 (6.71)
Compound Growth Rate (percent)	12.31	11.76	11.7	9.79	11.74	7.64	8.61

Note : Figures in parentheses are annual growth rates.
Source : Worked out from the data given in *World Development Indicators*: Various Issues.

Table 7.8
Growth of Labour among SAARC Nations

(Thousands)

Year	Bangladesh	Bhutan	India	Maldives	Nepal	Pakistan	Sri Lanka
(1)	(2)	(3)	(4)	(5)	(6)	(7)	(8)
1981	37273	178	286468	47	5975	28271	5883
1982	38405 (3.03)	181 (1.69)	291957 (1.92)	49 (4.26)	6090 (1.92)	29040 (2.72)	5964 (1.38)
1983	39573 (3.04)	184 (1.66)	296901 (1.69)	50 (2.04)	6208 (1.94)	29721 (2.35)	6059 (1.59)
1984	40723 (2.90)	188 (2.17)	302229 (1.79)	51 (2.00)	6329 (1.95)	30507 (2.64)	6143 (1.39)
1985	41852 (2.78)	191 (1.60)	307028 (1.59)	52 (1.96)	6453 (1.96)	31723 (3.94)	6250 (1.74)
1986	43010 (2.77)	195 (2.09)	312832 (1.89)	53 (1.92)	6581 (1.98)	32405 (2.15)	6305 (0.88)
1987	44028 (2.37)	199 (2.05)	318658 (1.86)	54 (1.89)	6712 (1.94)	33138 (2.26)	6552 (3.92)
1988	45006 (2.22)	204 (2.51)	323960 (1.66)	55 (1.85)	6847 (2.01)	33882 (2.25)	6788 (3.60)
1989	45935 (2.06)	207 (1.47)	329631 (1.75)	56 (1.82)	6977 (1.40)	34553 (1.98)	7031 (3.58)

1990	46931 (2.17)	210 (1.45)	335119 (1.66)	58 (3.57)	7124 (2.11)	35238 (1.98)	7267 (3.36)
1991	47932 (2.13)	209 (-0.48)	340399 (1.58)	60 (3.45)	7265 (1.98)	35939 (1.99)	7192 (-1.03)
1992	48747 (1.70)	206 (-1.43)	345786 (1.58)	62 (3.33)	7436 (2.35)	36652 (1.98)	7060 (-1.83)
1993	49504 (1.55)	202 (-1.94)	350660 (1.41)	65 (4.84)	7613 (2.38)	37416 (2.08)	7155 (1.35)
1994	50352 (1.71)	200 (-1.00)	355592 (1.41)	67 (3.08)	7799 (2.44)	38266 (2.27)	7350 (2.72)
1995	51164 (1.61)	199 (-0.01)	361991 (1.80)	70 (4.48)	7993 (2.49)	39346 (2.82)	7221 (-1.76)
1996	52011 (1.66)	199 0.00	368738 (1.86)	74 (5.71)	8220 (2.83)	40620 (3.24)	7407 (2.58)
1997	53257 (2.40)	202 (1.51)	375172 (1.74)	77 (4.05)	8444 (2.72)	42072 (3.57)	7572 (2.21)
1998	54610 (2.54)	205 (1.49)	381837 (1.78)	81 (5.19)	8677 (2.76)	43334 (3.00)	8151 (7.65)
1999	55899 (2.36)	210 (2.44)	389305 (1.96)	86 (6.17)	8931 (2.92)	44981 (3.80)	8090 (-0.74)
2000	57264 (2.44)	214 (1.90)	396216 (1.77)	90 (4.65)	9178 (2.76)	46702 (3.83)	8161 (0.88)
2001	58704 (2.51)	218 (1.87)	404399 (2.07)	94 (4.44)	9430 (2.75)	48577 (4.01)	7910 (-3.08)

(Contd.)

TABLE 7.8 (*Contd.*)

(1)	(2)	(3)	(4)	(5)	(6)	(7)	(8)
2002	60144 (2.45)	222 (1.83)	412542 (2.01)	97 (13.19)	9704 (2.90)	50533 (4.03)	8017 (1.35)
2003	61596 (2.41)	225 (1.35)	421337 (2.13)	101 (4.12)	9987 (2.83)	52384 (3.66)	8120 (1.28)
2004	62364 (1.25)	235 (4.44)	427166 (1.38)	112 (9.82)	10233 (2.46)	54476 (3.99)	8292 (2.12)
2005	63869 (2.41)	249 (5.96)	435036 (1.84)	117 (4.46)	10522 (2.82)	56532 (3.78)	8402 (1.33)
Compound Growth Rate (percent)	2.18	0.93	1.73	3.79	2.4	2.8	1.51

Note : Figures in parentheses are annual growth rates.
Source : Worked out from the data given in *World Development Indicators:* Various Issues.

TABLE 7.9

Effect of Real Gross Domestic Product, Real Foreign Capital Inflows and Integration on Investment

Country	Constant	Real Gross Domestic Real Foreign	Real Foreign Capital Inflows	D_1	D_2	R^2	F- Statistics Country
(1)	(2)	(3)	(4)	(5)	(6)	(7)	(8)
Bangladesh	-3.36**	1.59**	-0.01	0.02*	0.05**	0.88	36.67
	(19.19)	(34.85)	(0.44)	(2.08)	(3.06)		
Bhutan	-0.65	1.51**	-0.38	-0.05	-0.05	0.87	33.46
	(1.45)	(5.00)	(1.25)	(0.42)	(0.37)		
India	-2.62**	1.34**	3.06	0.01	-0.04	0.88	36.67
	(6.64)	(18.19)	(0.63)	(0.25)	(1.21)		
Maldives	2.26	-0.02	-0.29	0.33	0.68*	0.9	45
	(2.03)	(0.03)	(1.30)	(1.33)	(1.93)		
Nepal	-1.85**	1.24**	0.1	0.06	0.07	0.89	40.45
	(2.95	(7.12)	(0.78)	(1.43)	(0.93)		
Pakistan	0.57	0.74**	-0.02	0.03	0.01	0.89	40.45
	(1.53)	(7.61)	(0.63)	(1.28)	(0.04)		

(Contd.)

TABLE 7.9 (*Contd.*)

(1)	(2)	(3)	(4)	(5)	(6)	(7)	(8)
Sri Lanka	-0.44 (0.77)	0.98** (5.71)	0.04 (0.05)	-0.07* (2.38)	-0.05 (0.92	0.88	36.67
SAARC	-0.12 (0.30)	1.01** (8.40)	-0.17** (3.19)	0.01 (0.25)	0.08 (1.48)	0.9	147.6
Restricted F-test value	9.17* (6, 164)[a]						
Hausman test	3.23 (4)[a]						

Note : Figures in parentheses are t-values.
** Significant at one per cent level.
* Significant at five percent level.
[a] degrees of freedom.
Source : Based on data given in Tables 7.4 to 7.8.

foreign capital flows was significant and negative indicating that with increase in foreign capital inflows would decrease in gross capital formation of SAARC. This is due to the fact that foreign capital inflows has not been using for capital formation in developing economies. The coefficients of time Dummies, i.e. D_1 (from the formation of SAARC to the formation of SAPTA) and D_2 (after the formation of SAPTA) were non-significant and positive. This suggested that integration has positively and non-significantly affected the gross capital formation of SAARC nations.

Country-wise effects have also been estimated with the help of multiple regression equation. Real GDP had significantly and positively affected the gross capital formation in all SAARC nations (except Maldives) during 1981-2005. In Maldives, it had non-significantly and negatively affected the gross capital formation. The coefficient of real foreign capital inflows was non-significant and positive in case of only three SAARC nations, i.e. India, Nepal and Sri Lanka while for other SAARC nations (Bangladesh, Bhutan, Maldives and Pakistan), it was non-significant and negative. It indicates that real foreign capital inflows are not playing any role for capital formation in these economies. The time effect and integration coefficient (D_1) was significant and positive only for Bangladesh indicating that there was significant and positive impact on gross capital formation. While it was significant and negative for Sri Lanka indicating that integration had negative impact on capital formation of Sri Lanka during the same period. For remaining SAARC nations (except Bhutan), it was non-significant and positive indicating that integration had non-significant impact on capital formation of these economies. The integration effect after the formation of SAPTA has been captured by D_2. This was significant and positive only for Bangladesh and Maldives indicating that formation of SAPTA has significantly and positively affected the capital formation of these countries. While for other SAARC nations, i.e. Bhutan, India and Sri Lanka, it was non-significant and negative and for remaining SAARC nations, i.e. Nepal and Pakistan, it was non-significant and positive. Thus, integration has no impact on capital formation of SAARC.

Effect of Real Capital Stock, Labour and Integration on GDP

Table 7.10 reports the effect of real capital stock, labour and integration on GDP for SAARC as a whole and for SAARC nations during 1981-2005. For SAARC as a whole, regression equation has been estimated with the help of pooled (restricted) model and one-way fixed effects model (due to panel data). Then, a restricted F-test has been carried out to check for the pool ability of the data. Its value was 1.32 at (6,164) d.f. which was non-significant indicating OLS results are unbiased suggesting to select a model without individual effects. Therefore, there is no need to estimate the equation with the help of one-way random effects model. Highlighted row of Table 7.10 reports the results of pooled model. The value of coefficient of growth of capital stock of SAARC was -0.06 depicting that an increase by one percent in growth rate of capital stock will decrease in growth rate of gross domestic product by an average index of 0.06 percent. The coefficient of growth of labour had non-significantly and positively affected the growth rate of GDP. The coefficient of growth rate of labour was found to be 0.27 depicting that with one per cent increase in growth rate of labour will increase the growth rate of gross domestic product by an average index of 0.27 percent. Surprisingly, two time dummies had significantly and negatively affected the growth rate of GDP in SAARC suggesting that integration has decreased the rate of technological progress among member countries during 1981-2005. In other words, integration has reduced the rate of productivity growth.

Effect on productivity growth has also been estimated for country-by-country with the help of multiple regression equations. Growth rate of capital stock had non-significantly affected the growth rate of GDP in all SAARC nations during 1981-2005. It had positively affected in Bhutan, India, Nepal and Pakistan. While for Bangladesh, Maldives and Sri Lanka, it had negatively affected. Regarding the growth rate of labour, it had significantly and positively affected the growth rate of GDP for Sri Lanka only while for other SAARC nations, it had non-significantly affected the growth rate of GDP. It had negatively affected the growth rate of GDP in Bangladesh, India and Maldives while for other SAARC nations (Bhutan, Nepal and

TABLE 7.10

Effect of Real Capital Stock, Labour and Integration on Real GDP

Country	*Constant*	*Real Gross Domestic Real Foreign*	*Real Foreign Capital Inflows*	D_1	D_2	R^2	*F- Statistics Country*
(1)	*(2)*	*(3)*	*(4)*	*(5)*	*(6)*	*(7)*	*(8)*
Bangladesh	6.51**	-0.02	-0.63	-1	0.37	0.44	3.94
	(3.88)	(0.90)	(1.26)	(1.09)	(0.40)		
Bhutan	2.21	0.06	1.25	3.97	1.41	0.17	1.04
	(0.45)	(0.87)	(1.70)	(0.89)	(0.31)		
India	5.95	0.05	-1.42	1.31	2.72	0.09	0.5
	(1.38)	(0.78)	(0.54)	(0.68)	(1.18)		
Maldives	46.21**	-0.42	-0.84	-34.12*	-32.78*	0.3	2.08
	(2.78)	(-1.50)	(0.34)	(2.79)	(2.38)		
Nepal	0.84	0.08	0.07	2.88	2.52	0.09	0.52
	(0.12)	(1.25)	(0.02)	(1.06)	(0.62)		
Pakistan	2.48	0.03	0.96	0.37	-2.06	0.27	1.8/2
	(0.89)	(0.62)	(1.10)	(0.20)	(0.81)		
Sri Lanka	5.92*	-0.04	0.35	-2.03	-1.7	0.17	1.06
	(2.32)	(0.72)	(1.85)	(0.73)	(0.47)		

(Contd.)

TABLE 7.9 (*Contd.*)

(1)	*(2)*	*(3)*	*(4)*	*(5)*	*(6)*	*(7)*	*(8)*
SAARC	10.53** (3.71)	-0.06 (1.09)	0.27 (0.70)	-5.21* (2.22)	-5.45* (2.15)	0.04	1.68
Restricted F-test value	1.32 (6,164)[a]						

Note : Figure in parentheses are t-values.
** Significant at one per cent level.
* Significant at five percent level.
[a] degrees of freedom.
Source : Based on data given in Tables 7.4 to 7.8.

Pakistan), it had positively affected. The time dummies (D_1 as well as D_2) had significantly and negatively affected the growth rate of GDP in Maldives indicating that integration had significantly reduced the rate of productivity in Maldives. For Bangladesh and Sri Lanka, D_1 had non-significantly and negatively affected the growth rate of GDP while for other SAARC economies, it had non-significantly and positively affected the growth rate of GDP. It indicates that integration had a positive impact for many SAARC nations (Bhutan, India, Nepal and Pakistan) on technological progress but its role is not significant. After the formation of SAPTA, integration positively and non-significantly affected the growth rate of GDP in Bangladesh, Bhutan, India and Nepal as D_2 was positive. Thus, it is clear that SAARC integration has reduced the rate of technological progress in SAARC.

Thus it is clear that dynamic effects of SAARC in terms of investment and productivity are not so strong during 1981-2005. There is a need to strengthen the static effects firstly, and then dynamic effects will automatically be generated and powerful. But for this, growth of intra-regional trade is a necessary requirement. It has been expecting that SAFTA will generate this growth, then dynamic effects will come out in SAARC. Thus, the dynamic effects of SAARC integration cannot explain the rapid rates of growth experienced by members of regional integration and also these effects cannot serve as a rationale for integration. SAARC do not affect the growth of their member countries directly but it does have a significant positive influence on investment and investment has a strong and significant effect on growth.

8

A Gravity Model Analysis of India's Export Potential to Other SAARC Countries

This chapter examines the bilateral exports between India and SAARC members based on gravity model and analyses India's export potential to SAARC nations. The chapter has been divided into two sections. Section I deals with the empirical results of gravity model for India's exports while section II analyses the export potential of India.

I

THEORIES OF TRADE

Nowadays, countries are more closely linked through trade. Developed and developing countries are removing their trade barriers to expand more trade with each other. Different theories of trade have explained the reasons of trade in different ways. Classical trade theory and new trade theory explains the reasons, while gravity model answers the question of magnitude of trade between countries which cannot be explained by these theories of international trade.

The first, which is considered as basis of trade theory, is absolute advantage theory given by Adam Smith (1776). He explained that countries specializing in the production of goods according to their absolute advantage and then by trading with other, gain in international trade. However, his argument is convincing, only for country which has absolute advantage. It cannot explain the reason for trade for a country which does not have absolute advantage in international trade and has specialization in all commodities.

David Ricardo (1817) answered questions left by Adam Smith satisfactorily under the theory of comparative advantage. According to him, a nation gains from trade by exporting the goods or services in which it has its greatest comparative advantage in productivity and importing those in which it has the least comparative advantage (Linder, 1991). This model is still incomplete due to unrealistic assumptions of extreme degree of specialization, absence of economies of scale, intra-industry trade and income distribution.

Due to the several defects of classical model, Eli Hecksher (1919) and Bertil Ohlin (1933) has extended the Ricardo Model and developed an influential theory of trade known as Factor Endowment theory or Hecksher–Ohlin Model. The model predicts that "countries export products that use their abundant factor intensively and import the product using scarce factors intensively (Linder, 1991).

Thus classical theory implies that countries which are less similar tend to trade more. However, theory is unable to explain the huge proportion of trade between nations with similar factor endowments (i.e. intra-industry trade). This is the motivation for new trade theories which have been established in the 1980 by researchers like Krugman (1979), Lancaster (1981), Helpman (1990), Markusen (1990) and many others. New trade theory explains the world trade based on the economies of scale, imperfect competition and product differentiation which relax the strict assumptions of classical theory like constant returns to scale, perfect competition and homogenous goods. Under these assumptions, each country can specialize in producing narrow range of products at larger scale with higher productivity and lower costs. Thus, it can increase the variety of goods available to its consumers through trade. Trade occurs when countries do not differ in the resources or technology (Markusen, 1990 and Krugman and Maurice, 2005).

The classical and new trade theory can successfully explain the reasons for countries to join in world trade. However, they cannot answer the question of size of the trade flows. Another trade theory, the gravity model, which has been used intensively in analyzing patterns and performances of international trade in recent years, can be applied to quantify the trade flows empirically. This model of trade is similar to the Newton's Law. This model of trade is as follows, "the trade flow between two countries is proportional to the product of each country's economic mass", generally measured by GDP, each to the power of quantities to be determined, divided by the distance between the countries respective 'economic centers of gravity' generally their capitals raised to power of another quantity to be determined (Christie, 2002). Among the above mentioned trade theories, the gravity model has been chosen to quantify the India's exports with its six members of SAARC (Bangladesh, Bhutan, Maldives, Nepal, Pakistan and Sri Lanka).

Gravity Variables

The study has taken different variables to estimate the gravity model of India's exports. These are:

(a) *Gross Domestic Product of Exporter Country:* A high level of income in the exporting country indicates a high level of production which increases the availability of goods for exports. Therefore, it is expected that coefficient for this variable to be positive (Harris and Matyas (1998), Matyas *et. al.* (2000), Zorzoso and Lahman (2000), Abraham and Hove (2005) and Rahman (2005)).

(b) *Gross Domestic Product of Importer Country:* Since a high level of income in the importing country suggests higher imports, therefore, it is also expected that coefficient for this variable to be positive (Harris and Matyas (1998), Matyas *et. al.* (2000), Zorzoso and Lahman (2000), Abraham and Hove (2005) and Rahman (2005)).

(c) *Population of Exporter Country:* The coefficient estimate for population of the exporter may be positive or negative depending on whether the country exports less when it is big (absorption effect) or whether a big country export more than a small country (economies of scale) (Harris and Matyas (1998), Matyas *et. al.* (2000), Zorzoso and Lahman (2000), Abraham and Hove (2005) and Rahman (2005)).

(d) *Population of Importer Country:* The coefficient of the importing country's population has also an ambiguous sign due to above reasons (Harris and Matyas (1998), Matyas *et. al.* (2000), Zorzoso and Lahman (2000), Abraham and Hove (2005) and Rahman (2005)).

(e) *Real Exchange Rate of Exporter Country:* Real exchange rate is defined as local currency value of 1 unit in US $ multiplied by India's deflator and divided by US's deflator. It is expected to be positive as India's exchange rate depricates with respect to other and will have a positive impact on India's exports (Harris and Matyas (1998), Matyas *et. al.* (2000), Zorzoso and Lahman (2000) and Abraham and Hove (2005)).

(f) *Real Exchange Rate of Importer Country:* This rate is obtained by local currency value of 1 unit in US $ multiplied by importer country's deflator and divided by US's deflator. The coefficient for this variable is expected to be negative as import country's currency depreciates with respect to other countries, other country's exports will fall (Harris and Matyas (1998), Matyas *et. al.* (2000), Zorzoso and Lahman (2000) and Abraham and Hove (2005)).

(g) *Difference in Per Capita Income:* According to H-O theory, the sign of this coefficient would be positive as similar countries trade less than dissimilar ones. On the other hand, based on the Linder Hypothesis, the sign would be negative as similar countries trade more than dissimilar ones. (Zorzoso and Lahman (2000), Batra (2002), Rahman (2005) and Montanari (2005)).

(h) *Distance:* Distance between two countries is expressed as the distance (in km) between the capital cities. Distance has a negative impact on volume of exports.

As the distance between the exporting and importing country becomes longer, exports will fall. The distance is a factor which is used as a proxy to consider the impact of transport cost and other transaction costs. Therefore, the coefficient for this variables is expected to be negative (Zorzoso and Lahman (2000), Abraham and Hove (2005) and Rahman (2005)).

(i) *Border:* This is the dummy variable for a pair of countries sharing common border. As the sharing border increases the export between any given pair of countries, therefore, it is expected that coefficient for this variable to be positive (Zorzoso and Lahman (2000), Abraham and Hove (2005) and Rahman (2005)).

(j) *Language:* This is also dummy variable for a pair of counters sharing common language. It is also expected that coefficient for this variable to be positive as the exports (trade) will be more between two countries if language is well understood in both trading partners (Zorzoso and Lahman (2000), Abraham and Hove (2005) and Rahman (2005)).

Table 8.1 depicts the *growth of real GDP* among SAARC nations during 1981-2005. Growth of real GDP was maximum in Maldives (6.72 percent) followed by Sri Lanka (4.11 percent), Bhutan (3.66 percent), Pakistan (2.76 percent), India (2.56 percent), Bangladesh (2.49 percent) and Nepal (2.25 percent) during 1981-2005.

Table 8.2 depicts the *growth of population* among SAARC nations during 1981-2005. Growth of population was highest in Maldives (3.02 percent) followed by Pakistan (2.54 percent), Nepal (2.41 percent), Bangladesh (2.16 percent), India (1.87 percent), Bhutan (2.19 percent) and Sri Lanka (1.15 percent) during 1981-2005.

Table 8.3 depicts the *growth of difference in per capita GDP* between India and SAARC nations (in absolute terms) during 1981-2005. Table shows that growth of difference in per capita GDP between India and Sri Lanka was highest, i.e. 9.35 percent followed by Bhutan (6.22 percent), Maldives (6.04 percent), Bangladesh (1.70 percent) and Nepal (1.49 percent). For

TABLE 8.1
Growth of Real GDP among SAARC Nations

(US $ Millions)

Year	*Bangladesh*	*Bhutan*	*India*	*Maldives*	*Nepal*	*Pakistan*	*Sri Lanka*
(1)	*(2)*	*(3)*	*(4)*	*(5)*	*(6)*	*(7)*	*(8)*
1981	32350.17	243.74	311759.96	98.04	3725.16	45999.83	7229.26
1982	27065.11 (-16.34)	227.65 (-6.60)	295804.7 (-5.12)	99.79 (1.79)	3583.85 (-3.79)	45977.73 (-0.05)	7136.12 (-1.29)
1983	24197.67 (-10.59)	238.08 (4.58)	303490.44 (2.60)	118.25 (18.49)	3451.32 (-3.70)	40469.52 (-11.98)	7289.17 (2.14)
1984	27315.3 (12.88)	233.57 (-1.90)	284484.02 (-6.26)	220 (86.05)	3501.41 (1.45)	42131.95 (4.11)	8199.21 (12.48)
1985	28263.88 (3.47)	230.22 (-1.43)	300696.56 (5.70)	254 (15.45)	3425.77 (-2.16)	40728.77 (-3.33)	7818.01 (-4.65)
1986	26846.87 (-5.01)	260.46 (13.14)	312585.99 (3.95)	260.55 (2.58)	3617.44 (5.59)	40472.21 (-0.63)	8126.67 (3.95)
1987	29514.2 (9.94)	320.67 (23.11)	342548.34 (9.59)	231.15 (-11.28)	3669.78 (1.45)	41393.45 (2.28)	8293.18 (2.05)
1988	30965.46 (4.92)	342.8 (6.90)	354052.19 (3.36)	264.06 (14.24)	4211.4 (14.76)	46465.54 (12.25)	8427.66 (1.62)

(Contd.)

TABLE 8.1 (*Contd.*)

(1)	(2)	(3)	(4)	(5)	(6)	(7)	(8)
1989	31323.5 (1.16)	325.9 (-4.93)	342038.86 (-3.39)	279.41 (5.81)	4115.84 (-2.27)	46907.85 (0.95)	8158.95 (-3.19)
1990	33895.32 (8.21)	342.5 (5.09)	357153.54 (4.42)	302.82 (8.38)	4081.55 (-0.83)	45011.79 (-4.04)	9037.4 (10.77)
1991	33529.66 (-1.08)	273.93 (-20.02)	289759.63 (-18.87)	305 (0.72)	4246.71 (4.05)	49229.88 (9.37)	9748.42 (7.87)
1992	33184.45 (-1.03)	265.99 (-2.90)	256978.74 (-11.31)	313.19 (2.68)	3559.05 (-16.19)	50898.15 (3.39)	10154.73 (4.17)
1993	33928.94 (2.24)	243.53 (-8.44)	282378.86 (9.88)	322 (2.81)	3743.76 (5.19)	52660.63 (3.46)	10576.82 (4.16)
1994	33769 (-0.47)	275 (12.92)	323505.98 (14.56)	325.11 (0.97)	4067 (8.63)	51895 (-1.45)	11718 (10.79)
1995	37156.44 (10.03)	300.93 (9.43)	365061.48 (12.85)	341.03 (4.89)	4309.9 (5.97)	59383.4 (14.43)	12761.07 (8.90)
1996	39029.85 (5.04)	308.31 (2.45)	372722.1 (2.10)	365.85 (7.28)	4339.98 (0.70)	60772.94 (2.34)	13339.37 (4.53)
1997	39857.75 (2.12)	351.42 (13.98)	387017.27 (3.84)	390.77 (6.81)	4632.59 (6.74)	58802.26 (-3.24)	14214.41 (6.56)
1998	40845.34 (2.48)	355.88 (1.27)	385603.12 (-0.37)	412.21 (5.49)	4498.17 (-2.90)	57612.67 (-2.02)	14632.34 (2.94)

1999	41864 (2.49)	390.25 9.66	412721.5 (7.03)	486.78 (18.09)	4612.06 (2.53)	57696.16 (0.14)	14344 (-1.97)
2000	42534.96 (1.60)	404.8 (0.73)	415620.35 (0.70)	520 (6.83)	4961.85 (7.58)	66219.25 (14.77)	14749.42 (2.83)
2001	41500.25 (-2.43)	428.9 (5.95)	422747.52 (1.71)	508.13 (-2.28)	5309.25 (7.00)	63195.98 (-4.57)	13917.59 (-5.64)
2002	41007.42 (-1.19)	469.55 (9.48)	438375.33 (3.70)	510.76 (0.52)	5222.16 (-1.64)	61692.35 (-2.38)	14273.17 (2.55)
2003	43958.85 (7.20)	535.6 (14.07)	510492.47 (16.45)	560.32 (9.70)	5369 (2.81)	69846.52 (13.22)	15478.06 (8.44)
2004	47071.41 (7.08)	592.46 (10.62)	577924.84 (13.21)	641.32 (14.46)	6041.05 (12.52)	81388.78 (16.53)	16656.67 (7.61)
2005	48484.81 (3.00)	670.78 (13.22)	650730.64 (12.60)	595.28 (-7.18)	6606.16 (9.35)	89888.12 (10.44)	19010.06 (14.13)

Note : Figures in parentheses are annual growth rates.
Source : Worked out from the data given in *World Development Indicators*: Various Issues.

TABLE 8.2
Growth of Population among SAARC Nations

(Thousands)

Year	Bangladesh	Bhutan	India	Maldives	Nepal	Pakistan	Sri Lanka
(1)	(2)	(3)	(4)	(5)	(6)	(7)	(8)
1981	84196	434	702821	163	15509	85096	15010
1982	86289 (2.49)	445 (2.53)	718946 (2.29)	168 (3.07)	15868 (2.31)	87436 (2.75)	15196 (1.24)
1983	88441 (2.49)	456 (2.47)	734072 (2.10)	173 (2.98)	16237 (2.33)	89832 (2.74)	15417 (1.45)
1984	90624 (2.47)	467 (2.41)	749677 (2.13)	178 (2.89)	16616 (2.33)	92284 (2.73)	15603 (1.21)
1985	92818 (2.42)	480 (2.78)	765147 (2.06)	184 (3.37)	17003 (2.33)	94794 (2.72)	15841 (1.53)
1986	95012 (2.36)	496 (3.33)	781893 (2.19)	190 (3.26)	17398 (2.32)	97354 (2.70)	16127 (1.81)
1987	97212 (2.32)	514 (3.63)	798680 (2.15)	196 (3.16)	17803 (2.33)	99953 (2.67)	16373 (1.53)
1988	99437 (2.29)	530 (3.11)	815590 (2.12)	202 (3.06)	18220 (2.34)	102622 (2.67)	16599 (1.38)
1989	101710 (2.29)	542 (2.26)	832535 (2.08)	209 (3.47)	18656 (2.39)	105270 (2.58)	16825 (1.36)

1990	104047	547	849515	216	19114	107975	17017
	(2.30)	(0.92)	(2.04)	(3.35)	(2.45)	(2.57)	(1.14)
1991	106454	544	866530	223	19595	110750	17267
	(2.31)	(-0.5)	(2.00)	(3.24)	(2.52)	(2.57)	(1.47)
1992	108921	535	882821	230	20096	113562	17426
	(2.32)	(-1.7)	(1.88)	(3.14)	(2.56)	(2.54)	(0.92)
1993	111428	522	899329	237	20614	116444	17646
	(2.30)	(-2.4)	(1.87)	(3.04)	(2.58)	(2.54)	(1.26)
1994	113946	512	915697	244	21145	119402	17891
	(2.26)	(-1.9)	(1.82)	(2.95)	(2.58)	(2.54)	(1.39)
1995	116455	507	932182	252	21682	122375	18136
	(2.20)	(-1)	(1.80)	(3.28)	(2.54)	(2.49)	(1.37)
1996	118946	509	948759	259	22226	125410	18336
	(2.14)	(0.39)	(1.78)	(2.78)	(2.51)	(2.48)	(1.10)
1997	121426	517	965428	267	22776	128457	18567
	(2.08)	(1.57)	(1.76)	(3.09)	(2.47)	(2.43)	(1.26)
1998	123905	529	982182	275	23329	131582	18774
	(2.04)	(2.32)	(1.74)	(3.00)	(2.43)	(2.43)	(1.12)
1999	126398	543	999016	282	23881	134790	19043
	(2.01)	(2.65)	(1.71)	(2.55)	(2.37)	(2.44)	(1.43)
2000	128916	559	1015293	290	24431	138080	19351
	(1.99)	(2.95)	(1.63)	(2.84)	(2.30)	(2.44)	(1.62)
2001	131461	574	1032473	298	24975	141450	18732
	(1.97)	(2.68)	(1.69)	(2.76)	(2.23)	(2.44)	(-3.2)

(Contd.)

TABLE 8.2 (*Contd.*)

(1)	(2)	(3)	(4)	(5)	(6)	(7)	(8)
2002	134029 (1.95)	591 (2.96)	1048641 (1.57)	306 (2.68)	25515 (2.16)	144902 (2.44)	19007 (1.47)
2003	130615 (-2.5)	607 (2.71)	1064399 (1.50)	313 (2.29)	26053 (2.11)	148439 (2.44)	19253 (1.29)
2004	139215 (6.58)	623 (2.64)	1079721 (1.44)	321 (2.56)	26591 (2.07)	152061 (2.44)	19462 (1.09)
2005	141822 (1.87)	639 (2.57)	1094583 (1.38)	329 (2.49)	27133 (2.04)	155772 (2.44)	19625 (0.84)
Compound Growth Rate (Percent)	2.16	2.19	1.87	3.02	2.41	2.54	1.15

Note : Figures in parentheses are annual growth rates.
Source : Worked out from the data given in *World Development Indicators* : Various Issues.

TABLE 8.3
Growth of Difference in Per Capita GDP between India and SAARC Nations (Absolute Value)

(US $ Millions)

Year	Bangladesh	Bhutan	Maldives	Nepal	Pakistan	Sri Lanka
(1)	(2)	(3)	(4)	(5)	(6)	(7)
1981	5935.91	11802.01	15788.39	20339.06	9698.02	3804.58
1982	9778.55 (64.74)	10013.34 (-15.16)	18255.84 (15.63)	18558.85 (-8.75)	11440.23 (17.97)	5816.27 (52.88)
1983	13983.17 (43.00)	10867.06 (8.53)	27007.27 (47.94)	20087.54 (8.23)	3706.81 (-67.6)	5936.64 (2.07)
1984	7806.19 (-44.17)	12066.56 (11.04)	85647.96 (217.10)	16875.05 (-16)	7707.12 (107.92)	14601.36 (146.00)
1985	8848.32 (13.35)	8663.43 (-28.2)	98744.29 (15.29)	19151.14 (13.40)	3666.36 (-52.43)	10053.79 (-31.14)
1986	11721.8 (32.47)	12534.84 (44.69)	97153.72 (-1.611)	19185.85 (0.18)	1594.11 (-56.52)	10413.59 (3.58)
1987	12528.65 (6.88)	19497.24 (55.54)	75043.11 (-22.76)	22276.05 (16.10)	1476.39 (-7.384)	7762.25 (-25.46)
1988	12269.77 (-2.066)	21268.89 (9.09)	87313.45 (16.35)	20296.38 (-8.89)	1867.78 (26.51)	7361.54 (-5.162)

(Contd.)

TABLE 8.3 (*Contd.*)

(1)	(2)	(3)	(4)	(5)	(6)	(7)
1989	10287.15 (-16.16)	19044.74 (-10.46)	92605.82 (6.06)	19022.25 (-6.28)	3475.54 (86.08)	7408.96 (0.64)
1990	9465.11 (-7.991)	20571.74 (8.02)	98150.96 (5.99)	20688.31 (8.76)	354.81 (-89.79)	11066.03 (49.36)
1991	1942.22 (-79.48)	16916 (-17.77)	103332.2 (5.28)	11766.68 (-43.1)	11012.28 (3003.60)	23017.87 (108.00)
1992	1357.71 (-30.09)	20609.69 (21.84)	107059.4 (3.61)	11398.6 (-3.13)	15710.88 (42.67)	29164.64 (26.70)
1993	949.63 (-30.06)	15254.62 (-25.98)	104466.1 (-2.422)	13237.58 (16.10)	13825.15 (-12)	28540.04 (-2.142)
1994	5692.96 (499.50)	18382 (20.50)	97914.57 (-6.271)	16095.07 (21.60)	8133.48 (-41.17)	30167.68 (5.70)
1995	7255.77 (27.45)	20192.28 (9.85)	96165.6 (-1.786)	19284.27 (19.80)	9363.72 (15.13)	31201.14 (3.43)
1996	6472.14 (-10.8)	21286.23 (5.42)	101971 (6.04)	19758.64 (2.46)	9174.18 (-2.024)	33464.4 (7.25)
1997	7262.9 (12.22)	27884.33 (31.00)	106267.9 (4.21)	19747.85 (-0.05)	5688.19 (-38)	36469.73) (8.98)
1998	6294.79 (-13.33)	28013.99 (0.47)	110636.1 (4.11)	19978.4 (1.16)	4524.77 (-20.45)	38679.51 (6.06)

1999	8192.02 (30.14)	30555.61 (9.07)	131303.1 (18.68)	22000.11 (10.10)	1491.68 (-67.03)	34011.47)-12.07)
2000	7941.67 (-3.056)	31479.5 (3.02)	138374.3 (5.39)	20626.35 (-6.24)	7021.16 (370.69)	35284.44 (3.74)
2001	9376.65 (18.07)	33775.97 (7.30)	129568.3 (-6.364)	19686.88 (-4.55)	3732.11 (-46.84)	33353.31 (-5.473)
2002	11208.2 (19.53)	37645.61 (11.46)	125109.9 (-3.441)	21337.11 (8.38)	771.08 (-79.34)	33290.16 (-0.189)
2003	14305.34 (27.63)	40277.32 (6.99)	131056.6 (4.75)	27352.64 (28.20)	906.6 (17.58)	32432.36 (-2.577)
2004	19713.36 (37.80)	41573.27 (3.22)	146263.5 (11.60)	30806.99 (12.60)	1.61 (-99.82)	32060.2 (-1.147)
2005	25263 (28.15)	45522.75 (9.50)	121484.7 (-16.94)	35102.78 (13.90)	1745.16 (107.74)	37416.45 (16.71)
Compound Growth Rate (Percent)	1.7	6.22	6.04	1.49	-10.28	9.35

Note : Figures in parentheses are annual growth rates.
Source : Worked out from the data given in *World Development Indicators*: Various Issues.

TABLE 8.4

Growth of Real Exchange Rate among SAARC Nations

Year	*Bangladesh*	*Bhutan*	*India*	*Maldives*	*Nepal*	*Pakistan*	*Sri Lanka*
(1)	*(2)*	*(3)*	*(4)*	*(5)*	*(6)*	*(7)*	*(8)*
1981	43	19.21	22.16	13.48	21.65	19.82	20.55
1982	42.26 (-1.721)	18.5 (-3.696)	22.21 (0.23)	12.16 (-9.792)	20.5 (-5.312)	23.78 (19.98)	21.32 (3.75)
1983	44.52 (5.35)	18.7 (1.08)	22.5 (1.31)	12.07 (-0.74)	19.61 (-4.341)	24.06 (1.18)	25 (17.26)
1984	53.32 (19.77)	20.88 (11.66)	25.41 (12.90)	12.12 (0.41)	22.44 (14.43)	22.21 (-7.69)	26.28 (5.12)
1985	59.13 (10.90)	20.7 (-0.862)	25.78 (1.46)	13.68 (12.87)	50.86 (126.65)	28.38 (27.78)	27.408 (4.29)
1986	47.47 (-19.72)	18.12 (-12.46)	22.67 (-12.1)	11.03 (-19.37)	40.85 (-19.68)	25.65 (-9.62)	28.52 (4.06)
1987	44.89 (-5.435)	16.84 (-7.064)	20.93 (-7.68)	13.09 (18.68)	36.45 (-10.77)	25.41 (-0.94)	30.763 (7.87)
1988	45.38 (1.09)	19.1 (13.42)	23.84 (13.90)	11.98 (-8.48)	40.27 (10.48)	26.17 (2.99)	33.03 (7.37)
1989	49.4 (8.86)	21.24 (11.20)	26.21 (9.94)	12.7 (6.01)	42.89 (6.51)	28.99 (10.78)	40 (21.10)
1990	53.17 (7.63)	22.21 (4.57)	26.14 (-0.27)	13.25 (4.33)	42.87 (-0.047)	29.03 (0.14)	40.24 (0.60)

1991	47.8	28.99	36.85	11.17	54.97	28.98	42.58
	(-10.1)	(30.53)	(41.00)	(-15.70	(28.23)	(-0.17)	(5.82)
1992	43.15	27.23	30.49	11.4	44.99	27.32	46
	(-9.728)	(-6.071)	(-17.3)	(2.06)	(-18.16)	(-5.73)	(8.03)
1993	40.15	31	31.38	11.1	49.24	30.07	49.56
	(-6.952)	(13.85)	(2.92)	(-2.632)	(9.45)	(10.07)	(7.74)
1994	37.59	28.63	29	10.86	46.73	27.49	49.98
	(-6.376)	(-7.645)	(-7.58)	(-2.162)	(-5.097)	(-8.58)	(0.85)
1995	37.73	30.32	31	10.43	51	27.67	54
	(0.37)	(5.90)	(6.90)	(-3.959)	(9.14)	(0.66)	(8.04)
1996	39.53	28.01	30.27	10.2	49.58	30.33	56
	(4.77)	(-7.619)	(-2.35)	(-2.205)	(-2.784)	(9.61)	(3.70)
1997	39.77	27.22	31.36	9.65	51.03	29.88	61
	(0.61)	(-2.82)	(3.60)	(-5.392)	(2.92)	(-1.48)	(8.93)
1998	40.33	26.9	30.05	9.3	51.18	27.84	68
	(1.41)	(-1.176)	(-4.18)	(-3.627)	(0.29)	(-6.83)	(11.48)
1999	42.79	25.18	30.04	10.21	55.2	30.23	72
	(6.10)	(-6.394)	(-0.03)	(9.78)	(7.85)	(8.59)	(5.88)
2000	45.69	27.1	33.26	10.89	52.86	34.54	82
	(6.78)	(7.63)	(10.70)	(6.66)	(-4.239)	(14.26)	(13.89)
2001	45.67	26.16	31.37	10.71	51.6	28.77	93
	(-0.044)	(-3.469)	(-5.68)	(-1.653)	(-2.384)	(-16.7)	(13.41)
2002	44.59	25.28	30.19	11.17	48.87	30.08	95
	(-2.365)	(-3.364)	(-3.76)	(4.30)	(-5.291)	(4.55)	(2.15)

(Contd.)

TABLE 8.4 (*Contd.*)

(1)	(2)	(3)	(4)	(5)	(6)	(7)	(8)
2003	46.88 (5.14)	23.9 (-5.459)	28.82 (-4.54)	11.87 (6.27)	52.93 (8.31)	29.29 (-2.63)	96 (1.05)
2004	49.86 (6.36)	23.52 (-1.59)	27.98 (-2.910	12.9 (8.68)	56.95 (7.59)	30.43 (3.89)	104 (8.33)
2005	52.1 (4.49)	23.94 (1.79)	29.07 (3.90)	12.9 0.00	66.18 (16.21)	30.51 (0.26)	102 (-1.923)
Compound Growth Rate (Percent)	-0.2	1.56	1.53	-0.59	3.78	1.26	7.23

Note : Figures in parentheses are annual growth rates.
Source : Worked out from the data given in *World Development Indicators*: Various Issues.

Pakistan, it is negative (-10.28 percent) due to very low difference between per capita GDP in 2004.

Table 8.4 explains the *growth of real exchange rates* among SAARC nations during 1981-2005. Growth of real exchange rate was maximum in Sri Lanka (7.23 percent) followed by Nepal (3.78 percent), Bhutan (1.56 percent), India (1.53 percent), Pakistan (1.26 percent), and Maldives (0.59 percent). For Bangladesh and Maldives it was negative, i.e. -0.20 percent and -0.59 percent respectively.

Table 8.5 explains the non-time variant variables of gravity model of India's exports. The simple distance calculated following the great circle formula which uses latitudes and longitudes of the most important city (in term of population) or of its official capital (www.CEPII.com). These distances were expressed as the distance (in kms) between the capital cities. The distance between India and Maldives is maximum, i.e. 2750.04 kms, followed by Sri Lanka (2431.215 kms), Bangladesh (1421.938 kms), Bhutan (1236.124 kms), Nepal (801.1845 kms) and Pakistan (683.3699 kms). The language dummy value is zero for all SAARC nations except Pakistan shows that Indian and Pakistan language is well understood by both countries. Border's dummy value is zero for Maldives and Sri Lanka showing that their borders are not shared by India.

TABLE 8.5

Non-time Variant Variables of Gravity Model (Distance (Kms.), Language and Border)

Country	*Distance (kms.)*	*Language*	*Border*
Bangladesh	1421.938	0	1
Bhutan	1236.124	0	1
Maldives	2750.04	0	0
Nepal	801.1845	0	1
Pakistan	683.3699	1	1
Sri Lanka	2431.215	0	0

Note : 0 and 1 represents values of dummy variables.
Source : www.cepII.org

Estimation Results of Gravity Model

The estimation results of bilateral exports of India with six SAARC members (Bangladesh, Bhutan, Maldives, Nepal, Pakistan and Sri Lanka) have been reported in Table 8.6. The gravity model of India's exports has been estimated by restricted (pooled) model, fixed effect model and random effect model. The restricted model is the pooled model with the restrictive assumptions of single intercept and with the same parameter over time and across trading partners. The unrestricted model (fixed effect model), however is the same behavioural equation but allows the intercept to vary across trading partners. Formally, F-test has been carried out to test for the null hypothesis that the country specific effects are jointly zero. In Table 8.6, the value of F-test was 63.23 at (5, 137) d.f. which was far larger than tabulated value and supported the alternate hypothesis indicating SAARC countries had different propensities to export with India. The pooled estimation gives biased results due to omitted variables. Next, the Hausman test has also been performed to compare the fixed and random effect estimators. The statistic result had a value of 60.01 at 7 d.f. which was also far larger than the critical value. This suggested that the fixed effect is a better choice than the random effect. Therefore, the direction of the study focuses on the fixed effects estimation.

Exports equation has run through above mentioned three estimation methods. Estimated coefficients had nearly all the expected signs except for population of importer country, real exchange rate of importer country and per capita difference. However, the magnitudes of the coefficients in pooled and random effect estimation were notably different from those in the fixed effect method suggesting that there might be biased results due to ignoring country individual effects in pooled estimation and inconsistent estimates because of correlation between the individual effects and other regressors in random effect method. Even F-test and Hausman test had also supported the same argument for the present data. Gravity model results given in Table 8.6 shows that economic size (GDP) of exporter country (India) as well as importer countries (SAARC nations other than India) came out to be significantly and positively affecting India's exports showing that India tends

TABLE 8.6

Results of Gravity Model

Variable	*Restricted/Pooled Estimation*		*Fixed Effects Estimation*		*Random Effects Estimation*	
	Coefficient	*Z-statistics*	*Coefficient*	*Z-statistics*	*Coefficient*	*Z-statistics*
(1)	*(2)*	*(3)*	*(4)*	*(5)*	*(6)*	*(7)*
Constant	-35.07**	-3.82	-71.29**	-10.67	-41.38**	-5.62
Gross Domestic Product of Exporter Country	0.54	0.49	1.19*	1.98	0.66	0.76
Gross Domestic Product of Importer Country	0.19	0.78	0.83*	1.96	0.62	1.18
Population of Exporter Country	4.80	1.94	17.31**	8.63	6.15**	3.21
Population of Importer Country	0.60**	2.69	-9.90**	-7.48	0.09	0.19
Real Exchange Rate of Exporter Country	0.0004	0.02	0.02	1.23	0.001	0.54
Real Exchange Rate of Importer country	0.009**	2.85	-0.02**	-6.45	-0.01	-1.78
Per Capita Difference	0.42**	4.09	-0.08	-1.19	0.001	0.02
R^2	0.75		0.92		0.65	
Restricted F-test			63.23** (5,137)			
Hausman Test					60.01 (7)	

**Significant at one per cent level.
*Significant at five per cent level.
Figures in parentheses are degrees of freedom.
Source : Based on data given in Tables 8.1 to 8.5.

to exports with larger economies. An increase by one percent of India's GDP will go in increasing India's exports by an average index of 1.19 percent and an increase by one percent of SAARC member's GDP (other than India) will go in increasing India's exports by an average index of 0.83 percent. But market size (population) of India had highly significantly and positively affected the India's exports, one percent increase in market size of India will increase the India's exports up to 17.31 per cent on average. Market size (population) of SAARC members (other than India) had highly significantly and negatively affected the India's exports showing absorption effect, i.e. country exports less when it is big. One percent increase in market size of SAARC members (other than India) will decrease the India's exports up to 9.90 per cent on average. Surprisingly, real exchange rate of exporter country (India) had non-significant and positive effect on India's exports. One percent increase in country's value of exchange rate (depreciation of the exporter currency) will increase the India's exports by two percent on average only. (The effect of currency depreciation is two-fold. Firstly, exports would be instantaneously cheaper. However, this effect will be negated to the extent that imported raw materials would now be costlier. Overall, though it seems sensible to assume that the former effect will dominate.) Thus, non-significance of this variable is possible suggesting that the two conflicting effects (supply and demand) are canceling each other out. While real exchange rate of importer country had highly significant and negative effect on India's exports. One per cent increase in currency of SAARC nations (other than India) will decrease in India's exports up to two per cent only. The coefficient of difference in per capita income was non-significant and negative suggesting that Linder effect dominated in India's exports. According to Linder trade model, bilateral trade will be greater, when the per capita GDPs of the trading countries are more similar. The coefficient value was -0.08 percent implies that India's exports with SAARC increase as difference in per capita GDP between India and SAARC decreases.

As the fixed effect model is better, therefore only fixed effect model's country effects are reported in Table 8.7 and these effects are ranked. Bangladesh followed by Pakistan, Sri Lanka and Nepal had the highest propensity with India's exports and

Maldives and Bhutan had the lowest propensity with India's exports during 1981-2005.

TABLE 8.7
Country Effects

Country	*Fixed effects*
Bangladesh	11.10(1)
Bhutan	-12.91(5)
Maldives	-15.96(6)
Nepal	4.22(3)
Pakistan	9.94(2)
Sri Lanka	3.62(4)

Source : Based on the results of gravity model.
Figures in parentheses are ranks.

Table 8.8 reports the results obtained when the fixed effects from model are regressed on the distance variables and dummies which are fixed over time (Border and Language). According to the results, all the non-time variant variables (Distance, Border and Languages) were found to be non-significant and had expected sign. A very low R^2 coefficient (0.28) means that there were other determinants of the trading pair effects (which have not keen included in the analysis).

TABLE 8.8
Cross-Section Regression Results (Individual Effects Regressed over Distance and Dummies for Language and Border)

Variables	*Coefficient*	*t-statistics*
Constant	46.334	0.163
Language	5.830	0.229
Border	1.385	0.041
Distance	-15.385	-0.184

D.W = 1.71j R^2 = 0.28
Source : Based on Tables 8.5 and 8.7.

II

EXPORT POTENTIAL

The gravity model is not only useful to find out determinants of bilateral exports flows. It can also be used to predict future trade flows or export flows. In particular, it is used to calculate trade potentials, i.e. difference between the predicted and the actual bilateral export flows. Predictions are based on the gravity model estimates. The study had estimated the export potentials by fixed effect model only since fixed effect model had been proved as better model than random effect model.

Table 8.9 reports the export potential by calculating the difference between the potential (P) and actual level of exports (A), i.e. value of P-A. A positive value indicates future possibilities of export expansion while a negative value shows India has exceeded its export potential with the particular SAARC countries (Batra, 2004). The average of export potential had been calculated to find out the export potentials of SAARC members with India over a period of time. The average of P-A was highest for Bangladesh (187.32) followed by Sri Lanka (2.08) during 1981-2005 showing that for Bangladesh and Sri Lanka, India had export potential with these nations where for other SAARC members, it was negative showing that India has exceeded its export potential with these nations.

Export potential had also been calculated with the help of ratio method. The ratio of export potential (P) as predicted by the model and actual trade (A) was also used to analyze the future direction of export for India. If the value of P/A exceeds one, there is a potential expansion of exports with the respective country (Batra, 2004). The results of this ratio are given in Table 8.10. The average of this ratio was maximum for Maldives (2.59) followed by Bhutan (1.58), Nepal (1.17), Pakistan (1.11), Bangladesh (1.08) and Sri Lanka (1.07) indicating that India had the highest potential of exports with Maldives and Bhutan during 1981-2005.

TABLE 8.9

Export Potential between India and SAARC Members using (P-A)* Approach

(US $ Millions)

Year	*Bangladesh*	*Bhutan*	*Maldives*	*Nepal*	*Pakistan*	*Sri Lanka*
1981	-13.35	-0.034	-0.54	-68.79	9.05	-61.75
1982	3.99	-0.010	-0.30	-43.40	6.45	-47.82
1983	-34.28	0.0259	0.08	-67.65	8.26	-65.17
1984	-66.95	0.0385	-0.18	-40.72	1.65	-85.30
1985	-82.30	0.0788	1.63	-74.89	0.003	-0.54
1986	-55.38	0.119	0.77	-48.54	3.08	18.31
1987	-53.04	0.191	0.64	-10.46	8.71	35.81
1988	-32.96	0.2493	0.84	3.12	8.68	63.08
1989	-26.94	0.275	4.70	-144.16	-17.78	26.97
1990	-138.87	0.418	-0.25	78.62	-6.08	112.21
1991	6.15	-0.501	1.55	19.68	0.032	100.92
1992	-34.36	-1.421	-3.47	23.31	-20.16	-20.67
1993	66.71	-4.00	-0.11	29.87	-19.83	25.41
1994	49.46	-4.616	-9.18	57.72	-6.84	46.43
1995	-162.75	-7.86	-3.40	53.53	4.20	117.39
1996	81.08	-3.14	-39.17	32.41	-61.57	148.24
1997	292.94	-5.43	2.90	52.27	-49.86	209.05
1998	238.18	-0.17	3.69	81.99	-9.85	150.40
1999	531.98	4.93	7.32	72.25	22.52	160.51
2000	527.72	10.76	-1.71	158.47	-39.75	-25.44
2001	391.04	11.37	-16.64	189.88	-54.44	69.86
2002	511.47	-11.52	-9.91	110.51	-12.86	-141.03
2003	1322.20	-45.04	-14.22	-110.72	-26.80	-245.11
2004	518.69	-45.75	-11.41	-169.52	41.37	-337.25
2005	842.61	-45.39	-23.39	-288.01	-217.67	-202.46
Average (1981-2005)	187.32	-5.86	-4.39	-4.13	-17.18	2.08

*P = predicted by gravity model, A = actual values.

Source : Based on the results of gravity model.

TABLE 8.10
Export Potential between India and SAARC Members using (P/A)* Approach

(US $ Millions)

Year	*Bangladesh*	*Bhutan*	*Maldives*	*Nepal*	*Pakistan*	*Sri Lanka*
1981	0.83	0.79	0.67	0.47	2.84	0.42
1982	1.07	0.93	0.80	0.61	2.07	0.52
1983	0.63	1.18	1.06	0.55	2.46	0.47
1984	0.45	1.28	0.93	0.68	1.11	0.46
1985	0.39	1.60	2.24	0.30	1.00	0.99
1986	0.61	1.94	1.31	0.53	1.18	1.21
1987	0.71	2.54	1.26	0.88	1.58	1.38
1988	0.84	3.06	1.23	1.03	1.38	1.58
1989	0.87	3.36	41.21	0.43	0.64	1.19
1990	0.58	4.72	0.96	2.75	0.87	1.98
1991	1.02	0.54	1.29	1.24	1.00	1.53
1992	0.91	0.32	0.59	1.31	0.62	0.91
1993	1.15	0.22	0.98	1.39	0.66	1.10
1994	1.09	0.34	0.43	1.68	0.88	1.14
1995	0.83	0.36	0.72	1.49	1.06	1.30
1996	1.10	0.67	0.20	1.21	0.55	1.34
1997	1.39	0.63	1.34	1.32	0.64	1.47
1998	1.27	0.98	1.47	1.65	1.91	1.36
1999	1.80	1.66	2.05	1.54	1.26	1.36
2000	1.66	5.41	0.91	2.22	0.73	0.95
2001	1.41	5.29	0.49	2.36	0.72	1.14
2002	1.52	0.57	0.62	1.41	0.92	0.81
2003	1.97	0.31	0.58	0.78	0.88	0.76
2004	1.38	0.35	0.67	0.71	1.11	0.70
2005	1.64	0.41	0.53	0.57	0.58	0.87
Average (1981-2005)	1.08	1.58	2.59	1.17	1.11	1.07

*P = Predicted by gravity model, A = Actual values.
Source : Based on the results of gravity model.

Speed of Convergence

There is a convergence if growth rate of potential is lower than that of actual exports and the computed speed of convergence is negative. There is a divergence in the opposite case. The argument for the prominent efficiency of this method over the point estimated method is that the speed of convergence exploits the dynamic structure of the data during estimation, which offers more reliable than the analysis of point estimates.

The results of potential exports using speed of convergence are reported in Table 8.11. India's exports with six SAARC members presents an interesting situation separating trade partners into two groups, the first group characterized by an overtrade situation and the second one reflecting potentials to develop export. India had convergence in exports with four SAARC members (Bhutan, Maldives, Nepal and Pakistan) and divergence with two SAARC members (Bangladesh and Sri Lanka). In other words, India had not exploited all the export potentials in trading with six SAARC members. There is a large scope for export expansion for Maldives, Bhutan, Pakistan and Nepal. Speed of convergence for Sri Lanka was maximum, i.e. 26.88 percent showing that Sri Lanka had over-exported by India. The increasing FDI can help to explain the over-utilized export potential between India and Sri Lanka. For Bangladesh, it was 17.15 percent depicting that Bangladesh had also over-

TABLE 8.11

Speed of Convergence

(Percent)

Country	*Potential Growth of Exports*	*Actual Growth of Exports*	*Speed of Convergence*
Bangladesh	18.69	15.95	17.15
Bhutan	28.06	93.58	-70.01
Maldives	15.66	234.65	-93.33
Nepal	11.37	17.48	-34.98
Pakistan	16.30	27.39	-40.50
Sri Lanka	16.82	13.26	26.88

Source : Based on the results of gravity model.

exported by India. For diverging economies, Maldives's speed of convergence was negative showing that in Maldives, maximum export potentials are under-utilizing. And also, in case of Bhutan, Pakistan and Nepal, the India's exports potential are not fully utilized.

The Convergence of India's Actual Exports towards Potential Exports

It is worth examining whether the estimated exports flows represent an empirical equilibrium as well, in other words, whether there is convergence of the actual data towards the estimated equilibrium. For this purpose, the study has estimated a model regressing the change in actual export values on the difference between the actual and potential export values in the previous period. Certainly for convergence, the estimated coefficient should be negative. The results for this model have been reported in Table 8.12. Table 8.12 shows that the coefficient of the explanatory variable was -0.01 and significant. Thus the results indicated that there was presence of convergence in India exports with SAARC countries and in the other words, actual India's exports to SAARC countries converged towards the estimated export potential.

TABLE 8.12
The Convergence of India's Actual Exports Towards Potential Exports

Variable	*Coefficient*	*t-Test*
Constant	26.89**	4.16
Difference between actual and potential exports	-0.01*	2.15

D.W. = 2.31, R^2 = 0.34
Source : Based on the results of gravity model.

Thus the study reveals that among SAARC countries, India's export potential exists for Maldives, Bhutan, Pakistan and Nepal.

9

Conclusions and Implications

Regional integration among various countries, particularly among developing countries has assumed increasing significance during the last two decades. By the time, WTO was established on 1st January 1995, almost all the members of the WTO belonged to one or more regional trade agreements (RTAs). About 380 RTAs have been notified to the GATT/WTO till July 2007. South Asia Association Regional Cooperation (SAARC) is one of these RTAs for which present study has been undertaken.

Trade retains a marginal character in South Asian region but it can play a crucial role in the development of region by promoting the welfare of the world's down-trodden and poverty stricken people living in this region. European Union (EU) constituted 38.2 percent share in total world exports followed by North American Free Trade Arrangement (NAFTA) with 13.9 percent, Association of South East Asian Nations (ASEAN) with 6.3 percent, MERCOSUR with 1.6 percent and SAARC with just 1.3 percent (World Bank, 2007). Thus the share of exports of SAARC in World's exports is least as compared to other regional trading blocs.

Keeping in view the magnitude and seriousness of the problem regarding trade of SAARC region, a comprehensive study is needed of SAARC region in relation to other forms of regional integration and to suggest measures to increase intra-regional trade in SAARC. As India is major trading partner in SAARC, so comprehensive study is needed to analyze trade trends as well as trade potentials of India with SAARC nations. The present study has been undertaken with the following specific objectives:

(1) To examine positive as well as negative effects of regional trading agreements.
(2) To study competitiveness or complementarities in production and trade among SAARC nations and pattern of intra-regional trade in SAARC.
(3) To analyze India's trade trends with the other member countries of SAARC.
(4) To study static trade effects (in terms of trade creation and trade diversion) and dynamic effects (in terms of investment and technical change) of SAARC.
(5) To examine the potential of India's exports with the other member countries of SAARC.
(6) To analyze various problems faced by member countries in enhancing the trade of South Asian region.
(7) To suggest a coordinated strategy of development of trade in the region.

HYPOTHESES OF THE STUDY

In the light of above mentioned objectives, the study attempts to test the following hypotheses:

1. Complementarities in production and trade exist among SAARC countries.
2. Trade of SAARC nations is geographically diversified.
3. India's trade is not intense with all other SAARC nations.

4. The dynamic effects in terms of investment and technical change of regional integration, i.e. SAARC explain the rapid rates of growth experienced by members of regional integration.
5. There exists sufficient potential of India's exports to other SAARC nations.
6. Indian exports to SAARC countries have converged towards the estimated export potential.

PLAN OF THE STUDY

To meet the objectives, the study had been organized into nine chapters including introduction. Second chapter examines positive as well as negative effects of regional trading agreements. The third chapter reviews the empirical studies. Fourth chapter explains the data base and methodology of the study. Fifth chapter deals with production and trade structure among SAARC nations, while sixth chapter explains growth and performance of India's trade with other SAARC nations. Seventh chapter explores the static as well as dynamic effects of SAARC nations while eighth chapter explores the India's export potential to other SAARC nations using gravity model. The last chapter presents the summary and brings out policy implications of the study.

DATA BASE AND METHODOLOGY

The nature of the study was such that it required secondary data. The data were collected mainly from World Bank publications such as World Development Indicators, IMF Directory of Trade Statistics Year Book, UNCTAD's Handbook of Statistics and Key Indicators of Asia and Pacific Countries.

The study mainly covered the period of 1981-2005. However, to see the impact of WTO on intra-regional trade of SAARC, whole period had been divided into two sub-periods, i.e. pre-WTO period (1985-94) and post-WTO period (1995-2005). The study computed annual growth rates and compound growth rates to study the growth of different variables like exports, imports, etc. To study complementarities in production and trade of SAARC countries, percentage shares, trade competitiveness indices and revealed comparative advantage indices were used. Percentage shares were used to study direction of India's trade with SAARC nations, SAARC and World. Moreover, trade intensity indices were used to study bilateral trade flows of SAARC nations, concentration indices to find out the degree of market concentration of SAARC nations and diversification indices to calculate the extent of the difference between the structure of trade of the SAARC nations and world average. To compute dynamic effects (in terms of investment and technical change) of SAARC, panel data methodology (pooled model, fixed effect model and random effect model) was being used. India's export potential to other SAARC nations was calculated with the help of gravity model of exports using panel data methodology (pooled model, fixed effect model and random effect model). To find out the convergence and divergence of India's exports to SAARC members, speed of convergence was used.

MAIN FINDINGS

SAARC countries accounted for about 22 percent of world population but their share in world GDP was merely 2.77 percent, in world exports was about 1.32 percent and in imports share was about 1.87 percent in 2006. Within SAARC, India alone represented 76 percent of the region's population and 80 percent of its gross domestic product of the region. Not only India is a strong country in terms of GDP, population but also in terms of FDI inward flows, exports and imports (having share of 68 percent, 77 percent and 74 percent respectively) of the region.

Complementarities in production measured in terms of *structure of production* showed that in 1985, GDP of all SAARC countries except Bhutan and Nepal had been dominated by *service sector*. In Bhutan and Nepal, GDP had been dominated by *agriculture sector* (the share being 52.6 percent and 51.7 percent). The share of *service sector* in GDP was maximum in Pakistan (49 percent) followed by Sri Lanka (48.8 percent) and Bangladesh (47.0 percent). In 1995, in all SAARC countries share of *agriculture* in GDP had decreased and share of *manufacturing industry* and *service sector* (except Nepal) in GDP had increased

(The rapid decline in share of *agriculture* in GDP was in case of Bhutan and Nepal (share declined from 52.6 percent and 51.7 percent in 1985 to 34.0 percent and 40.8 percent in 1995 respectively)) and the rapid increase in share of *service sector* in GDP was in case of India (share increased from 38.8 percent in 1985 to 43.6 percent in 1995). In 2005, GDP of all SAARC countries (except Bhutan) again had been dominated by *service sector*. In Bhutan, share of *industry* in GDP was maximum, i.e. 48.8 percent. Share of *service sector* in GDP was maximum in Maldives (i.e. 73.7 percent followed by Sri Lanka (54.7 percent), Pakistan (53.5 percent) and Bangladesh (51.6 percent), As compared to pre-WTO period (1985), share of all SAARC members had decreased in *agriculture sector* and it had increased in *industry* (except India) in post-WTO period. Similar production structure of SAARC nations indicated lack of complementarities in production at sectoral level.

Complementarities in trade measured in terms of *trade structure of SAARC* countries revealed that in 1990, export basket for all SAARC countries had been dominated by *manufactured goods*. In Nepal, *manufacturers* accounted for 83 percent of total exports, 79 percent in Pakistan and 78 percent in Bangladesh. *Fuels* accounted for minimum share in export basket for all of the SAARC countries. In 1995, the situation remained same. The maximum share of *manufactures* in total exports was of Bangladesh (85.2 percent) followed by Nepal (83.7 percent) and Pakistan (83 percent). In 2005, export basket of the SAARC countries except Maldives had been dominated by *manufactured goods*. Among SAARC nations, again Bangladesh constituted major share in *manufactures*, i.e. 89.6 percent in total exports. In Maldives, *all food items* accounted for 66.7 percent share in total exports. As compared to pre-WTO period share of exports of *manufactures* of all SAARC nations except India, Maldives and Nepal had increased in post-WTO period. Import basket for all SAARC nations had been dominated by *manufactured goods* in 1990. In imports, maximum share was of Sri Lanka (64.8 percent) followed by Bangladesh (55.8 percent) and Pakistan (54.1 percent). In 1995, all SAARC nations' share of *manufactured goods* in import basket had increased. However, the rapid increase was found in Bangladesh (share increased from 55.8 percent in 1990 to 69.1 percent in 1995). In 2005, import basket for all of the SAARC countries again had been dominated by *manufactured goods*. The maximum share was of Sri Lanka (68.9 percent) followed by Maldives (63.0 percent) and Bangladesh (62.0 percent). Thus the huge complementarities in trade had been found lacking at section level.

To find out complementarities further, *Revealed Comparative Advantage (RCA)* indices of ten top export items of each nation had also been measured for the latest years (2002 and 2005). In 2002, of the 32 export commodities with highest revealed comparative advantage, Sri Lanka, India and Maldives had revealed comparative advantage in narrow range of commodities (4 or 5 out of 10 top exported items). Countries namely, Bangladesh, Nepal and Pakistan had revealed comparative advantage in 6 (out of 10) range of commodities. Most of items with highest revealed comparative advantage entered under *manufactured goods* section (11 out of 32) followed by *food and live animals* (8 items). In *food and live animals*, Sri Lanka had highest revealed comparative advantage in *tea and mate*, Maldives in *fish salted, dried as smoked*, Pakistan in *rice* and Bangladesh in *shell fish, fresh and frozen*. In *miscellaneous manufactured goods*, RCA of Bangladesh was highest in *under garment non-knit men's outwear knit* and Nepal in *textile clothing accessories*. In *manufactured goods*, Nepal had highest revealed comparative advantage in *floor coverings*, Pakistan in *textile articles, cotton fabrics, woven and textile yarn* and India *in pearl prec. stones* indicating extent of complementarities in export structure in 2002. In 2005, of 46 export commodities with highest revealed comparative advantage, Sri Lanka had revealed comparative advantage in 9 (out of 10) range of commodities while number was 4 in 2002. Other SAARC country's condition also improved because all countries had revealed comparative advantage in at least 7 (out of 10) range of commodities. Most of the items with highest revealed comparative advantage entered under *miscellaneous manufactured goods* (23 out of 46) followed by *machinery and transport* (11) and *food and live animals* (7). In *food and live animals*, Sri Lanka again had highest revealed comparative advantage in *tea and mate*, Maldives *in fish, dried salted or smoked* and Pakistan in *rice* (same position as in 2002). In *miscellaneous manufactured articles*, Bangladesh had highest comparative advantage in *male clothing, knitted crocheted,* Pakistan in *male clothing knitted crocheted,* Maldives and Sri Lanka in *female clothing in knitted crocheted* indicating existence of complementarities in export structure at commodity level in 2005

The study has calculated *trade competitiveness* of different sections of the commodities under Standard International Trade Classification (SITC Rev. 2) with the help of *Balassa's index* at three points of time 1985, 1995 and 2005. The study revealed that India had competitive gain in *food and live animals, beverage and tobacco,* and *miscellaneous manufactured articles,* Bangladesh and Nepal in *miscellaneous manufactured articles,* Bhutan in *crude materials, inedible except fuels; mineral fuels, lubricants and related materials* and *chemicals-related products,* Sri Lanka in *food and live animals* and Pakistan in *machinery and transport equipment* in 1985, 1995 as well as in 2005. Maldives had modest competitive losses for all commodities sections during the study period. For *crude materials, inedible except fuels,* Nepal, Pakistan and Sri Lanka had competitive loss in 1995 and 2005. Competitive loss was also seen for *food and live animals* in Nepal and for *unclassified goods* in Bangladesh. Thus Nepal, Pakistan and Sri Lanka should specialize in production *of crude materials* (Nepal in *food and live animals* also) while Bangladesh in *unclassified goods*. In the form of trade potential, this index depicted that for *food and live animals* and *miscellaneous manufactured articles,* maximum number of SAARC countries were the potential exporters in 1985, 1995 and 2005.

To see *direction of exports* of SAARC nations, the study found that for Bangladesh and Sri Lanka, Pakistan constituted main export market with share being 4 percent and 2 percent while for India and Pakistan, Bangladesh constituted main export market with share being 1.14 percent and 2.37 percent respectively and for Nepal, India constituted main market with share being 28.12 percent in 1985. In 1995, all SAARC country's main export market remained same except Bangladesh and India. The share of Bangladesh in India's exports has increased from 1.14 percent in 1985 to 3.14 percent in 1995. In 2005, for most of the countries namely, Bangladesh, Bhutan, Nepal, Pakistan and Sri Lanka, India constituted main market with share being 1.28 percent, 27.76 percent, 40.68 percent, 2.10 percent and 10.78 percent respectively. For Maldives and India,

Sri Lanka constituted main market with share being 11.60 percent and 1.88 percent, respectively in 2005 indicating lack of market diversification of exports of SAARC countries.

Changes in bilateral trade flows had also been calculated with the help of *trade intensity index*. It was revealed that in 1985, trade intensity index of Nepal with SAARC was maximum, i.e. 23.93 percent followed by Maldives (13.05 percent) and Bangladesh (6.82 percent). Country-wise analysis showed that Bangladesh's trade was most intense with Pakistan (24.69 percent), of India with Nepal (39.67 percent), of Maldives with Sri Lanka (189.85 percent), of Nepal with India (35.5 percent), of Pakistan with Bangladesh (18.70 percent), and of Sri Lanka with Maldives (148.29 percent). As compared to 1985, intensity index of Bangladesh, Nepal, Pakistan and Sri Lanka with SAARC experienced decline in 1995. Nepal witnessed a rapid decline from 23.93 percent in 1985 to 8.09 percent in 1995. In 2005, index of Nepal with SAARC was maximum, i.e. 23.93 percent followed by Bhutan (18.12 percent) and Sri Lanka (7.16 percent). Country-wise analysis showed that Bangladesh's trade was most intense with Bhutan (6.42 percent), of Bhutan with Bangladesh (26.45 percent), of India with Nepal (47.18 percent), of Maldives with Sri Lanka (140.66 percent), of Nepal with India (31.25 percent), of Pakistan with Sri Lanka (11.61 percent) and of Sri Lanka with Maldives (73.28 percent). Heavy dependence on either one or two markets led to reduction in intra-SAARC exports of countries like Bhutan, Maldives and Nepal.

To find the degree of market concentration of the exports and imports among SAARC nations, *the market concentration index* for exports as well as market concentration index for imports of SAARC countries has been calculated with the help of Herfindhal-Hirchmann index at three points of time 1985, 1995 and 2005. In 1985, its value was less than 0.50 in all SAARC nations indicating that exports are geographically diversified. It was 0.22, 0.25 and 0.28 for Pakistan, Nepal and Bangladesh respectively. In 1995, export market concentration index of SAARC countries namely Bangladesh, Bhutan, India and Sri Lanka had decreased depicting the market diversification of their exports. While in case of Maldives, Nepal and Pakistan, it had increased. As compared to 1985, export market concentration index of all SAARC countries except Bangladesh and Maldives had decreased in 2005 depicting the geographic diversification of their exports. In case of import market concentration index, all SAARC nations had value less than 0.25 in 1985. The import market concentration of Nepal was 0.11 per cent followed by Bangladesh (0.13 per cent) and Maldives (0.14 per cent). In 1995, all SAARC nations except Bangladesh and Nepal experienced a decrease in index. But as compared to 1985, only Bhutan and Nepal experienced an increase in import concentration index in 2005 indicating the increasing geographic concentration of import items of these countries.

The extent of the difference between the structure of trade of the country and world average measured in terms of *commodity diversification index* showed that the export diversification index of Pakistan, India and Sri Lanka was 0.63, 0.61 and 0.59, respectively in 1985 showing that a difference between the structure of export of these countries and world average. In 1995, only two SAARC nations namely, India and Nepal's export diversification Index had decreased while for other SAARC nations, it had increased depicting the increasing difference of the structure of the export from world average. As compared to pre-WTO period (1985), this index had increased for all SAARC nations (except India) in post-WTO period (2005) indicated that India's export structure is getting closer to world's structure. In the case of import diversification index, all SAARC nations had less than 0.50 in 1985. In 1995, only Bhutan's index had decreased, i.e. from 0.42 in 1985 to 0.37 in 1995. While for other SAARC nations, it has increased. In 2005, the picture was something different. This index had increased for all SAARC nations in 2005 as compared to 1985 indicating the increasing large difference of the structure of import of SAARC nations from world average.

In the chapter entitled *"Indo-SAARC Trade : Trends and Growth"*, an attempt was made to examine India's trade performance with SAARC countries and world in terms of growth rate of exports, imports, trade and trade instability indices during pre-WTO period (1985-94), post-WTO period (1995-2005) and entire period (1985-2005). The comparative analysis of India's trade with SAARC and world depicted that India's growth rate of trade with SAARC was higher than her growth with world during pre-WTO period, post-WTO period and entire study period. Share of SAARC in India's trade has increased to 2.73 percent in 2005 from 1.55 percent in 1985 exhibiting increased role of SAARC in India's trade. India's exports to SAARC had exhibited growth rate of 13.07 percent during post-WTO period which was less compared to pre-WTO period (16.61 percent). Country-wise analysis showed that India's exports to Bhutan increased at highest rate (25.41 percent) followed by Maldives (20.15 percent) and Pakistan (19.61 percent) respectively during the study period (1985-2005). Maldives was the major export partner of India while Nepal was the minor export partner of India during pre-WTO period (on the basis of growth rates). In post-WTO period, Bhutan was the major export partner of India and Nepal was the minor export partner of India. Regarding the performance of imports, India's imports from SAARC witnessed growth rate of 5.00 percent during pre-WTO period which was less than growth rate of post-WTO period (19.00 percent). Country-wise analysis showed that India's imports from Maldives increased at a highest rate (23.94 percent), followed by Sri Lanka (20.49 percent) and Nepal (18.71 percent) during the study period (1985-2005). Period-wise analysis showed that Maldives was the major import partner of India and Bhutan was the minor import partner of India during pre-WTO period. While during post-WTO period, Nepal was the major import partner of India while Bangladesh was the minor import partner of India.

By *calculating variations* in export, import and trade with world, SAARC and SAARC nations, the study revealed that the variations in India's exports with SAARC were higher (46.70 percent, 51.44 percent and 86.92 percent) than world (33.13 percent, 44.87 percent and 70.29 percent) during pre-WTO period, post-WTO period and entire study period. India's export variations with SAARC were higher than world due to large variations in India's exports with Bhutan, Pakistan and Nepal during post-WTO period and entire study period while with Maldives and Sri Lanka during pre-WTO period. As compared to pre-WTO period, trade instability index with SAARC increased during post-WTO period due to increase in index witnessed by Nepal and Pakistan. During pre-WTO period, post-WTO period and entire study period, the variations in India's imports with SAARC was higher (35.27 percent, 62.13

percent and 106.16 percent) than world (17.28 percent, 52.75 percent and 74.74 percent). During pre-WTO period, India's import variations with SAARC were higher than world due to large variations in India's imports with Maldives, Bhutan and Pakistan. While during post-WTO period it was due to large variations in India's imports with Sri Lanka, Maldives, and Bhutan. During entire study period, it was due to variations with Sri Lanka, Maldives and Bhutan. During pre-WTO period, post-WTO period and entire study period, variations in India's trade with SAARC was higher (42.07 percent, 55.42 percent and 85.07 percent) than the variations with world (23.66 percent, 49.25 percent and 72.61 percent). These higher trade variations were due to large variations in India's trade with Bhutan, Maldives, Nepal and Sri Lanka during entire study period (with Bhutan, Maldives, and Pakistan during pre-WTO period and with Bhutan, Nepal and Sri Lanka during post-WTO period). As compared to pre-WTO period, trade instability index with SAARC increased during post-WTO period due to large trade variations with Bhutan, Nepal, Maldives and Pakistan.

An analysis of *commodity composition of India's exports* of all commodity sections (SITC Rev. 2) to SAARC revealed that in pre-WTO period, *machinery and transport equipment, chemical and related products, commodities and transactions not classified* and *beverage and tobacco* were the main commodity groups of India's exports. But in post-WTO period, *food and live animals, mineral fuels, lubricants and related materials, machinery and transport equipment* and *beverage and tobacco* were the main commodity groups. Regarding *commodity composition of India's imports* from SAARC, in pre-WTO period, *food and live animals, crude materials inedible except fuels* and *commodities and transactions not classified* were the main commodity groups of India's import basket. But in post-WTO period, *food and five animals, beverage and tobacco, manufactured goods classified chiefly, animals and vegetables oils, chemical and related products* and *miscellaneous manufactured articles* were the main commodity groups. Thus, there was structural shift in commodity groups in post-WTO period.

The *direction structure of India's exports* of commodity sections (SITC Rev. 2) to SAARC nations revealed that Bangladesh, Nepal and Sri Lanka were major destinations for most of the India's exports in pre-WTO period. In post-WTO period, these countries again remained as major destinations. Section-wise analysis showed that in India, Bangladesh became important market for *mineral fuel lubricants and related materials, crude materials inedible except fuels, manufactured goods classified chiefly by materials, machinery and transport equipment, miscellaneous manufactured articles* and *commodities and transactions not classified;* Nepal for *beverage and tobacco and commodities and transactions not classified* and Sri Lanka for *food and live animals and chemical and related products* in pre-WTO period, in India. While in post-WTO period, Bangladesh became main export market for *food and live animals, crude materials, inedible except fuels, mineral fuel lubricants and related materials, animals and vegetable oils* and *manufactured goods classified chiefly by materials,* Nepal for *beverage and tobacco, mineral fuel lubricants and related materials* and *commodities and transactions not classified* and Sri Lanka for *mineral fuel lubricants and related materials, machinery and transport equipment* and *miscellaneous manufactured articles.* Thus, it is clear that though major export partners (Bangladesh, Nepal and Sri Lanka) among SAARC nations remained same in post-WTO period, but there was structural shift in direction of India's exports to SAARC.

An analysis of *direction structure in imports of commodity* sections (SITC Rev. 2) revealed that Nepal, Pakistan and Bangladesh were major destinations for most of India's imports in pre-WTO period. In post-WTO period, these countries remained as major destinations but Sri Lanka also emerged as important import market for most of the commodities in India. Section-wise analysis showed that Nepal became important import market for *food and live animals, beverage and tobacco, chemical and related products, miscellaneous manufactured articles* and *commodities and transactions not classified;* Bangladesh *for manufactured goods classified chiefly* and Pakistan for *crude materials inedible except fuels* and *machinery and transport equipment* during pre-WTO period (1985). While in post-WTO period (2004), Nepal became important import market for *animals and vegetable oils, chemical and related products, machinery and transport equipment* and *miscellaneous manufactured articles,* Bangladesh for *commodities and transactions not classified,* Pakistan for *food and live animals* and *mineral fuel lubricants and related materials* and Sri Lanka for *crude materials inedible except fuels* and *manufactured goods classified chiefly*. Thus it is clear that, major import partners (Bangladesh, Nepal, Pakistan) among SAARC nations remained same in post-WTO period and one more import partner namely (Sri Lanka) also emerged as new import market for India in post-WTO period. With this change, there was also structural shift in direction of India's imports from SAARC.

In the chapter entitled *"Static and Dynamic Effects of SAARC"*, an attempt was made to quantify static effects (trade creation and trade diversion) and dynamic effects in terms of investment and technical change. The average growth of exports expansion measured in terms of average growth of total exports of SAARC increased at rate of 9.65 percent during pre-WTO period and 12.21 percent during post-WTO period depicting that growth of total exports in SAARC was greater than pre-WTO period. The average growth of exports creation measured in terms of intra-SAARC exports was 8.37 percent in pre-WTO period and 16.99 percent in post-WTO period depicting that growth of intra-regional exports of SAARC was more rapid in post-WTO period than in pre-WTO period. The average growth of exports diversion measured in terms of exports of SAARC with rest of the world was 9.75 percent in pre-WTO period and 12.03 percent in post-WTO period depicting that growth of SAARC exports diversion was more rapid in post-WTO period than in pre-WTO period. Thus, the average growth of exports expansion, exports creation and exports diversion in post-WTO period was more than in pre-WTO period. The comparative analysis also showed that the growth of exports creation was more rapid than the growth of exports expansion and growth of exports diversion in post-WTO period and entire study period while growth of exports diversion was more in pre-WTO period. Regarding the imports effects, the average growth of imports expansion measured in terms of average growth of total imports of SAARC increased at rate of 4.82 percent during pre-WTO period and 14.64 percent during post-WTO period depicting that growth of total imports in SAARC was greater in post-WTO period than in pre-WTO period. The average growth of imports creation measured in terms of intra-SAARC imports was 8.95 percent in pre-WTO period and 16.70 percent in post-WTO period depicting that growth of intra-regional imports of

SAARC was more rapid in post-WTO period than in pre-WTO period. The average growth of imports diversion measured in terms of imports of SAARC with rest of the world was 4.74 percent in pre-WTO period and 14.61 percent in post-WTO period depicting that growth of SAARC imports diversion was more rapid in post-WTO period than in pre-WTO period. Thus the average growth of imports expansion, imports creation and imports diversion in post-WTO period was more than in pre-WTO period. The comparative analysis also showed that the growth of imports creation was more rapid than the growth of imports expansion and growth of imports diversion in pre-WTO period, post-WTO period and entire study period.

To quantify dynamic effects of SAARC (effect of real gross domestic product, real foreign capital inflows and integration on investment and effect of capital stock, labour and integration on GDP), panel regression approach had been applied due to panel data of the study. Results were drawn with the help of pooled model, fixed effects model and random effects model and then applied different tests (restricted F-test and Hausman test) for selecting the model. In SAARC, foreign capital inflows significantly and negatively affected the gross capital formation of SAARC during 1981-2005 while gross domestic product significantly and positively affected the gross capital formation of SAARC. The coefficients of time Dummies, i.e. D_1 (from the formation of SAARC to the formation of SAPTA) and D_2 (after the formation of SAPTA) were non-significant and positive. This suggested that integration has positively and non-significantly affected the gross capital formation of SAARC nations. Country-wise these effects have also been estimated with the help of multiple regression equation. Real GDP had significantly and positively affected the gross capital formation in all SAARC nations (except Maldives) during 1981-2005. In Maldives, it had non-significantly and negatively affected the gross capital formation. The coefficient of real foreign capital inflows was non-significant and positive in case of only three SAARC nations, i.e. India, Nepal and Sri Lanka while for other SAARC nations (Bangladesh, Bhutan, Maldives and Pakistan), it was non-significant and negative. It indicates that real foreign capital inflows are not much playing role for capital formation in these economies. The time effect and integration coefficient (D_1) was significant and positive only for Bangladesh indicating that there was significant and positive impact on gross capital formation. While it was significant and negative for Sri Lanka indicating that integration had negative impact on capital formation of Sri Lanka during the same period. For remaining SAARC nations (except Bhutan). It was non-significant and positive indicating that integration had non-significant impact on capital formation of these economies. The integration effect after the formation of SAPTA has been captured by D_2. This was significant and positive only for Bangladesh and Maldives indicating that formation of SAPTA has significantly and positively affected the capital formation of these countries. While for other SAARC nations, i.e. Bhutan, India and Sri Lanka, it was non-significant and negative and for remaining SAARC nations, i.e. Nepal and Pakistan, it was non-significant and positive. Thus, integration has little impact on capital formation of SAARC.

Effect of capital Stock, labour and integration on GDP had revealed that growth of capital stock had non-significantly and negatively affected the growth of GDP while labour had non-significantly and positively affected the growth of GDP. Surprisingly, two time dummies had significantly and negatively affected the growth rate of GDP in SAARC suggesting that integration has decreased the rate of technological progress among member countries during 1981-2005. In other words, integration has reduced the rate of productivity growth. Effect on productivity growth has also been estimated for country-by-country with the help of multiple regression equations. Growth rate of capital stock had non-significantly affected the growth rate of GDP in all SAARC nations during 1981-2005. It had positively affected in Bhutan, India, Nepal and Pakistan. While for Bangladesh, Maldives and Sri Lanka, it had negatively affected. Regarding the growth rate of labour, it had significantly and positively affected the growth rate of GDP for Sri Lanka only while for other SAARC nations it had non-significantly affected the growth rate of GDP. It had negatively affected the growth rate of GDP in Bangladesh, India and Maldives while for other SAARC nations (Bhutan, Nepal and Pakistan) it had positively affected. The time dummies (D_1 as well as D_2) had significantly and negatively affected the growth rate of GDP in Maldives indicating that integration had significantly reduced the rate of productivity in Maldives. For Bangladesh and Sri Lanka, D_1 had non-significantly and negatively affected the growth rate of GDP while for other SAARC economies, it had non-significantly and positively affected the growth rate of GDP. It indicates that integration has a positive impact for many SAARC nations on technological progress (Bhutan, India, Nepal and Pakistan) but its role is not significant. After the formation of SAPTA, integration positively and non-significantly affected the growth rate of GDP in Bangladesh, Bhutan, India and Nepal as D_2 was positive. Thus it is clear that SAARC integration has reduced the rate of technological progress in SAARC. Dynamic effects of SAARC in terms of investment and productivity are not so strong during 1981-2005. There is a need to strengthen the static effects firstly then dynamic effects will automatically be generated and powerful. But for this, growth of intra-regional trade is a necessary requirement. It has been expecting that SAFTA will generate this growth and then dynamic effects will come out in SAARC. Thus the dynamic effects of SAARC integration cannot explain the rapid rates of growth experienced by members of regional integration and also these effects cannot serve as a rationale for integration. SAARC do not affect the growth of their member countries directly but it does have a significant positive influence on investment and investment has a strong and significant effect on growth.

In the chapter entitled *"A Gravity Model Analysis : India's Export Potential to other SAARC Countries"*, an attempt was made to quantify India's export potential to SAARC countries using *gravity model*. Due to panel data structure for this model also, the study had used restricted model, fixed effects model and random effects model and then applied different tests (restricted F-test and Hausman test) for selecting the model which had suggested that fixed effect model was better for the present data. The gravity model for India's exports had been fitted for the time period 1981-2005. The study revealed that the economic size (GDP) of exporter country (India) as well as importer countries (SAARC members other than India) had significantly and positively affected India's exports. Market size (population) of India had highly significantly and positively affected the

India's exports. But market size of SAARC members (other than India) significantly and negatively affected the India's exports showing presence of absorption effect (country exports less when it is big). Real exchange rate of exporter country non-significantly and positively affected India's exports. Non-significance of this variable was due to currency deprecation effect which can be explained in two ways. Firstly, exports would be instantaneously cheaper. However, this effect will be negated to the extent that imported raw materials would now be costlier. Overall though it seems sensible to assume that the former effect will dominate. The non-significance of this variable has suggested that the two conflicting effects are canceling each other out. While real exchange rate of importer country had highly significant and negative effect on India's exports. The coefficient of difference in per capita income was non-significant and negative suggesting that Linder effect dominates in India's exports. The country effects showed that Bangladesh followed by Pakistan, Sri Lanka and Nepal had the highest propensity with India's exports and Maldives and Bhutan had the lowest propensity with India's exports. To see the effect of the variables and dummies which are fixed over time (distance, border and language), the fixed effects obtained from fixed effects model were regressed on these variables. These variables were found to be non-significant and had expected signs. Low value of R^2 (0.28) had suggested that there are other determinants of the trading pair effects, different from the ones traditionally included in the analysis, which should be investigated.

The study not only found out determinants of bilateral exports flows of India but also *predicted future export flows* (export potential). For this, the study had used point estimates as well as interval estimate. The point estimate (P-A) showed that the average of P-A (Predicted–Actual) was highest for Bangladesh (187.36) followed by Sri Lanka (2.08) while for other SAARC nations, it was negative indicating that over a period of time (1981-2005), India had exceeded its export potential with these SAARC nations. Other point estimate (P/A: Predicted/ Actual) had also been used by the study. The average of this ratio was maximum for Maldives (2.59) followed by Bhutan (1.58), Nepal (1.17) and Pakistan (1.11) during 1981-2005 indicating India had highest potential of exports with these nations. The interval estimate i.e. the speed of convergence showed that India had convergence in exports with four SAARC members (Bhutan, Maldives, Nepal and Pakistan) and divergence with two SAARC members (Bangladesh and Sri Lanka). In other words India has not exploited all the export potential in trading with six SAARC members. There is a large room for export expansion for Maldives, Bhutan, Pakistan and Nepal. Speed of convergence for Sri Lanka was maximum i.e. 26.88 percent showing that Sri Lanka had over-exported by India. The increasing FDI can help to explain the over-utilized export potential between India and Sri Lanka. For Bangladesh, it was 17.15 percent depicting that Bangladesh had also over-exported by India. In case of Maldives, Bhutan, Pakistan and Nepal, India's export potential were under utilized during the study period (1981-2005).

The study also estimated that whether there was convergence of actual data towards the estimated equilibrium. The study found that there was presence of convergence in Indian exports with SAARC countries. In other words, India's exports to SAARC countries converged towards the estimated export potential.

On the basis of the analysis carried out in the study, following hypotheses are accepted:

1. Trade of SAARC nations is geographically diversified.
2. India's trade is not intense with all other SAARC nations.
3. There is a potential of India's exports to other SAARC nations.
4. India's exports to SAARC nations have converged towards the estimated equilibrium.

The hypothesis, i.e. complementarities in production and trade exists among SAARC nations is not conclusively accepted or rejected as complementarities in production and trade among these nations do not exist at broad level. However, at commodity level, complementarities are found. Another hypothesis, i.e. dynamic effects of SAARC can explain the rapid rates of growth experienced by its members is not accepted as these effects can not explain the rapid rates of growth experienced by members of SAARC.

POLICY IMPLICATIONS

1. Intra-regional SAARC trade is low as compared to other regional blocks (NAFTA, EU). To increase intra-regional trade, regional exports processing zones should be developed. SAARC countries should arrange trade fairs and exhibitions. Trade delegations should be exchanged on bilateral and multilateral basis. SAARC countries should provide adequate line of credit to expand intra-regional trade. Further, to encourage capacity building and to improve productivity and competitiveness in terms of both quality and cost, domestic and foreign investments must be attracted through appropriate government policies of SAARC nations. Greater stability in the international exchange system would also help to increase prospects for trade and investments of SAARC countries.
2. SAARC nations face low intra-industry trade, but the potential for widening the scope of this type of trade with in the region is rather large. This can only be realized if the import duties are low. Intra-industry trade is largely driven by product differentiation and increasing returns to scale. Therefore, regional countries should develop technological capacity to produce different product varieties at declining average cost to achieve an increased level of intra-industry trade. Formation of SAFTA can be helpful in increasing intra-industry trade. To ensure the success of SAFTA, all countries must have very small negative list. If the list is large, the SAFTA would become redundant. There should be a firm basis to exclude product and ground rules should be laid down and be transparent.
3. There exists lack of complementarities at section level in SAARC nations. So trade complementarities can be developed within the region if countries achieve vertical specialization through production sharing

arrangements. Vertical specification would not only allow the regional trading partners to strengthen their trade ties but also enable them to reap economies of scale by concentrating on a specific production process in the value addition chain.

4. Services sector also offers large potential for trade between SAARC nations. In particular, educational institutes, financial and IT enabled services, tele communication, information exchanges and tourism (including medical) are the service sectors where bilateral trade can benefit the SAARC nations. A Research and Policy Group should be set to improve trade composition and trade imbalance between India and SAARC nations. R & D Facilities should be widened in SAARC nations specifically for Quality Improvement, Designing, Innovation and Product Development.
5. To capture the dynamic effects of SAFTA, there is need to take into account the positive relationship among trade, investment and growth which in turn depends upon the strengthening the trade relationship among the SAARC nations.
6. Country-wise analysis showed that trade potentials between India and Pakistan are bright. For this purpose, India can consider import of pulses, fruits and nuts (excluding cashew nuts), textile and textile products and chemicals from Pakistan, India on the other hand, has developed a competitive advantage in certain manufactured exports as auto-mobiles, pharmaceuticals and agricultural implements, etc. So, in addition to import of agricultural products, Pakistan can consider import of these manufactured items from India at much cheaper rates. Both the governments of India and Pakistan must take necessary steps to dismantle the political barriers. The opening of rail route can bring dividends only if more rail wagons are permitted and for the land route to be more beneficial, the present cargo clearance systems at Wagah border

need to be upgraded. In addition, Pakistan should consider import of more items via land route.

7. Moreover, as India has strengths in the information technology and its software industry is growing at a higher rate, it can establish joint ventures with SAARC nations. There are big opportunities for the joint ventures with SAARC countries in the textile sector as this sector is the leading sector in the exports of India as well as other SAARC nations. There is a need for a well coordinated integrated textile strategy at the national and regional level to fasten the competitive strength in the highiy competitive quota free international market system in the post-MFA period.
8. The policy implications of the results obtained from the gravity model are that all kinds of trade barriers in countries involved must be removed in order to enhance the India's exports. Adoption of SAFTA is a step in this direction.
9. Proper quality of the goods and services must be maintained as well as the varieties of goods and services must be increased as the India's exports largely depend on the foreign demand.

India is the only SAARC member that shares land border with four members and sea border with two. No other SAARC country shares a common border with each other. In terms of trade, commerce, investments, etc., India is a source of potential investment and technology and a major market for products from all other SAARC members. Therefore, it is essentially in India's interest to put her weight behind SAARC.

Bibliography

Abraham, F. and Janvan Hove (2005), *The Rise of China: Prospects of Regional Trade Policy*, Discussion Paper Series, Centre for Economic Studies, DPS 2005-06.

Achay, L. (2006), *Assessing Regional Integration in North Africa*, National Institute of Statistics and Applied Economics, Robot Morocco.

Aggarwal, M. and P. Pandey (1992), "Prospects of Trade Expansion in the SAARC Region", *The Developing Economies*, Vol. 30 (1), pp. 3-23.

Ahmed, Mudabber (2002), "Money-Income and Money Price Causality in selected SAARC Countries: Some Econometric Exercises", *The Indian Economic Journal*, Vol. 50, No. 1, pp. 55-60.

Ahujan, Shoaba and Rina Bhattacharya (1989), "Trade Complementarities and Prospects for Regional Import Substitution among SAARC-ASEAN Countries", *Foreign Trade Review*, Jan.-March, Vol. 23(2), pp. 186-99.

Amjad, Faiza and Naheed Zia Khan (2004), "Determinants of Growth and Growth Projections: SAARC and Pakistan", *Pakistan Development Review*, Vol. 43, No. 4 (2), pp. 737-55.

Arghyrow, M.G. and Evelyn Bazina (2003), "Competitiveness and the External Trade of Greece in the 1990s: A Cross Sectoral Investigation", *Journal of Economic Integration*, pp. 763-93.

Asher, Mukul G. and Sadhana Srivastava (2003), *Indian and the Asian Economic Community*, RIS Discussion Papers, RIS-DP# 51, 2003.

Asian Development Bank, *Key Indicators of Asia and Pacific Countries:* Various Issues.

Badinger, Herald (2005), "Growth Effects of Economic Integration," *Review of World Economy*, Vol. 141(1), pp. 50-78.

Balassa, Bela (1965), "Trade Liberalization and Revealed Comparative Advantage", *The Manchester School of Economics and Social Studies*, Vol. 33, No. 2, pp. 90-123.

Baltagi, B.H. (1995), *Econometric Analysis of Panel Data*, Chichester, Wiley, England.

Banik, N. (1998), "Indo-Srilankan Trade: With Special Reference to Indian Exports", *Asian Economic Review*, Vol. 34(2), pp. 38-47.

Basu, Suprana and Debabrata Datta (2007), "India-Bangladesh Trade Relation: Problem of Bilateral Deficit", *Indian Economic Review*, Vol. 47, No. 1.

Batra, Amita (2004), *India's Global Trade Potential: The Gravity Model Approach?* ICRIER Working Paper, No. 151, Indian Council for Research as International–Economic Relations.

Bergsten, C.F. (1996), *Competitive Liberalization and Global Free Trade: A Vision for the Early 21st Century*, Asia Pacific Working Paper Series, No. 96-116, Institute for International Economics, Washington.

Bhagwati, J. (1993), "Regionalism and Multilateralism: An Overview", in Melo and Pangariya (eds.), *New Dimensions in Regional Integration*, Cambridge University Press, Cambridge.

Bhatt, R.P. (2000), "Foreign Direct Investment in ASEAN Economies", *Indian Journal of Economics*, Vol. 34, No. 3, pp. 207-25.

Bhattacharya, B. and Somasri Mukhopadhyay (1996), *Duty Free Access to Indian within SAPTA Framework*, Occassional Paper, No. 5, Indian Institute of Foreign Trade, New Delhi.

Bhattacharya, R. and T. Benerjee (2004), *Does the Gravity Model Explain India's Direction of Trade: A Panel Data Approach*, IIMA Working Paper, No. 2006-09-01.

Bhattacharya, Swapan K. (2004), "Does Bangladesh Benefit from Preferential Trade with India: A Gravity Analysis", *Economic and Political Weekly*, Vol. 39 (48), pp. 5152-62.

Boillot, J.J. and M. Labbouz, (2006), "India-China Trade Lessons Learned and Projection for 2015", *Economic and Political Weekly*, Vol. 41(26), pp. 2893-2943.

Brada, C. Josef and Mendez A. Jose (1985), "Economic Integration among Developed, Developing and Centrally Planned Economics: A Comparative Analysis", *The Review of Economics and Statistics*, Vol. 67, No. 4, pp. 549-56.

———, (1988), "An Estimate of Dynamic Effects of Economic Integration", *The Review of Economics and Statistics"*, Vol. 70, Issue 1, pp. 163-68.

Braga, C.A.P., Raed Safadi and Alexander Yeats (1994), *NAFTA's Implications for East Asian Exports*, World Bank Policy Research Working Paper, No. 1351, World Bank

Cernat, Lucian (2003), *Assessing South-South Regional Integration: Same Issue, Many Metrics*, UNCTAD Policy Issues in International Trade and Commodities, Study Series No. 21.

———, (2003), *Assessing RTA: Are South-South RTAs More Trade Diverting*, Policy Issues in International Study Series, No. 16, UNCTAD, Geneva.

Chadha, Rajesh and Davendar Partap, (2007), "Titanic FTAs: Is It Time to Establish a Pan Asian FTA?", *Margin*, Vol. 1, No. 1, pp. 23-45.

Chand, R. (2004), *Preferential Trading Agreement and Regional Trade: Implication for Asia*, Working Paper, Institute of Economic Growth, Delhi (www.iegindia.org/workpap/wp240.Pdf, accessed 8 June 2007).

———, (2006), *Free Trade Area in Asia*, Academic Foundation, New Delhi.

Chang, I.M. and H.J. Wall (2005), "Controlling for Heterogeneity in Gravity Models of Trade Integration", *Federal Reserve Bank of St. Louis Review*, Vol. 87, Issue 1, pp. 49-63.

Chaudhary, M.A. and Abe Kiyoshi (2000), "Pakistan, Japan and ASEAN Trade Relations and Economic Development: A Comparative Analysis", *Pakistan Economic and Social Review*, Vol. 38, No. 2, pp. 193-214.

Chaudhri, K. (1997), "Purchasing Power Party: Evidence from South Asian Countries", *Indian Journal of Economics*, Vol. 79, No. 308-9, pp. 2-15.

Chawla, K.L. (1991), *Economic Cooperation among Developing Countries with Special Reference to SAARC*, RBSA Publishers, Jaipur.

Chowdhury, Mamta (2005), "Trade Reforms and Economic Integration in South Asia", *Applied Econometrics and International Development*, Vol. 5, Issue 4.

Christie, E. (2002), *Potential Trade in South East Europe: A Gravity Model Approach*, Working Paper, The Vienna Institute For International Economic Studies-WIIW.

CMIE, *Foreign Trade and Balance of Payments*, 2006 (Sept.).

Corden, W. Max (1970), "The Efficiency Effects of Trade and Protection", in I.A Mc Dougall and R.H. Snape (eds.), *Studies in International Economics*.

Debroy, Bibek (1989), "Intra-Regional Trade in the SAARC Region", *Foreign Trade Review*, Vol. XXIII, Jan.-March 1989, No. 4.

Devi, Nirmla (1989), *Regional Economic Cooperation in South Asia*, Chugh Publications, Allahabad.

Devlin, R. and F. Richard (1998), *Towards and Evaluation of Regional Integration In Latin America in The 1990s*, WP2 INTAL-ITD Series, IDB-Intal.

Doganlar, Murat (1998), "Testing Long Run Validity of Purchasing Power Parity for Asian Countries", *Indian Journal of Economics*, Vol. 79, No. 312-13.

Drysdale, Peter and Ross Gamaut (1982), "Trade Intensities and Analysis of Bilateral Trade Flows in a Many Country World: A Survey", *Hitosubashi Journal of Economics*, Vol. 22, No. 2.

Easton, Stephens and Herbert G. Grubel (1982), "The Costs and Benefits of Protection in a Growing World", *Kyklos* 36, pp. 213-30.

Egger, P. and M. Pfaffermayr (2002), "The Pure Effects of European Integration on Intra-EU Core and Peripherry Trade", *University of Innsbruck Economics Working Paper No. 02/01*, Austrian Institute of Economic Research and University of Innsbruck, Department of Economics.

Egger, P. (2002), "An Econometric View on Estimation of Gravity Models and the Calculation of Trade Potentials", *World Economy,* Vol. 25, Issue 2, pp. 297-312.

Fayez, Al Hahib (1986), "Saudi Trade Relationship with the EEC Countries: An Analytical Study (1966-82)", *Asian Economic Review,* Vol. 28, August 86, No. 2, pp. 35-40.

Fernandez, Raquel (1997), *Returns to Regionalism: An Evaluation to Non-Traditional Gains from Regional Trade Agreements,* World Bank Policy Research Working Paper, No. 1816, World Bank.

Fillpini, C. and Vasco Molini (2003), "The Determinants of East Asian Trade Flows: A Gravity Equation Approach", *Journal of Asian Economics,* Vol. 14(5), pp. 695-711.

Francis, Ng and Alexander Yeats (2003), *Major Trade Trends in East Asia: What are Implications for Regional Corporation and Growth,* World Bank Policy Research Working Paper, No. 3084, World Bank .

Frankel, J. (1997), *Regional Trading Blocks in the World Economic System,* Institute for International Economics, Washington DC.

Frankel, J.E. Stein and S. Wei (1995), "Trading Blocks and the Americas: The Natural, The Unnatural and The Super Natural", *Journal of Development Economics,* Vol. 47, pp. 61-96.

Fukao, Kyoji, Toshihiro Okubo and Mstern Robert (1999), *An Econometric Analysis of Trade Diversion under NAFTA,* Discussion Paper No. 491, School of Public Policy, The University of Michigan (www.sppumich.edu/rsie/workingpapers/wphmtl, accessed 9 August 2007).

Garnaut, Ross (1998), "ASEAN and Regionalization and Globalisation of World Trade", *ASEAN Economic Bulletin,* 14, pp. 215-23.

Geda, A. and H. Kebret (2002), "Regional Economic Integration in Africa: A Review of Problems and Prospects with a Case Study of COMESA", *Journal of African Economics,* Vol. 17(3), pp. 357-94.

Ghuman, R.S. and Madaan, D.K. (2000), "Indo SAARC Trade Scenario: Emerging Trend and Trade Off", *Indian Economic Journal,* Vol. 47, No. 3, pp. 97-104.

Goto, Junichi (1997), *Regional Economic Integration and Agricultural Trade*, World Bank Policy Research Working Paper, No. 1805, World Bank.

Gould, D. (1998), "Has NAFTA Changed North American Trade?" *Economic Review*, Federal Research Bank of Dallas, First Quarter, pp. 12-23.

Gujarati, D.N. (2003), *Basic Econometrics*, McGraw Hill, Higher Education, New York.

Guru Gharana, K.K. (2000), "Macro-Economic Modeling of South Asian Economies with Intra-SAARC Trade Link", *A Report: South Asian Network of Economic Institutes*, Institute for Integrated Development Studies. (www.saneinetwork.net/pdf/SANEI-I/Macromodelling-fin-PDF, accessed 12 June 2008).

Hapsari, I.M. and C. Mangunsong (2006), *Determinants of AFTA Member's Trade Flows and Potential for Trade Diversion*, Asia Pacific Research and Training Network on Trade, Working Paper Series, No. 21, November 2006.

Hasan, M.K. (2001), "Is SAARC a Viable Economic Block? Evidence from Gravity Model", *Journal of Asian Economics*, Vol. 12, pp. 263-90.

Helpman, E. (1981), "International Trade in the Presence of Product Differentiation, Economies of Scale and Monopolistic Competition", *Journal of International Economics*, pp. 305-40.

Heng T. and V. Gayathri (2004), "Impact of Regional Trade Liberalization on Emerging Economies: The Case of Vietnam", *ASEAN Economic Bulletin*, Vol. 21, No. 2.

Hirantha, Seeknwa Wasani (2003), "From SAPTA to SAFTA: A Gravity Analysis of South Asian Free Trade?", *Paper presented at the European Trade Study Group.*

Iglesias, E.V. (2000), "Twelve Lessons from Latin America and the Caribbean", *Paper Presented at the Conference of the Institute for the Integration of Latin America and the Caribbean.*

IMF, *Direction of Trade Statistics Year Book*: Various Issues.

Jakab, Z.M., M.A. Kovacas and K.A. Oszlay (2001), "How Far has Trade Integration Advanced? An Analysis of Actual and Potential Trade of Three Central and Eastern European Countries", *Journal of Comparative Economics*, Vol. 29, pp. 276-92.

Janssen, L.H. (1961), *Free Trade, Protection and Custom Union*, Economisch Sociologisch Institute, Tilburg, Leiden.

Jayarama, T.K. (1978), *Economic Cooperation in the Indian Sub-continent*, Orient Longman, Bombay.

Jha, S.C. (1991), "Changing Pattern of Intra-Regional Trade in Asia", *Indian Economic Journal*, Vol. 44, No. 3, pp. 45-60.

Joshi, P.K., A. Gulati, P. Birthal and L. Tewari (2004), "Agriculture Diversification in South Asia: Patterns, Determinants and Policy Implications", *Economic and Political Weekly*, June, pp. 2457-68.

Kalbasi, H. (2002), "The Gravity Model and Global Trade Flows", *Asian Economics Review*, Aug., Vol. 44, No. 2, pp. 225-43.

Kannan, R. and A. Mukherjee (2007), "Is East and South-East Asia including India an Optimum Currency Area", *Economics and Political Weekly*, pp. 953-964.

Karaman, F.M. and N.L. Ozkale (2006), "Static Effects of the EU-Turkey Custom Union", *Paper presented at the eighth meeting of European Trade Study Group, Vienna* (www.etsg.org/ETSG2006/papers/Karaman/pdf, accessed 12 October 2007).

Khan, A.H. and Mahmood (1998), "Trade and Regional Economic Integration", *Pakistan Journal of Applied Economics*, Vol. 14, Nos. 1 and 2, pp. 28-41.

Kim, J. (2003), "Sub-Regionalisms, Regionalism, Trans-regionalism: Implications for Economic Integration and International Trade Policies", *Asia Europe Journal*, Vol. 1, No. 2, pp. 183-96.

Kreinin, Mordichai E. and Michael, G. Plummer (1992), "Structural Change and Regional Integration in East Asia", *International Economic Journal*, Vol. 8(2), pp. 1-12.

Kritzinger, L. (2005), *Regional Integration: Concepts Advantages, Disadvantages and lessons of Experience*, SARPN (Southern African Regional Poverty Network) Publications, World Bank.

Krueger, A.O. (1980), "Importance of General Policies to Promote Economic Growth", *The World Economy 8*, pp. 93-108 (June).

———, (1980), "Trade Policy as an Input to Development", *American Economic Review*, pp. 288-92.

Krueger, A.O. (1999), *Trade Creation and Trade Diversion under NAFTA*, National Bureau of Economic Research, Working Paper, No. 7429, Cambridge, M.A.

Krugman, P. (1979), "Increasing Returns, Monopolistic Competition and International Trade", *Journal of International Economics*, Vol. 9, pp. 469-79.

———, (1991), "Is Bilateralism Bad?", in E. Helpman and A. Razin (eds.), *International Trade and Trade Policy*, Mass : MIT Press, Cambridge.

Lan, S. Kim, Y. Zulkornain and Lawsiong Hook (2006), "China and ASEAN-5 Bilateral Trade Relationship", *Sunway Academic Journal*, 4.

Lancaster (1980), "Intra-Industry Trade under Perfect Competition", *Journal of International Economics*, pp. 90-110.

Laurenceson, James (2003), "Economic Integration between China and ASEAN-5", *ASEAN Economic Bulletin*, Vol. 20, No. 2, pp. 103-11.

Linders, P.H. (1991), *International Economics*, 9th Edition, Homewood, Irwin.

Linders, Gert. Jan, Henri L.F.De Groot (2006), *Estimation of the Gravity Equation in the Presence of Zero Flows*, Tinbergen Institute, Discussion Paper No. 06-072/3.

Linneman, H. (1966), *An Econometrics Study of International Trade Flows*, North Holland, Amsterdam

Lipsey, R.G. (1957), "The Theory of Custom Union: Trade Diversion and Welfare", *Economica*, Vol. 24, pp. 40-46.

———, (1960), "The Theory of Custom Unions: A General Survey", *Economic Journal*, 60 (Sept), pp. 496-573.

Lizano, E. (2000), "Regional Integration and International Integration", *Paper Presented at the Policy Forum*, INTAL, Thirty-five Years of Commitment to Regional Integration, during the celebration of the Thirty-fifth Anniversary of Institute for the Integration of Latin America and the Caribbean, Buenos Aires.

Lloyd, P.J. and Macleren, D. (2004), "Gains and Losses from Regional Trading Agreements: A Survey", *Economics Record*, 80, pp. 445-67.

Madaan (1998), *SAARC: Economic and Trade Development*, Encyclopedia of SAARC Countries, Deep & Deep Publications, New Delhi.

Madani, H. Dorsati (2001), *South-South Regional Integration and Industrial Growth: The Case of the Andean Pact,* World Bank Policy Research Working Paper, No. 2614, World Bank.

Majumdar, S. and Debesh Chakraborthy (2001), "A Study on Production Structures of the SAARC Countries", *Indian Journal of Economics,* Vol. 81, No. 322-23, pp. 73-92.

Mansifield and Reinhardt (2003), "Multilateral Determination of Regionalism: The Effect of GATT/WTO on the Formation of Preferential Trading Arrangements", *International Organization, 57*(4), pp. 829-62.

Martin, John, P. (1978), "X–efficiency, Managerial Effort and Protection", *Economica,* Vol. 45, pp. 273-86.

Matthews, Alan (2003), *Regional Integration and Food Security in Developing Countries, Food and Agriculture Organization of the United Nations,* Rome.

Matyas, L., L. Kenya and M.N. Harris (2000), *Modelling Export Activity of Eleven APEC Countries,* Melbourne Institute Working Paper No. 5/00.

———, (1997), *Modelling Export Activity in a Multicountry Economic Area: The APEC Case,* Monash Econometrics and Business Statistics Working Paper: 1/97.

Meade, J.E. (1968), *The Theory of Custom Unions,* Amsterdam, North Holland.

Melo, De Jaime, Claudio Montengro and Arvind Pangariya (1992), *Regional Integration: Old and New,* World Bank Policy Research Working Paper, No. 985, World Bank.

Modwel, S.K. and R.K. Pandey (1987), "South Asian-ASEAN Trade: Possibilities of Expansion and Diversification", *Foreign Trade Review,* Vol. 21(4), Jan.-March, pp. 343-68.

Montanari, M. (2005), "EU Trade with Balkans: Large Room for Growth", *Eastern European Economics,* Vol. 43, No. 1, pp. 59-81.

Mukherji, I.N. (1997), "India's Exports to South Asia Identifying Products for Sustainable Development", *Foreign Trade Review,* Vol. 30.

Mundell, Robert (1964), "Tariff Preferences and Terms of Trade", *Manchester School of Economic and Social Studies,* Vol. 1(1), pp. 1-13.

Musleh-ud-Din (2004), "Exports, Imports and Economic Growth in South Asia: Evidence Using Multivarate Time Series Framework", *The Pakistan Development Review,* Vol. 43, No. 2, pp. 105-24.

Nag, B. and A. Nandi (2006), "Analyzing India's Trade Dynamics *vis-à-vis* SAARC Members using Gravity Model", *South Asia Economic Journal,* Vol. 7, No. 1, Jan.-June, pp. 83-98.

Nanda, P. and P.S. Raikhy (2004), "Complementarities in Production and Trade among Asian Countries—Prospects of Asian Economic Union", *Indian Journal of Quantitative Economics,* Vol. 19, Nos. 1-2, pp. 39-63.

———, (2004), *India's Trade with SAARC Countries: Emerging Opportunities,* Unpublished paper.

Naqvi, M.B. (1986), "South Asian Co-operation", *Pakistan Horizon,* Vol. 36, No. 3, pp. 21-36.

Nayak, Parmananda and Avijit Mandal (2007), "Indo-Thai FTA: Sensitivity Analysis of Textiles and Clothing Industry", *Business Perspective,* Vol. 8, No. 2, pp. 11-24.

Nori, Usha and Shankar Patnaik (2002), *Globalisation and Trade between Blocks: A Study of SAARC and EU with Special Reference to India,* University of Hyderabad, India.

Pal, Parthapritam (2006), "Regional Trade Agreements in a Multilateral Trade Regime: A Survey of Recent Issues", *Foreign Trade Review,* pp. 27-45.

Panagariya, A. (1996), "The Free Trade Area of the Americas: Good for Latin America?" *World Economy,* 19, No. 5, September, pp. 485-515.

———, (2000), "Prèferential Trade Liberalization: The Traditional Theory and New Developments", *Journal of Economic Literature,* June 2000.

Polachek, S.W. (1999), "Conflict and Trade: An Economic Approach to Political International Interactions", *Peace Economics, Peace Science and Public Policy,* Vol. 5, Issue 2.

Pomfort, Richard (1997), "The Eco Current Status and Future Prospects", *Europe Asia Studies,* Vol. 49, No. 4, 1997.

Prabir De and Buddhadeb Ghosh (2003), "India in the BIMST-EC : Some Issue", *India Quarterly,* Vol. 59 (3 and 4), July-December 3, pp. 1-25.

Raballand, G. (2003), "Determinants of the Negative Impact of Being Landlocked on Trade: An Empirical Investigation through the Central Asian Case", *Comparative Economic Studies*, 45, pp. 520-36.

Rahman, A. (1980), *A Custom Union in South Asia: Prospects and Problems*, Ministry of Finance, Govt. of Bangladesh.

Rahman, M.M. (2005), "Possibility of Trade Expansion among SAARC Countries: Evidence from the Macro Economics and Regional Trade Blocs", School and Economics and Political Science, *Working Paper*, University of Sydney, Sydney, Australia.

———, (2005), *The Determinants of Bangladesh's Trade: Evidence from the Generalized Gravity Model*, School and Economics and Political Science, Working Paper ECON 2005-3, The University of Sydney, Australia.

Ram, Mangat (1979), *Regional Cooperation in South Asia*, S. Chand and Company, New Delhi.

Ramos, L. and M. Zarzoso (2005), "Does Heterogeneity Matter in the Content of the Gravity Model", *Economic Bulletin*, Vol. 6, No. 17, pp. 1-7.

Rault, C., R. Sova and A. Sova (2007), "An Empirical Examination of the Evolution of Trade Flow Configuration of Easter European Countries", *Paper presented in European Applied Business Research Conference*, Venice.

Reddy, K.C. and T.N. Devi (1984), "Revealed Comparative Advantage among the South Asian Countries", *Asian Economic Review*, Vol. 26, No. 3.

Santis Roberta and Claudia Vicarelli (2007), "The Deeper and the Wider EU Strategies of Trade Integration: An Empirical Evaluation of EU Common Commercial Policy Effects", *Global Economy Journal*, Vol. 7, Issue 4 (works.brepress.com/Roberta_de_santis/2, accessed 18 October 2007).

Sarkar, Amal (2004), "Impact of Free Trade in South Asia with Reference to India", *Foreign Trade Review*, Vol. 38, No. 1-2, April-Sep, pp. 39-43.

———, (2004), "A Trade Linkage System for SAARC", *Foreign Trade Review*, Vol. 39, No. 2, pp. 3-40.

———, (2004), "An Economic Modeling of Trade Flows between SAARC and ASEAN", *Foreign Trade Review*, Vol. 39, No. 1, pp. 65-76.

Schiff, M., Y. Wang and M. Olarrega (2002), *Trade Related Technology Diffusion and Dynamics of North-South and South-South Integration,* World Bank Policy Research Working Paper, No. 2861, World Bank.

Schiff, Maurice (2000), *Multilateral Trade Liberalization Political Disintegration and Choice of Free Trade Agreements versus Customs Unions,* World Bank Policy Research Working Paper, No. 2350, World Bank.

Schott, Jeffrey (2004), "More Free Trade Area Policy Analyses", *International Economics,* 27, Institute for International Economics, Washington, D.C.

Scitovsky, T. (1958), *Economic Theory and West European Integration,* M.A: Allen and Unwin, Winchester.

Shepherd, B. (2008), *Dealing with Zero Trade Flows,* Niehaus Princeton University, GEM.

Sikdar, C. (2006), "Prospects of Bilateral Trade between India and Bangladesh", *Foreign Trade Review,* Vol. 41, No. 1, April-June, pp. 27-43.

———, (2008), "Free Trade Arrangement between India and EU-15—A Theoretical and Empirical Analysis", *ICFAI Journal of Applied Economics,* (January).

Simwaka, Kisu (2006), *Dynamics of Malawi's Trade Flows: A Gravity Model Approach,* MPRA Paper, No. 1122.

Sinha, Dipendra and Tapen Sinha (2001), "Openness, Investment and Economic Growth in Asia", *Indian Economics Journal,* Vol. 49, No. 4.

Srinivasan, T.N. (1994), "Regional Trading Arrangements and Beyond: Exploring Some Options For South Asia: Theory Empiric and Policy", *Report No. IDP-142,* South Asia Region, World Bank, Washington, D.C.

Sriwardna, Mahindra (2003), "Trade Liberalization in South Asia: Free Trade Area or Custom Union", *Journal of South Asia Studies,* Vol. 26, No. 3.

Summers, L. (1991), *Regionalism and the World Trading System: Policy Implications of Trade and Currency Zones,* Edited by The Federal Reserve Bank of Kansas City, pp. 295-301.

Todaro, Michael P. and C. Stephen Smith (2004), *Economic Development,* 8th Edition, p. 580, Pearson Publications.

UN, *UN COMTRADE Statistics*: Various Issues.

UN, *UNCTAD Hand Book of Statistics*: Various Issues.

Upadhyaya, Kamal, Franklin, C.P. Mixon, and Dharmendra Dhakal (1998), "Do Devaluation Improve Trade Balances: Evidence from South Asian Countries", *The Indian Economic Journal*, Vol. 46, No. 3, pp. 15-23.

Vanbergeijk, P.A.G. and H. Oldersma (1990), "Détente, Market-oriented Reform and German Unification: Potential Consequences for the World Trade System", *Kuklos*, 43, pp. 599-609.

Venables, A.J. (1997), *Regional Integration Arrangement: A Force for Convergence and Divergence*, World Bank Policy Research Working Paper, No. 2260, World Bank.

Verbeek, M. (2004), *A Guide to Modern Econometrics*, second edition, Chichester, Wiley.

Verma, Satish (2006), "India and Pakistan: Macro Economics, Trade and Potentials", *Indian Journal of Economics*, Vol. 87, No. 346.

Viner, Jacob (1950), *The Custom Union Issues*, Carnegie Endowment for International Peace, New York.

Vlachos, Liliana (1995), "The Interaction between the Australian Economy and the Economics of the ASEAN", *The Indian Economic Journal*, Vol. 44, No. 3, pp. 485-92.

Wang, Z.K. and L.K. Winters (1991), The Trading Potential of Eastern Europe, CEPR Discussion Paper 61.

Wemelsfelder, J. (1960), "The Short-term Effect of Lowering Import Duties in Germany", *Economic Journal*, pp. 94-104.

World Bank, *World Development Indicators:* Various Issues.

Yahya, F. (2003), "BIMSTEC and Emerging Patterns of ASIAN Regional and Inter-Regional Cooperation", *Australian Journal of Political Science*, Vol. 40, No. 3.

Yeats, Alexander (1997), *Does MERCOSUR's Trade Performance Raise Concerns about the Effects of RTAs*, World Bank Policy Research Working Paper, No. 1729, World Bank.

Zarzoso, M. (2003), "Gravity Model: An Application to Trade between Regional Blocs", *Atlantic Economic Journal*, pp. 200-21.

Zarzoso, M. and F.N. Lehmann D. (2000), "Augmented gravity Model: An Empirical Application to Mercosur-European Union Trade Flows", *Journal of Applied Economics*, Vol. 6, No. 2, pp. 291-316. (Nov).

Zhang, J. and G. Kristensen (1995), "A Gravity Model with Variable Coefficients: The EEC Trade with Third Countries", *Geographical Analysis*, Vol. 27, pp 307-20.

WEBSITES

1. *www.unctad.org* (accessed 15 June 2007).
2. *www.uncomtrade-un-org* (accessed 9 July 2007).
3. *www.saarc-sec.org* (accessed 9 January 2009).
4. *www.cepII.org* (accessed 12 March 2008).
5. *www.wto.org* (accessed 18 April 2009).

Index